Advance Praise for
The Genesis Enterprise

"*The Genesis Enterprise* is a treasure chest of information and ideas for visionary leaders. Tompkins puts together a comprehensive map to guide leaders beyond the buzzwords of the nineties. A guide for those struggling with 'empowerment,' 'teams,' 'vision,' and other essentials for survival."
—DONNA R. NEUSCH, PH.D.
Coauthor, *The High Performance Enterprise: Reinventing the People Side of Your Business*

"Results, that is what one gets from Jim Tompkins. This book is another illustration of the practical, commonsense approach that Jim Tompkins brings to the workplace. Refreshing. A must read."
—VIRGIS W. COLBERT
Senior Vice President, Operations
Miller Brewing Company

"With *The Genesis Enterprise,* Jim Tompkins has made a significant contribution to understanding and applying the principles of leadership in business today. I heartily recommend it."
—DONALD T. PHILLIPS
Author, *Lincoln on Leadership*

"Becoming a team-based peak-to-peak organization was not easy. By following the process defined in this book, we were able to significantly improve quality, reduce new product introduction time, increase schedule attainment and reduce costs. A must-read by all organizations who want to achieve their potential and more."
—DONALD M. LORTON
President, Diversified Operations
Maytag Cleveland Cooking Products

"Jim Tompkins is a leader who through his own experience has come to understand the principles of achieving peak-to-peak performance. This book must be read by organizations dedicated to achieving productivity and quality excellence."
—D. SCOTT SINK
Professor and Director
The Quality and Productivity Center at Virginia Tech

The Genesis Enterprise

Creating Peak-to-Peak Performance

Jim Tompkins

McGraw-Hill, Inc.

New York   San Francisco   Washington, D.C.   Auckland   Bogotá
Caracas   Lisbon   London   Madrid   Mexico City   Milan
Montreal   New Delhi   San Juan   Singapore
Sydney   Tokyo   Toronto

Library of Congress Cataloging-in-Publication Data

Tompkins, James A.
    The genesis enterprise : creating peak-to-peak performance / Jim
Tompkins.
       p. cm.
    Includes index.
    ISBN 0-07-065103-5 (acid-free paper)
    1. Industrial management. 2. Personnel management.
3. Leadership. 4. Success in business. I. Title.
HD31.T636 1995
658.4—dc20   94-47476
                                            CIP

1 2 3 4 5 6 7 8 9 0 DOC/DOC 9 0 0 9 8 7 6 5

ISBN 0-07-065103-5

*The sponsoring editor for this book was James H. Bessent, Jr., the editing
supervisor was Jane Palmieri, and the production supervisor was Suzanne W. B.
Rapcavage. It was set in Baskerville by Inkwell Publishing Services.*

Printed and bound by R. R. Donnelley & Sons Company.

McGraw-Hill books are available at special quantity discounts to use as pre-
miums and sales promotions, or for use in corporate training programs.
For more information, please write to the Director of Special Sales,
McGraw-Hill, Inc., 11 West 19th Street, New York, NY 10011. Or contact
your local bookstore.

 This book is printed on recycled, acid-free paper containing a
minimum of 50% recycled de-inked fiber.

To my family who have lived through my peaks and valleys and allowed me to grow to become a Genesis Leader.
Thank you Shari, Tiffany, Jamie, and Jimmy. I love you.

Contents

v

Preface

Peak performance doesn't necessarily lead to success. In fact, peak performance often leads to failure. This is true both for individuals and for organizations, and due to today's turbulent times, when the definition of peak performance changes daily. What was yesterday's peak performance is merely good performance today, average performance next week, and poor performance next month. Once an individual or organization has achieved peak performance, the tendency is to stop getting better. Thus begins the journey to failure.

Therefore the key to long-term success is not the achievement of peak performance, but rather the continuous process of beginning anew and climbing to a new peak, and the next peak, and the next peak. A Genesis Leader is one who is able to continuously climb to new peak after new peak. A Genesis Enterprise is an organization that is able to continuously climb to new peak after new peak by creating a culture that continuously improves relationships with its employees and partners.

This book is a guidebook for you as an individual and for you as a member of an organization as you seek to achieve peak-to-peak performance. This book is based upon my experiences and my observations. As an individual I have gone from success to failure, from failure to success, and from success to success. As the founder, chairman, and president of an engineering-based consulting firm, I have actively participated in taking my organization from success to failure, from failure to success, and from success to success. As a consultant to some of the world's largest organizations, smallest organizations, and everything else in between, I have watched and actively participated as these organizations have gone from success to failure, from failure to success, and from success to success. I have learned from the thrill of victory and the agony of defeat. I have been down headed up, up headed down, and up heading higher. Personally and professionally I have learned many lessons from these experiences. This book presents my discoveries, as well as a roadmap for you to follow to reach the Genesis Enterprise and to achieve peak-to-peak performance.

I have consciously been learning the principles of the Genesis Enterprise for over 20 years, and I can track my subconscious awareness of the Genesis principles to more than 40 years ago. We all have been successful at something, then subsequently been unsuccessful at the same thing. That's life. The success of life has a lot to do with our ability to learn from our successes as well as failures, and to use this knowledge to travel to new levels of success. This process of peak-to-peak evolution has always been at the core of every successful individual and organization.

For your organization to become a Genesis Enterprise, four major shifts must occur. I became aware of the first shift by watching great leaders lead. The problem today is that most organizations don't have great leaders. Therefore, *the first shift required to become a Genesis Enterprise is an organizational shift from management to leadership.* The second and third shifts involve relationships. Whle many organizations understand the importance of these shifts, few understand how to successfully implement them. *The second shift has to do with relationships* within *organizations—a shift from individuals to teams. The third shift has to do with the relationships* between *organizations—a shift from the traditional customer/supplier relationships to true partnerships. The fourth shift has to do with how we reward and recognize people for their efforts in achieving peak-to-peak performance,* thus assuring the continuous evolution to new peaks. This last shift is the shift from traditional compensation to what I call Genesis Compensation. It is only by creating all four shifts that your organization may become a Genesis Enterprise and truly achieve peak-to-peak performance.

This book is practical; not a theoretical treatise on organizational evolution but a how-to on becoming a Genesis Enterprise where peak-to-peak performance is a reality. Many organizations have allowed Tompkins Associates, Inc., to help them become Genesis Enterprises. I am indebted to these clients, because it is through their confidence that the Genesis Process has evolved and continues to evolve. It is these clients that deserve the credit for this book.

The last three words of the last chapter of this book are *Go, Go, Go.* In concert with this ending, allow me to strongly encourage you now to *Begin, Begin, Begin.*

Acknowledgments

Many people have worked hard on this book and for their support I am most appreciative. At Tompkins Associates, many thanks go to Paulette Becoat, Sheila Bennett, Luz Davila, Latrelle Dechene, Blessing Eni, Rap McBurney, Kimberly McClain, Christopher Simmons, and Lin Wu. Special thanks to the Tompkins Associates Publications Coordinator, Rhonda Price, and our Leader of Organizational Excellence, Rob Haynes. At Martin Public Relations, thanks are due to the Genesis Team of Joe Slay, Tom Morris, Alan Crawford, Chris Love, and Windy Campbell. Finally, at McGraw-Hill, my thanks to the senior editor, Jim Bessent, and copy editor, Peter Roberts.

James A. Tompkins, Ph.D.
Raleigh, NC
January 1995

PART 1

Creating Peak-to-Peak Performance

Organizations are not truly successful when they achieve peak performance, as their achieving peak performance is often the beginning of failure. More often than not, success leads not to success, but to failure. True organizational success occurs when the organization understands that today's peak performance is tomorrow's good performance, next week's average performance, and next month's poor performance. True organizational success occurs only when an organization understands that it must continuously evolve from one level of peak performance to a higher level, to a higher level, and still higher. It is this process of continuously creating peak-to-peak performance that defines the Genesis Enterprise and true success. Chapter 1 sets the stage for becoming a Genesis Enterprise by creating peak-to-peak performance.

1

The Ultimatum to Become a Genesis Enterprise

Success has ruined many a man.   BENJAMIN FRANKLIN

Each success only buys an admission ticket to a more difficult problem.
                                          HENRY KISSINGER

We cannot solve today's problems with the same level of thinking that
created the problems in the first place.   ALBERT EINSTEIN

These are the worst of times and the best of times. The worst of times,
because we are faced with more problems than we can possibly solve. The
worst of times, because everyone is playing king of the mountain. It matters not what business you are in: As you are celebrating your climb to the
top of the mountain, many are planning to topple you. Business is difficult. In fact, as M. Scott Peck says in the opening words of his *The Road
Less Traveled,* "Life is difficult."

At the same time, these are the best of times. There has never been a
time, in all of recorded history, when it has been clearer than today that
there is no lasting solution to the problems we face. In fact, every solution
brings with it more problems. There is no paradigm shift that will make
us whole for the long term. You say, "How can these be the best of times
if I cannot solve the problems in front of me?" Because maybe we will once
and for all figure out that it is not our job to solve problems, that there is
no new program that will make us whole. We don't need a new program
that fixes problems by treating our symptoms. It is my hope that we will

3

face reality, that we will understand that there is no magic, no quick fix, and no solution that will stop the flow of problems. Sure, implementing new programs may change the problems, but the problems will never go away. There will always be more problems. In fact the more success we have, the more problems we have. So you ask again, how can these be the best of times if I am and I will continue to be bombarded with problems? The answer is sobering, but the timing has been predestined, and it is now time for us all to realize that we do not need another program, but rather a fundamental shift in the way we do business. We need not a solution to the immediate problems, but a new way of doing business that realistically faces the facts that there is no solution, that problems are continuous and that the only way to win is to change our approach to business, to install a process that anticipates and solves problems before they *are* problems and to continuously transform our organization into a championship organization that is nevertheless the underdog.

You see, we fight and fight and fight to get to the top, to achieve peak performance, then just as we start to celebrate, we begin our decline. This decline may be subtle at first, but nevertheless it is a decline. When we get to the top we are no longer the underdog, some other organization is, and it is in part a result of our success that the underdogs believe they too can climb the mountain and knock us off. Yes, business is difficult, and it will become even more difficult, but the question you must answer is "What am I going to do about it?" In fact, a possible title for this book that I liked was, *How Are You Gonna Get to Where You Gotta Go?* You have two choices: You can either cycle through the success/failure routine, or you can decide to change the way you do business and move from one level of peak performance to a higher level of peak performance, to a higher level of peak performance, etc. Today, with all the downsizing, rightsizing, delayering, restructuring, repositioning, demassing, and reengineering, it is clear that many organizations have decided it is their time in the cycle to begin to fail.

This book is not for those who have decided to fail and who are now on a downward trend. This book is for the organizations who have decided that they want to climb to the top of the mountain, achieve peak performance, and from this peak continue their success pattern to reach the next peak, the next, and the next. This book is for those organizations who don't want to retreat but to continue to win. This book is for all the organizations who have decided that instead of resorting to cutbacks and layoffs, they will continue to be successful. Why not just become better than the best? Why not grow? Why not be successful today, tomorrow, and into the future? This is why it is the best of times: Each organization now has the opportunity to become the best and then to become better than the best, to achieve peak performance, and then to continue to evolve to new peaks. This is the definition of being a Genesis Enterprise. Let's just do it!

NO MORE MIRACULOUS RECOVERIES

Robert Eaton, as the new chairman of Chrysler, was very upbeat as he read to his management team a *Wall Street Journal* article about the "miraculous recovery" of Chrysler in the early 1990s. He shocked his managers, however, when he reminded them that the same Chrysler miraculous recovery story had been written in 1956, then again in 1965, 1976, and again in 1983. Eaton told his managers, "I've got a better idea. Let's stop getting sick. My personal ambition is to be the first chairman never to lead a Chrysler comeback."

1.1 Why Is Success So Dangerous?

Success and failure are both a part of life. No matter what you do, you will need to learn to deal with both success and failure. These are the following four modes you must understand:

1. FAIL/FAIL. You fail and you fail some more. You have not been successful, you lose confidence, and so you fail again. This results in further lack of confidence, more failure, and a resignation to failing. You stop trying, you fail.

2. FAIL/SUCCEED. You fail, you learn, and you succeed. You have not been successful, but you learn from your lack of success. You love the underdog role and are motivated by this role. Your motivation to be successful uses the failures as building blocks to your becoming successful. You succeed.

3. SUCCEED/FAIL. You are successful, you become content with your success, and you stop getting better. Your dreams come true, and you don't replace them with new dreams. You become invincible in your own mind, you protect what you have instead of pushing forward, your decline accelerates, you blame others, and you fail.

4. SUCCEED/SUCCEED. You are successful, but you realize that since you are no longer the underdog you *are* in fact the underdog. You are dedicated to getting better, you define new dreams, and you focus all your energies on getting better than better. In fact, you no longer want to be the best of the best, you want to be better than the best in a category all by yourself. You continue to succeed. You believe in creating peak-to-peak performance. You are a Genesis Leader.

Why is success so dangerous? Because most organizations cycle through time by alternating between the FAIL/SUCCEED and SUCCEED/FAIL modes.

They begin with a surge of entrepreneurial energy and climb the mountain to success; the organization achieves peak performance., They become smug, stop being entrepreneurial, protect their success, decline and fail, their performance falls, and they find themselves in a valley. They bring in new people, reorganize, reignite the entrepreneurial fires, and once again climb the mountain to success, peak performance. Unfortunately they become smug, stop being entrepreneurial, and return to the valley, etc. This cycle goes on and on. An outsider may not see these cycles at work in many big organizations, because different portions of the organizations are at different phases of their FAIL/SUCCEED, SUCCEED/FAIL cycles, and so in the aggregate they appear to be stable. But they are *not* stable, just cycling out of a phase and giving the appearance of stability. This FAIL/SUCCEED, SUCCEED/FAIL cycling will generally continue over time until an organization has too great a swing to succeed, at which point it loses touch with its own mortality and cycles from a SUCCEED/FAIL into a FAIL/FAIL mode, and everyone asks, "What happened?" and "How could such a great company go out of business?"

Well, there is another way. Not many have found this way, but it is captured in a few quotes of the few people who were the SUCCEED/SUCCEED pioneers. These SUCCEED/SUCCEED pioneers, who truly understood how to create peak-to-peak performance, were the original Genesis Leaders, and built the prototypical Genesis Enterprises. Consider John Wooden, the greatest college basketball coach of all time, who said:

> It's what you learn after you know it all that counts.

Or consider the words of Jerry Garcia, leader of the most successful concert rock group of all times, The Grateful Dead:

> You don't just want to be considered the best of the best. You want to be considered the only one who does what you do.

Or, from Oliver Cromwell:

> He who stops being better, stops being good.

The topic of this book is how your organization can create peak performance and from this peak move on to an even higher peak, and on, and on. How your organization can get into a neverending loop of SUCCEED/SUCCEED, SUCCEED/SUCCEED, SUCCEED/SUCCEED.... How your organization can become a Genesis Enterprise.

IT ISN'T MAGIC

If it isn't magic, what makes corporations disappear? The caption to a figure in the *Fortune* article "Dinosaurs" was, "Some Leaders in Market

Value Do a Disappearing Act." In 1972 the company with the world's highest stock market valuation was IBM, with a value of $47 billion. Again in 1982, IBM led the world with a value of $57 billion. However, in 1992, IBM didn't even make the top 25 and had a value of only $29 billion. Similarly, General Motors was in 4th place in 1972 with a value of $23 billion, 5th place in 1982 with a value of $19 billion, but in 1992 fell all the way to 40th place with a value of $22 billion. Also, Sears Roebuck in 1972 was in 6th place, with a value of $18 billion, in 1982 in 13th place at $10 billion, and in 1992 in 81st place with a value below $16 billion. The key fact to keep in mind here is, during these same twenty years (1972–1992) the Standard & Poor's 500 was up 269 percent. What happened? How could these three giants all fall? At GM the most common explanation is "Inability to execute," at IBM "When a company gets to the top, the process of how decisions are made becomes all-consuming. The focus is on how decisions are made rather than what you decide." At Sears they created a "whole library of bulletins that spell out procedures for dealing with almost any problem." Lots of procedures, but no action. Will these giant companies disappear? It isn't clear. It *is* clear that in a big way they went from success to failure; the next phase is up to the present leadership. They can cycle from failure back to success, or to their ultimate failure. The choice is theirs. If they become a Genesis Enterprise, they certainly can go from failure to success, to success, to success, etc. Or they may totally disappear. Either way, it will not be magic.

1.2 Where Are We Today?

In some ways it's almost scary to pick up a newspaper or watch the news. So much is happening. Business is crazy, and the world is crazy. The dismantling of the Berlin Wall in 1989 marked the beginning of a revolution. Absolutely nothing is stable; everything is in transition. In the business world we have been shocked by layoff after layoff, bankruptcy after bankruptcy, and merger after merger, to the point that we aren't shocked anymore. In the political arena we have been shocked by unstable currencies, public debt, and political unrest—to the point that we're not shocked anymore. We have become calloused, and our senses have been deadened to the permanent white water in which we live. The only constant today, and into the future, is an increasing rate of change. In today's organization, change is occurring at such a rate that before an organization has adapted to the last change, a new change has already occurred. There is no steady state. Organizations must not only learn to live with constant change, but learn to embrace change and to harness the energy of change to become better and better. Genesis Enterprises are organizations that use the energy of change to continuously move to new peaks of performance, evolving into the future at a record-setting pace.

CHANGE—CHANGE—CHANGE—CHANGE—CHANGE

- In 1956 there were 7000 periodicals published in the United States. Today there are over 22,000.
- In 1989 the average supermarket stocked 25,000 items. Today there are over 30,000.
- From 1892 to 1982, there was only one Coke. Today there are seven varieties.
- In today's automobile, there are more dollars in its microelectronics than its steel.
- When I was a boy, you could buy either tennis shoes or basketball shoes. By 1980, you could buy tennis, basketball, running, walking, aerobic, and cross-training styles. Today one company sells 10 versions of their walking shoes, including one to only walk uphill!

In the early 1990s the philosophy of paradigm-shifting was popular, to keep pace with change. What now must be realized is that when you shift from one paradigm, you go on to another. What is needed is not just a single shift in paradigms, but a realization that we must *continuously* shift from paradigm to paradigm. Today's rate of change cries out for a process of continuous paradigm-shifting. Today's rate of change demands a continuous escalation to new levels of peak performance.

It is the paradigm-shift mentality that has caused businesses to shift from one program to another. Many of these programs were valid, but since they were viewed *as* programs they were destined to fail. It is interesting to view the life of a program as it travels through the phases:

Phase I   Skepticism

Phase II   Excitement

Phase III   Acceptance

Phase IV   Questioning

Phase V   Disillusion

Phase VI   Dismissal

It matters not which program one is talking about (Malcolm Baldrige National Quality Award, Just-In-Time, Total Quality Management, Reengineering, etc.), one can read the headlines (Table 1.1) and define the

Table 1.1   Headlines Relating to Programs during a Program's Life

Phase	Headline
I Skepticism	"A Need for Change" "How to Fix _____"
II Excitement	"The Hot New Management Tool" "Using _____ for Organizational Excellence"
III Acceptance	"Avoiding Failure With _____" More Than a Dying Fad"
IV Questioning	"On Trial Again _____" "Losing the Luster With _____"
V Disillusion	"Fatally Flawed or Simply Unfocused" "Success Limited With _____"
VI Dismissal	"Business Sours on _____" "Just Another Fad"

applicable phase of a program's life. There is a place for these programs, but they can't be viewed as independent pieces of a puzzle which, when implemented, will miraculously bring an organization long-term success. The problem lies in the success/fail evolution of organizations as they move from program to program. It's okay to pursue these programs, but only within the context of an ongoing, continuous *process* of discovery, learning, growing, evolving, improving, and performing. It is the adoption of this process that defines a Genesis Enterprise.

1.3   Becoming a Genesis Enterprise

When change was slow and the world was stable and predictable, there came into being a style of management, an organizational hierarchy, a relationship with outside organizations, and a method of compensation that worked. Top management defined the tasks of subordinates, the rules for dealing with suppliers and customers, and how they were to be compensated. Life went on. Then everything went nuts. The rate of change, the turbulence, the chaos, the white water, and the high velocity of everything resulted in the obsolescence, almost overnight, of how we do business. Unfortunately, many organizations today haven't changed, and are still attempting to apply yesterday's rules to today's game. This hasn't worked, and can never be made to work. What is needed is a basic shift in how organizations function. This basic shift demands that we leave behind many of the paradigms of the past and shift to a new way of evolving.

All organizations realize that a new rate of change is upon us. Most organizations believe that to adapt to this change we must change how we do business. Unfortunately, most don't understand that what is needed is not a further moving down our present path, but rather a shift to new paths. If all your organization does is improve its present position by improving what it now does, your organization will fail. It must make a fundamental shift in how it functions. This shift has its foundation, not in a stable shift to a new path, but in an ongoing process of renewal, a continuous shifting from path to path to path. Only when your organization implements these fundamental Genesis Enterprise shifts will it be able to become better than the best, and to be even better still tomorrow.

A Genesis Enterprise is an organization that understands the process of continuous renewal, of success/success–success/success–success/success, of being the underdog *because* you are on top, and of nonstop evolution to higher levels of peak performance. A Genesis Enterprise is an organization that is dedicated to growing, to prospering, to being successful, and to building more success. A Genesis Enterprise is an organization that

1. Shifts from management to leadership

2. Shifts from individuals to teams

3. Shifts from traditional customer/supplier relationships to partnerships

4. Shifts from traditional compensation to Genesis Compensation

There are books out there that will help you to make one of these shifts. But this book is different because it tells you how to make all *four* shifts, and explains how the *integration* of these four shifts is essential if you are to become better than the best. This book is your organization's guide to becoming all you can be and more. This book is your guide to becoming a Genesis Enterprise, and to continuing to achieve new levels of peak performance.

1.4 Conclusion

Life is difficult, and the ever-increasing rate of change continues to make life even more difficult. We need to realize that solving today's problems is not a solution. Problems are continuous, and what is needed is a shift in how we do business. We must adopt a process of continuous renewal. Genesis Enterprises must

1. Build upon success by getting better

2. Use the energy of change to move to new levels of peak performance

3. Adopt the ongoing, continuous process of discovering, learning, growing, evolving, improving, and performing

4. Shift from management to leadership
5. Shift from individuals to teams
6. Shift from traditional customer/supplier relationships to partnerships
7. Shift from traditional compensation to Genesis Compensation

Part 2 of this book provides the road map for shifting from management to leadership, Part 3 for shifting from individuals to teams, Part 4 for shifting from the traditional customer/supplier relationships to partnerships, and Part 5 for shifting from traditional compensation to Genesis Compensation. Part 6 concludes the book with some thoughts on how to make your organization a Genesis Enterprise.

Think of your organization as a train. Think of this book as the railroad tracks. Your train is moving. You are encouraged to jump on-board and to lead the train to success and then to more success. This continual renewal, progress, and evolution of your organization will result in peak performance, then a higher level of peak performance, then a higher level of peak performance, and ever onward and upward. When this occurs, you will be a Genesis Enterprise.

References

Blumenthal, B. and P. Haspeslagh, "Toward a Definition of Corporate Transformations," *Sloan Management Review,* Spring 1994.

Dessler, G., *Winning Commitment: How to Build and Keep a Competitive Work Force,* McGraw-Hill, New York, 1993.

Gordon J., "Into the Dark: Rough Ride Ahead for American Workers," *Training,* July 1993.

Goss, T., R. Pascale, and A. Athos, "The Reinvention Roller Coaster: Risking the Present for a Powerful Future," *Harvard Business Review,* November–December 1993.

Huey, J., "The New Post-Heroic Leadership," *Fortune,* February 21, 1994.

Loomis C. J., "Dinosaurs," *Fortune,* May 3, 1993.

Johnson, H. J., *Relevance Regained: From Top-Down Control to Bottom-Up Empowerment,* The Free Press, New York, 1992.

Pritchett, P., *Culture Shift,* Pritchett Publishing Company, Dallas, Texas, 1993.

——, *Firing Up Commitment During Organizational Change,* Pritchett Publishing Company, Dallas, Texas, 1994.

Riley, P., *The Winner Within: A Life Plan for Team Players,* G.P.Putnam's Sons, New York, 1993.

Smith, L., "Burned-Out Bosses," *Fortune,* July 25, 1994.

Stewart, T. A., "Welcome to the Revolution," *Fortune,* December 13, 1993.

——, "The Information Age in Charts," *Fortune,* April 4, 1994.

PART 2

The Evolution of Leadership

There have been many, many pages written, and speeches given, on the management-versus-leadership challenge. Is management more important, or is leadership? Do we need both management and leadership? It must be said at the outset that Genesis Enterprises must have both good management and good leadership. Today's challenge lies in the fact that we have an abundance of management and a shortage of leadership. To create the required management/leadership balance, a shift from management to leadership is required. This unit sets forth the key leadership tasks that must be addressed if a leader is to position his or her organization to be a Genesis Enterprise.

First, a Genesis Leader must shape an organization's culture to make it consistent with peak-to-peak performance (Chap. 2). Second, a Genesis Leader must define an organization's direction and must achieve organizational alignment with the direction (Chap. 3). Third, the Genesis Leader must assure the motivation of people within their organization, to maintain progress in peak-to-peak performance (Chap. 4). To do these things, the Genesis Leader must go through a personal transformation (Chap. 5). The Genesis Leader must evolve first, and only then can his or her organization evolve into a Genesis Enterprise.

2
Leaders Shape Culture

Culture is the foundation upon which organizations are built. Culture permeates all organizational activities and events, and allows one to interpret all that occurs. All organizations have a unique culture that plays an important role in their organization's success.

An important early task for an organization, in beginning the journey of peak-to-peak performance, is the transformation of its culture. Genesis Leaders will fail if the culture within which they are working does not embrace peak-to-peak performance. Therefore, the first task of a Genesis Leader is to shape the organization's culture.

An organization's culture is the perception of the people within the organization of how things work. Culture is intangible, unseen, and undefined. To the contrary, the manifestations of culture are tangible, visible, and often well defined. Cultural manifestations include

- Company cars
- Time clocks
- Neckties
- Starched white shirts
- Executive lunch room
- Windows in offices
- Reserved parking
- Founder's picture in hall
- Seating arrangements

Culture may also be perceived in an organization's language, jargon, stories, expectations, rewards, ceremonies, and titles.

YOU CAN'T SEE IT, BUT YOU CAN HEAR IT

My formal title is James A. Tompkins, Ph.D. This is the name that appears on my business card and is typed at the bottom of my letters. However, I always introduce myself to everyone as Jim Tompkins. Nevertheless, in various organizations where I work, I am called by various people Jim, Mr. Tompkins, Dr. Tompkins, Dr. Jim, Mr. T., Dr. T, and Jimbo.

I receive correspondence addressed to all of these handles plus JAT, Dr. James A. Tompkins, Dr. J.A. Tompkins, and Mr. Jim Tompkins. Interestingly, even what we are called is a result of culture.

2.1   The Cultural Evolution

Culture is initially created in an organization in the minds of the people who begin the organization. The essence of this early culture results from the homes, families, friends, schools, church, and business experiences of the organization's founders. Certainly, the culture of a start-up organization of three surfers in California will be different from a start-up organization of three Harvard MBAs in New York, as well as a start-up organization of three Ph.D. scientists in Japan. These early differences have to do with the differences between a surfer, a Harvard MBA, and a Japanese Ph.D. scientist. It is from these individual differences that the organization's cultural differences will evolve. As shown in Fig. 2.1, it is the organization's founders and the culture they created that will screen employees. Employees conforming to the culture will behave in accordance with the culture. It is this conformed behavior that determines the organization's performance—for better or worse.

All aspects of the organization are impacted by the continuing evolution of its culture. For a Genesis Leader to transform an organization's culture, he/she must transform the rules, habits, procedures, standards, norms, rewards, language, jargon, stories, expectations, ceremonies, and titles that impact the screening of employees, the cultural conformance, the organization's behavior, and thus, the organizational performance. A Genesis Leader must realize that an organization's existing culture will work to stifle the move to a Genesis Enterprise. Existing cultures work to maintain existing cultures. There are many examples of ambitious leaders who desired to transform an organization, but due to the routine of the existing culture were not successful in achieving transformation. The Genesis Leader must understand that existing cultures will always work to

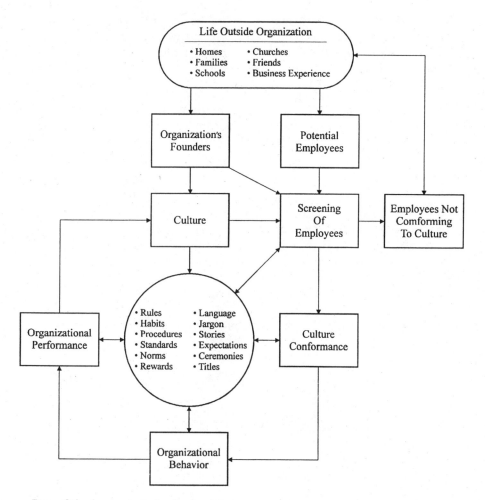

Figure 2.1 An organization's cultural evolution

maintain the status quo and to resist change. If the culture is not transformed, the Genesis Leader will be consumed. The Genesis Leader must go beyond changes in cultural manifestations and perceptions and truly transform the organization's culture in order to shape the organization's performance.

LEE IACOCCA: A GENESIS LEADER

In Lee Iacocca's autobiography, he entitles the chapter in which he joins Chrysler "Aboard a Sinking Ship." In this chapter, Iacocca says that what he found when he arrived at Chrysler was not a company but

35 "mini-empires." The problem was not just with the executives, but arose from the fact that "nobody was doing anything right." The organization had adopted a Chrysler culture that did not work and could not be made to work. Iacocca states:

> There was so much to do and so little time! I had to eliminate thirty-five little duchies. I had to bring some cohesion and unity into the company. I had to get rid of the many people who didn't know what they were doing. I had to replace them by finding guys with experience who could move fast.

Chrysler had engineering, financial, manufacturing, quality, marketing, and public relations problems. However, at the heart of all these problems was the culture of Chrysler. Iacocca had to transform the rules, habits, procedures, standards, norms, expectations, ceremonies, and titles of Chrysler, and then and only then was he in a position to begin the recovery. Five years later, after an unbelievable chain of events, Chrysler had a whole new culture and a whole new way of doing business. After all he had been through, he writes, "Now that we were out of danger, it was time to think about having fun again." What an exciting story! What an unbelievable turnaround! What a Genesis Leader!

2.2   A Genesis Culture

Two excellent questions that we all would like to answer now are

1. What is a Genesis Culture?

2. How can you shape your organization so as to create a Genesis Culture?

These questions are fair and good. Unfortunately, they cannot be answered. In fact, these questions are directly related to the following leadership questions, asked often in the 1980s, that also could not be answered:

1. What is good leadership?

2. How can you shape your personality to establish good leadership?

The difficulty is that leadership is not a set of personality traits. Culture is not a set of organizational traits. Many different types of personalities make good leaders. Many different organizational traits can be found in Genesis Cultures. In fact, the research on the shaping of organizational cultures does not begin to define the organizational traits of a Genesis Culture. In the book *Corporate Culture and Performance*, the authors conclude:

> The single most visible factor that distinguishes major cultural changes that succeed from those that fail is competent leadership at the top.

This obviously takes us right back to the unanswerable "What is good leadership?" question.

Although we cannot define a Genesis Culture, we can describe some cultural characteristics that are found in Genesis Cultures as opposed to those that are dying. A symbol for the culture of a dying organization is a dinosaur. Dinosaurs, although once very powerful and rulers of all the Earth, don't live here anymore. Crocodiles existed before dinosaurs, and still exist today. Crocodiles are survivors. Crocodiles know how to adapt to new circumstances. Whereas the dinosaur is a symbol of an obsolete, failing culture, the crocodile is a symbol of a surviving, winning, prospering culture, a Genesis Culture.

The objective of a dinosaur is to know what is happening, to make all decisions, and to be in control. Control is comfort for a dinosaur. To the contrary, the objective of a crocodile is growth. Control is less important to a crocodile. Growth is comfort for a crocodile. A crocodile is driven by stretching, pushing, pulling, and improving. The foundation of a dinosaur organization is analysis. Dinosaur organizations have task force after task force, analyzing every possible alternative. And even after every alternative has been analyzed, there is always one more meeting with one more set of alternatives that need to be analyzed. The decision process in dinosaur organizations is excruciatingly slow. To the contrary, in crocodile organizations the foundation is a shared consistent vision of where the organization is headed. The rightness of a path is measured more by its consistency with the overall vision than by analysis. Whereas dinosaur organizations often have analysis paralysis, crocodile organizations are able to take decisions and make progress because everyone in the organization shares the vision of where they are headed. Whereas dinosaur organizations wish to implement a solution next year, crocodile organizations want to do something *today* to be better *tomorrow*.

The process that is pursued in a dinosaur organization is the process of *optimization*—to maximize or minimize some objective—to define the ultimate solution so that the problem may be resolved once and for all and never have to be addressed again. The crocodile organization understands that this does not work. The crocodile organization has a total focus on peak-to-peak performance. The crocodile organization understands that today's optimal solution is next month's okay solution and next year's mediocre solution. In fact, the reason the crocodile organizations don't get hung up on excessive analysis is that they know today's solution will be continuously improved. Crocodile organizations spend more time focusing on the solution-after-next than they do on the next solution, as they truly understand the process of continuous, neverending peak-to-peak performance.

The result achieved in a controlled, highly analytical, optimization-seeking dinosaur organization is a culture of authoritarian bureaucracy. This bureaucracy has a life of its own; in fact, we often find that not individuals but "the system" makes decisions. To the contrary, in a crocodile organization, the result is a culture not of authoritarian bureaucracy but of learning, where the daily mandate is to continuously try hard to do better, where we learn from both our successes and our failures, where political nonsense is minimized, and where every opportunity is viewed as an opportunity to improve, to become better prepared to face tomorrow, to strive for a new level of peak performance. Whereas dinosaurs seek authoritarian bureaucracy, crocodiles seek learning.

So, as can be seen in Table 2.1, dinosaurs have as their objective *control*; they use *analysis* to pursue *optimization,* and the result is a culture of *authoritarian bureaucracy.* Crocodiles seek the process of *peak-to-peak performance,* and the desired result is a culture of *learning.* Which is the culture of your organization—dinosaur or crocodile? Genesis Leaders are crocodiles. You need to pursue a crocodile culture.

Another indication of the culture of an organization is the attitude the organization exhibits toward change. Three attitudes exist:

Type I   Static Consistency

Type II   Dynamic Inconsistency

Type III Dynamic Consistency

A Type I attitude is an indication of a dying culture. Type I organizations resist change. Type I organizations pride themselves on maintaining the status quo, and seldom realize it when there is an opportunity to improve. Statements that will be heard in a Type I organization are

Table 2.1   Characteristics of Organizational Culture

Dying Culture	*Genesis Culture*
Control	Growth
Analysis	Vision
Slow decision making	Progressiveness
Optimization	Peak-to-peak performance
Authoritarian bureaucracy	Learning

1. "We have optimized our operations, and there is no room for improvement."
   Or, "If it ain't broke, don't fix it."

2. "We have always been profitable, so why should we change anything?"
   Or, "Don't rock the boat."

A Type II attitude is once again an indication of a dying culture, but in this case the dying is occurring with less finesse. Type II organizations realize that they aren't successful, and they actively install new programs. They are busy organizations. Everyone is on a task force or two, but no one has a chance to *work* as the entire day is spent in meetings. There is no shared direction of where they are headed. Each person has his or her own direction. Although there are islands of success, the organization as a whole is not improving. Statements that will be heard in a Type II organization are

1. "We have been working hard implementing new programs, but everyone is marching to a different drummer. Maybe the next program will work."

2. "This too will pass. Don't pay attention to all these new programs; our management is a bunch of frogs that keep jumping from program to program."

A Type III attitude is the attitude of an organization that has a Genesis Culture. Type III organizations truly understand the meaning of the term *dynamic consistency*. They are driven by a *dynamic,* "improve–improve–improve" mentality, based upon a clear, shared, *consistent* vision of where the organization is headed. Type III organizations understand the difference between "change, change, change" and "improve, improve, improve," and endorse Abraham Lincoln's thought: "Let us not mistake change for progress." Type III organizations will be focused on achieving peak-after-peak-after-peak performance. Statements that will be heard in a Type III organization are

1. "Our leadership encourages us to take risks and to either enjoy the success or learn from the mistake."

2. "We value diversity, for it is by listening and understanding others that we are able to learn, grow, improve, and achieve the next level of peak performance."

2.3   Shaping a Genesis Culture

As was said earlier, existing cultures work to maintain existing cultures. As was seen in Fig. 2.1, an organization's culture will evolve, but unless there is a significant external influence, this evolution will be very slow. The most common external influences that facilitate the shaping of a Genesis Culture are

1. A crisis

2. A pending crisis

3. A new direction

A crisis is the ideal motivator for creating a Genesis Culture. It is commonplace during a crisis for the impossible to be accomplished. We all have seen a six-week job be taken care of in one day, in time of crisis. In time of crisis, it is expected that rules, habits, procedures, standards, and norms will be put to the side. It is, in fact, the style of some leaders who are not faced with a crisis to create a crisis. This can work for a while, but after a time the crisis leader will be treated like the boy who cried wolf. Therefore it is not recommended that leaders create crises. If a crisis truly exists, then the Genesis Leader's job is to shine a light on it, and use this book as a guide to making his or her organization a Genesis Enterprise. If a crisis doesn't exist, the Genesis Leader doesn't want to create a crisis, but it's certainly acceptable to identify, research, and document a pending crisis. There is no question that in today's dynamic business environment there are pending crises for all organizations. Of course the pending crisis must be valid and believable, and then the Genesis Leader's job is to document the pending crisis, to shine a light on the pending crisis, and to use this book as a guide to become a Genesis Enterprise.

The third external influence that facilitates the shaping of a Genesis Culture is when a Genesis Leader defines a new path, a new direction for an organization. In this case, the Genesis Leader must wipe the slate clean and begin anew. If too many of the cultural manifestations of the past are allowed to remain, the organization may not see the new direction as being truly a new direction, but rather as the continuation of an old one. Once the Genesis Leader has truly made the case for the new direction, it is his or her job to shine a light on this new direction, to create a sense of urgency, and to use this book as a guide to become a Genesis Enterprise.

JACK WELCH: A GENESIS LEADER

In 1981, Jack Welch became the CEO of General Electric. GE did not have a crisis. GE was profitable, had a very strong balance sheet, and to most of the organization was doing just fine. However, Welch was concerned with the slow-moving GE bureaucracy, slow growth, a lack of innovation, and the fact that GE was a non-global business. Welch didn't have a crisis, but he certainly had a *pending* crisis. He didn't wait. He went into action. What did he do? According to *Fortune,* Welch pursued a three-stage revolution:

Stage 1   Awakening: Documenting the pending crisis, and shining a light it.

Stage 2   Envisioning: Everyone in the GE organization understands the pending crisis, and is positioned to be a transformer.

Stage 3   Re-architecting: the transformation process.

Although the words are different, this book sets forth a proven process for awakening/envisioning/re-architecting. GE, today, is one of the most successful organizations in the world. What a Genesis Leader!

2.4   Conclusion

Culture is the foundation upon which organizations are built. A Genesis Leader will fail if the culture within which he/she is working does not embrace peak-to-peak performance. Therefore the first task of a Genesis Leader is to shape the organization's culture.

The culture of an organization evolves with the organization. A Genesis Leader must understand that an organization's existing culture will work to maintain the existing culture. To transform an organization, a Genesis Leader must understand that the culture first must be transformed.

Although we cannot define a Genesis Culture, we know that the following are characteristics of Genesis Cultures:

- Growth, not control
- Vision, not analysis
- Progressiveness, not slow decision making
- Continuous progression of peak-to-peak performance, not optimization
- Learning, not authoritarian bureaucracy

In addition, we know that Genesis Cultures readily accept change and exhibit an attitude of dynamic consistency.

A Genesis Culture may be adopted as a result of a crisis, a pending crisis, or a new direction. A Genesis Leader should shine a light on the need for transformation, then move swiftly (with this book as a guide) to become a Genesis Enterprise.

References

Iacocca, L. and W. Novak, *Iacocca: An Autobiography*. New York, Bantam Books, 1984.

Kotter, J. P., *A Force for Change: How Leadership Differs from Management*, New York, The Free Press, 1990.

Kotter, J. P. and J. L. Heshett, *Corporate Culture and Performance*, New York, The Free Press, 1992.

Kouzes, J. M. and B. Z. Posner, *The Leadership Challenge*, San Francisco, Jossey-Bass Publishers, 1991.

Ott, J. S., *The Organizational Culture Perspective*, Pacific Grove, California, Brooks/Cole Publishing Company, 1989.

Ticky, N. M., "Revolutionize Your Company," *Fortune*, December 13, 1993.

Tompkins, J. A., *Winning Manufacturing: The How-to Book of Successful Manufacturing*, Norcross, Georgia, IIE, 1989.

——, "Dinosaurs and Crocodiles: How-to Grow Your Business," *Network for Material Handling*, November 1992.

Westbrook, J. D., "Organizational Culture and Its Relationship to TQM," *Industrial Management*, January–February, 1993.

3
Leaders
Define Direction

The most important role of leadership is defining a company's vision and aligning the people in the company behind this vision. Consider the following quotations in support of this position:

> The leader's job is to create a vision. ROBERT SWIGGETT
> Chairman, Kollmorgen Corporation

> Action without vision is stumbling in the dark, and vision without action is poverty-stricken poetry. WARREN BENNIS
> Author, *On Becoming a Leader*

> There is no more powerful engine driving an organization toward excellence and long-range success than an attractive, worthwhile, and achievable vision of the future, widely shared. BURT NANUS
> Author, *Visionary Leadership*

> Vision is the beginning point for leading the journey. Vision focuses. Vision inspires. Without a vision, people perish. Vision is our alarm clock in the morning, our caffeine in the evening. Vision touches the heart. It becomes the criterion against which all behavior is measured. Vision becomes the glasses that tightly focus all of our sights and actions on that which we want to be tomorrow—not what we were yesterday or what we are today. The focus on vision disciplines us to think strategically. The vision is the framework for leading the journey.
> JAMES BELASCO and RALPH STAYER
> Authors, *Flight of the Buffalo*

> Without question, communicating the vision, and the atmosphere around the vision, has been, and is continuing to be, by far, the toughest job we face. JACK WELCH
> Chairman, General Electric

The first dictionary definition of a "leader" describes a primary shoot of a plant, the main artery through which the organism lives and thrives. In much the same way, organizations prosper or die as a result of their leaders' ability to embody and communicate the company's vision.

DONALD PHILLIPS
Author, *Lincoln on Leadership*

Many leaders have personal visions that never get translated into shared visions that galvanize an organization.... What has been lacking is a discipline for translating individual vision into a shared vision.

PETER SENGE
Author, *The Fifth Discipline*

No matter what it is called—personal agenda, purpose, legacy, dream, goal, or vision—the intent is the same. Leaders must be forward-looking and have a clear sense of the direction that they want their organization to take.

JAMES KOUZES AND BARRY POSNER
Authors, *The Leadership Challenge*

Vision without action is merely a dream. Action without vision just passes time. Vision with action can change the world.   JOEL BARKER
President, Infinity Limited, Inc.

In spite of this evidence in support of leadership's role in defining a vision and aligning people with this vision, there appears to be some debate. Consider the following quotations:

Take "this vision thing" for instance. Leaders are responsible to craft a vision. Leaders are responsible to implement that vision. Leaders are responsible for empowering their people to use the vision. That paradigm of leader responsibility for other people's performance, given today's circumstances, guarantees organizational failure.

JAMES BELASCO and RALPH STAYER
Authors, *Flight of the Buffalo*

Being a visionary is trivial.   WILLIAM GATES
Chairman, Microsoft Corp.

Vision may not exactly be dead in corporate America, but a surprising number of chief executive officers are casting aside their crystal balls to concentrate on the nuts-and-bolts of running their businesses in these leaner times.   DOUGLAS LAVIN
Reporter, *The Wall Street Journal*

Internally, we don't use the word vision.... This is a business of fundamentals. There isn't any magic.   ROBERT EATON
Chairman, Chrysler Corp.

One of the more ubiquitous forms of office decor these days is a suitably framed—and generally obtuse—vision statement. It always purports to speak to the driving sense of purpose underlying the organization. It's depressingly easy to point out that most of these statements are anything but visionary. In fact, if you picked 20 employees at random and asked them to recite the thing from memory, let alone make one up from scratch, chances are they wouldn't come anywhere near the happy horror hanging on the wall in your company lobby.

DICK SCHAAF
Author, *Pursuing Total Quality*

A lot of companies see this as a quick fix. These organizations use vision as a public relations tool, not as something to change the fundamental culture.   JAMES SHAFFER

Vice President, Towers Perrin

Although there appears to be a debate between the "visionaries" and the "nuts-and-bolts leaders," there really is no debate. What exists is a lack of understanding, a poor use of terminology, and many companies which have proven that if the vision thing is done poorly, there will be little positive benefit. This chapter will prove that, in fact, the most important role of leadership is to define direction.

WHICH IS IT?

In July of 1993, the new Chairman of IBM, Louis Gerstner, was quoted on the front page of *The Wall Street Journal* as saying, "The last thing IBM needs now is a vision." The cover story of the November 15, 1993 *Fortune* magazine proclaimed "Gerstner's New Vision for IBM." Well, which is it? In January of 1994, in an article on vision in *The Wall Street Journal,* an IBM spokesman explained:

> What Lou Gerstner was saying was that a 25- or 30-word sentence is simplistic and not realistic and not his first priority. But since then, Mr. Gerstner has distributed to employees a list of "IBM Principles" consisting of eight to eighteen words each. The principles pledge "a minimum of bureaucracy" and sensitivity to staff and others. And the spokesman says Mr. Gerstner does plan to articulate an explicit "vision" for the company some time in 1994.

The question remains: Which is it?

In 1982, in Tom Peters' book *In Search of Excellence,* there is no mention of the importance of vision. In his 1988 book, *Thriving on Chaos,* a company's vision is presented as being "essential" for directing the initiative and energy of front-line employees. Then in his 1992 book, *Liberation Management,* in a portion of the book entitled "The Vision and Values Trap," he sets the record straight when he says "All good ideas eventually get oversold. The importance of a corporate vision and values is no exception" and then concludes, "Values? Visions? Can't live without 'em....Can't live with 'em either." So...which *is* it?

3.1 What Is This "Vision Thing"?

The apparent "vision thing" debate is not a debate, but the result of combining doubletalk and doublethink. This is unfortunate, for we all already understand vision, have had personal experience of forming and pursuing a vision, and know the power of a vision. Think back to your childhood. What were your goals, your aspirations? You could daydream about those aspirations for hours, day after day. They couldn't be put down in a sentence or two, there were too many different elements to them. That's why it was so easy to lose yourself in your visualizations, to play make-believe and actually see yourself as achieving your aspirations. Those aspirations had a powerful impact on your life and functioned as a model of your future success. It is such aspirations that people refer to as "the Vision Thing." In this book, these aspirations, this "Vision Thing," is referred to as the Model of Success. It is the lack of understanding of the Model of Success that has resulted in the apparent vision debate.

To understand the fallacy of a one- or two-sentence Model of Success, one must consider what is expected to result from having a clear Model of Success. In a study done by Kouzes and Posner which asked people to explain when they performed at their best, it was found that when a Model of Success was effectively communicated, the result was significantly higher levels of job satisfaction, commitment, loyalty, esprit de corps, clarity about organizational values, pride in the organization, organizational productivity, and encouragement to be productive. Obviously, this can't be achieved just with a few sentences. Nanus believes that by presenting such a Model of Success

1. People will be committed and energized
2. Workers' lives will be made more meaningful
3. A standard of excellence will be established
4. The present will be bridged with the future

Further, Nanus believes that a powerful and transforming Model of Success has seven special properties:

1. It is appropriate for the organization and for the times.
2. It sets standards of excellence and reflects high ideals.
3. It clarifies purpose and direction.
4. It inspires enthusiasm and encourages commitment.
5. It is well articulated and easily understood.
6. It reflects the uniqueness of the organization.
7. It is ambitious.

So, if a Model of Success isn't just a few sentences, what is it? That's a question I found I couldn't easily answer. I didn't know how to define a Model of Success. To begin to shed some light on this issue, I read about Ford, Edison, Goodyear, Watson, Toyota, Kroc, Walton, and many others. The question constantly in my mind was, "What is it that these great leaders gave their organizations?" What was their Model of Success, which they communicated to their staff to obtain alignment and success? After much study, it became clear to me that what these great leaders did for their organizations was to answer the following five Model of Success questions:

1. Where are we headed?
2. How will we get there?
3. What is the science of our business?
4. What values shall be practiced?
5. How will we measure success?

Therefore, to define an organization's Model of Success, the following five elements must be defined:

1. *Vision:* A description of where you are headed.
2. *Mission:* How to accomplish the Vision.
3. *Requirements of Success:* The science of your business.
4. *Guiding Principles:* The values we practice as we pursue our Vision.
5. *Evidence of Success:* Measurable results that will demonstrate when our organization is moving toward its Vision.

A useful communications tool for illustrating the first four of those elements is presented in Fig. 3.1*a–e*. (Note that the Evidence of Success typically is not included on the bull's-eye, as different organizational elements may have different Evidences of Success.)

3.2 Understanding the Elements of the Model of Success

The first two elements of the Model of Success are intimately linked. Often these two elements are referred to as The Vision/Mission Set. The vision and mission are closely linked, as the vision addresses the *where* and the mission the *how*. The vision is a *goal* and the mission is a *strategy*. The word *vision* involves the "seeing" of the future. John Madden writes in his book, *Hey, Wait a Minute: I Wrote a Book,* about a conversation he had

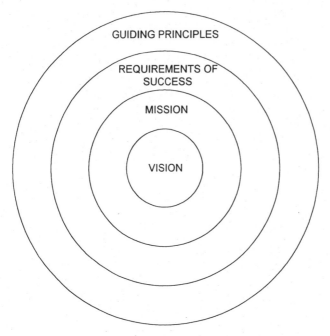

Figure 3.1a. Bull's-eye format

with Vince Lombardi about seeing the future and coaching. Lombardi said:

> The best coaches know what the end result looks like, whether it's an offensive play, a defensive play, a defensive coverage, or just some area of the organization. If you don't know what the end result is supposed to look like, you can't get there. All teams basically do the same thing. We all have drafts, we all have training camps, we all have practices. But the bad coaches don't know what the hell they want. The good coaches do.

In the same vein, I recall reading in a sports magazine that Larry Bird and Wayne Gretzky were described as follows:

> The difference between Larry [Wayne] and all the other players is that most players go to where the ball [puck] is, whereas Larry [Wayne] goes to where the ball [puck] is going to be. They actually see a play develop before it happens.

Leaders must work back from what they see in the future to the present. If, instead, leaders attempt to project from the present to the future, they will never reach their destination. You reach the future by focusing on where you are headed and not by looking at where you have been. In fact,

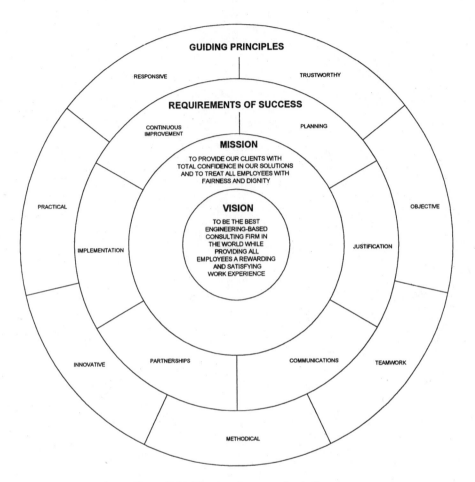

Figure 3.1b. Tompkins Associates, Inc. bull's-eye

a vision should be stated such that the present is described as a past condition of the future, not as a future condition of the past. As a mental picture of the future, visions should be expressions of optimism, hope, excellence, ideals, and breakthrough possibilities for the company of tomorrow. Each company vision must be unique, and appropriate only for that particular company.

The mission portion of the Vision/Mission Set presents the strategy that the company should follow as it pursues its vision. For example, the visions of both Tiffany's and Wal-Mart include total customer satisfaction. The methods, the strategies employed to achieve this vision, however, are very different. Tiffany's wishes to pamper, gratify, and entertain, whereas Wal-Mart wishes to provide friendly and fast service at the best price. The

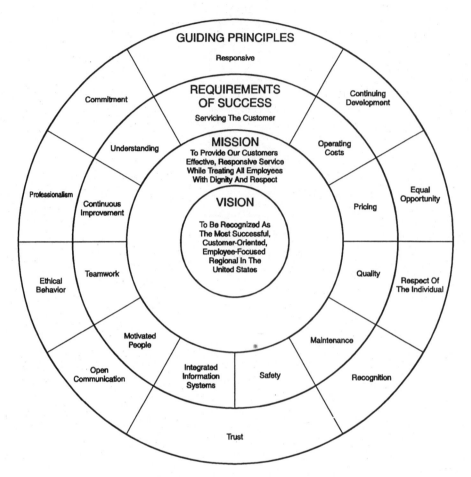

Figure 3.1c. Trucking firm bull's-eye

mission defines the strategic thrust of the company (Rolls-Royce or Chevrolet) and serves as a focal-point expression of the company's operating principles (McDonald's standardization versus Burger King's have it your way). The mission should be helpful to everyone in the company in providing guidance on how to respond to various day-to-day circumstances. For example at Tompkins Associates, Inc., where our mission is "to provide our clients with total confidence in our solutions and to treat all employees with fairness and dignity," I respond to all of the following questions with the question "What would give our clients the greatest confidence?"

Should we fax the report or send it overnight?

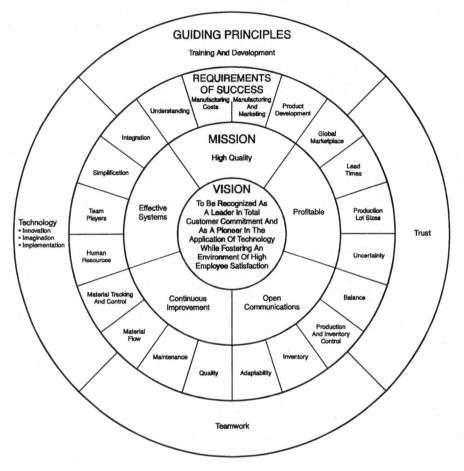

Figure 3.1*d.* Job shop bull's-eye

Do we invoice the client so that the invoice arrives on the due date, or so that it is mailed on the due date?

Should we have our logo or the client's logo on the bid specification?

Should we hand out the materials for the meeting before or after the presentation?

Should we stay at hotel X or hotel Y?

Who should attend a project update meeting?

Etc.

In this way, the mission becomes the organization's operating policy, in that it describes how it will be doing business.

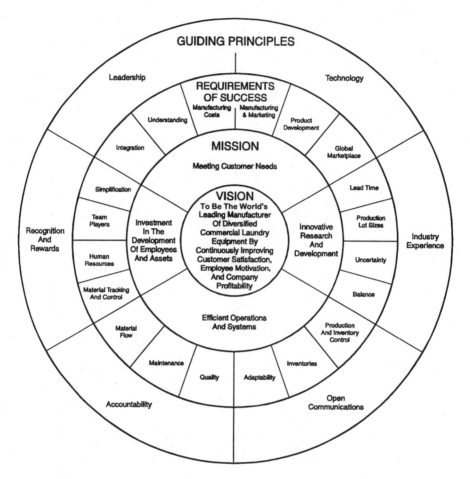

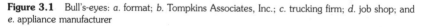

e. Appliance manufacturer bull's-eye

Figure 3.1   Bull's-eyes: *a.* format; *b.* Tompkins Associates, Inc.; *c.* trucking firm; *d.* job shop; and *e.* appliance manufacturer

---

DOES VISION ELECT PRESIDENTS?

George Bush was aware of the comments that said he had a problem with "this vision thing," but he was unable to step up to the problem. In fact, it is reported that he didn't want to hear about "the V word." The criticism followed Bush before he was President,

He does not have a clear, crisp, describable ideal for the country,

while he was President,

> Never has the lack of vision in Washington been more obvious. Ronald Reagan ran for President to do, George Bush to serve. Ronald Reagan knew where he wanted to move America; George Bush is unconceived about where America ends up.

and when he was defeated for reelection:

> Did the lack of vision defeat Bush? It certainly contributed to his loss. After the Gulf War, he seemed to be what *Newsweek* called him in its post-election analysis: "a man without a mission." Since he failed to articulate and communicate what he stood for, the electorate threw him over for a candidate who did. Bill Clinton convinced voters of at least one thing: the status quo will change.

The third element of the Model of Success answers these three questions:

1. What is the science of our business?
2. What are the rules of our game?
3. What are the paradigms in which we believe?

All of those questions are answered by an organization's statement of its Requirements of Success. It is absolutely critical that everyone in an organization have a clear understanding of the Requirements of Success. This means that, although what appears in the bull's-eye is a single word or a short phrase, there should exist, and be widely shared, an explanation of each Requirement of Success. Unlike the other four elements of the Model of Success, the Requirements of Success are not unique for each company. In fact, in the two industries where Tompkins Associates, Inc., practices most, manufacturing and warehousing, we have established and widely disseminated the Requirements of Success. In the manufacturing area, these Requirements of Success were the topic of the best-selling *Winning Manufacturing* book, the videotape *Manufacturing: Making a Difference,* and several articles, speeches, and seminars. The 20 manufacturing Requirements of Success, as defined fully in the book *Winning Manufacturing,* are

1. *Manufacturing costs* Manufacturing costs must be significantly reduced.
2. *Manufacturing and marketing* Manufacturing and marketing must become integrated and function as a team.
3. *Product development* Product development must become an integrated, iterative process.

4. *Global marketplace*   All manufacturing decisions must be made within the context of an integrated global strategy.

5. *Lead time*   Significant reductions in lead times must occur.

6. *Production lot sizes*   Production lot sizes and setup times must be minimized.

7. *Uncertainty*   All uncertainty must be minimized; discipline must be increased.

8. *Balance*   All manufacturing operations must be balanced.

9. *Production and inventory control*   The production and inventory control system must be straightforward and transparent.

10. *Inventories*   Drastic reductions in inventory must occur.

11. *Adaptability*   Manufacturing facilities, operations, and personnel must become more adaptable.

12. *Quality*   Product quality, vendor quality, and information quality must improve.

13. *Maintenance*   Manufacturing process failures must be minimized.

14. *Material flow*   Material flow must be efficient.

15. *Material tracking and control*   Material tracking and control systems must be upgraded.

16. *Human resources*   Every manager must be dedicated to creating an environment in which every employee is motivated and happy.

17. *Team players*   Everyone associated with manufacturing must work together as a team.

18. *Simplification*   All of manufacturing must be simplified.

19. *Integration*   All organizations and operations must be integrated.

20. *Understanding*   Manufacturing management must understand *Winning Manufacturing*.

In the warehousing area, these Requirements of Success were the topic of the videotape, *Warehouse Strategies,* as well as of several articles, speeches, and seminars. The 20 warehousing Requirements of Success are

1. *Professionalism*   Warehousing will be viewed as a critical step in the material flow cycle, not as a necessary evil.

2. *Customer awareness*   Successful warehouse operations will have a high regard for the customer, will know the customer's requirements, and will consistently meet those requirements.

3. *Measurement*   Warehouse standards will be established; performance will be measured against those standards, and timely actions will be taken to overcome any deviations.

4. *Operations planning* Systems and procedures will be put into effect that allow the warehouse manager to proactively plan the operations, as opposed to reactively respond to external circumstances.

5. *Centralization* The trend will be toward larger, centralized warehouses rather than smaller, decentralized warehouses.

6. *Public warehouses* More intelligent use of public warehouses, to handle peaks, will be commonplace.

7. *Pace* The reduction of lead times, shorter product lives, and increased inventory turnover will result in an increase in the pace of the warehouse.

8. *Variety* More different SKUs and more special customer requirements will result in an increase in the variety of tasks performed in the warehouse.

9. *Flexibility* Due to the increase in warehouse pace and variety, all warehouse systems, equipment, and people will be more flexible.

10. *Uncertainty* All uncertainty will be minimized; discipline will be increased.

11. *Integration* Activities within the warehouse (receive, store, pick, and ship) will be better integrated, and the warehouse will be better integrated within the overall material flow cycle.

12. *Inventory accuracy* Cycle counting will be used to manage inventory accuracy, and accuracy above 95 percent will be the norm.

13. *Space utilization* Space will be more efficiently and effectively utilized.

14. *Housekeeping* Quality housekeeping will be a priority and a source of employee pride.

15. *Order picking* The criticality of order picking will be understood, and procedures and layouts will be designed to maximize picking efficiency and effectiveness.

16. *Human resources* Every manager will be dedicated to creating an environment in which every employee is motivated and happy.

17. *Team players* Vendors, customers, and a wide variety of functions within the warehouse will be integrated into a single service-providing activity.

18. *Automation* Advanced technologies will be more easily embraced and economically justified.

19. *Automatic identification* Automatic identification systems will become the norm for data acquisition and transfer.

20. *Control systems* Real-time, paperless control systems will be used throughout all modern warehouses.

The explanations of the Requirements of Success, from the Tompkins Associates, Inc., Model of Success, are as follows:

Planning   Tompkins shall provide their clients with strategic, contingency, and detail planning of the highest quality. Internally, Vision, Goals, and Action Plans shall be used to lead and manage the affairs of our business.

Justification   Valid justification is the core of all of our recommendations. Through this technology, Tompkins shall assure wise expenditures of clients' funds. We shall apply the same vigor to the expenditure of our own funds as we do to our clients' funds.

Communication   High-quality written and oral communications are a prerequisite to a successful consulting relationship. Quality communications is mandatory for successful planning, justification, and implementation. We believe in open and honest communications. Every effort shall be made to assure employee involvement and participation through positive, ongoing communications.

Partnership   We are dedicated to the success and growth of our clients. We treat our clients' business with the same dedication and intensity as our own. We are dedicated to the success of our employees. We shall provide an environment in which all employees can enjoy working, develop professionally, be compensated fairly, and participate in company management.

Implementation   We are focused on improving our clients' businesses by implementing quality recommendations and implementing policies and practices that will result in happy employees, exceptional growth, and increasing profits.

Continuous   Continuous improvement is the key to success in today's
Improvement   dynamic world. We will address all client and company opportunities as being not only opportunities for improvement today, but a baseline upon which to build continuous improvement.

The Requirements of Success for an organization will most often be a compilation, revision, and/or adaptation of the requirements presented in this chapter. The Requirements of Success should present the basic truths of the company, in the language of the company, so that all company employees gain a knowledge of the underpinnings of their company.

The fourth element of the Model of Success, The Guiding Principles, presents a set of standards about how people should be treated. These values are deep-seated, pervasive standards that influence all that we do: our judgments, opinions, attitudes, desires, fears, responses, and actions. These values give direction to the company and define the spirit within which things in the company should be accomplished. As an individual contemplates different actions, he/she consciously and subconsciously compares the alternatives to these values so as to define the right path. Genesis Enterprises always demonstrate a set of Guiding Principles that present a strong commitment to the people in the company. This commitment flows from values such as trust, fairness, openness, teamwork, development, continuous improvement, respect, participation, pride, dignity, security, accountability, responsiveness. Because of the company's commitment to its people, the employees, in turn, become committed to the company.

The last element of an organization's Model of Success defines how an organization will measure its movement toward its Vision. There is power to be gained by defining an organization's measures. And *what* gets measured becomes important. An old leadership principle that I learned many years ago is still relevant today: "If you want it, measure it. If you can't measure it, forget it." Measurement is a tool that leadership should use to help focus their organization on the bull's-eye. Measurement is what provides leaders with the information they need to provide organizational feedback, and it is this feedback which serves as the basis for celebration or correction. Without the feedback of these measurements, you don't know if you should redouble your efforts, or change your course.

Unfortunately, in many companies, the traditional accounting-based measures used in the 1980s are still being used today. Accounting-based

---

WE *WILL* MEET GOAL THIS MONTH!

At one of the largest beverage manufacturers in the world, achieving corporate accounting-based goals is the norm. Jumping through hoops, internal chaos, and performance suicide is also the norm. The practice of playing ridiculous games with order placement, and when these orders are shipped, is widely known within the company. Orders are scheduled to be shipped throughout the month.

However, as the month ends, orders are stolen from next month so as to satisfy monthly financial goals. This action causes the next month to be short, so orders are stolen from even further out to meet goal. As obvious a problem as this is, the vicious cycle continues. Customers are dissatisfied by receiving unwanted product, production scheduling constantly juggles orders and production, packaging efficiencies and schedule attainment drops, inventories rise, obsolete product is prevalent, and employee morale spirals downward.

Why? Because the company has decided, "We *will* meet goal this month, no matter how much it costs!"

measures drive employees to play games so as to achieve cost and revenue targets, without regard to the actual performance of the business. Accounting-based measures attempt to control how a business functions. This is a real problem, as routine accounting data does not reflect customer satisfaction, market share, quality, employee development, company growth, and hundreds of other measures that are more important than whether Region X has achieved its budget. Effective Evidence of Success must be real-time, meaningful to an organization entity, based upon the metric of the organizational entity being measured, and accurate. Without effective Evidence of Success, an organization won't know if it's moving closer to its Vision or not.

To define the Evidence of Success, one must define the organizational entity to be measured, the perspective of measurement, and the performance to be measured. The definition of the organizational entity could be very broad (a whole company or division) or very narrow (a department or a team). The perspective of measurement could be the employees, owners (stockholders), partners (customers and suppliers), community/environment, and/or operations. The performance to be measured could be

1. Effectiveness

2. Efficiency

3. Quality

4. Relationships

5. Innovation

6. Financial

What should exist, then, is a series of Evidence of Success for each organizational entity. Figure 3.2 shows an example of the Evidence of Success for the organizational entity of the Distribution Improvement Team. Figure 3.3 provides an example of the Evidence of Success for the organizational entity of the Manufacturing Team.

3.3   How to Develop a Model of Success for Your Organization

I have seen organizations spend months, and in one case more than a year, developing a Vision. I have heard of companies who have spent over $100,000 to develop a Vision. This is ridiculous. The total duration from the beginning of the development of a Model of Success to its completion should be less than a month, and should require less than 15 hours of time

Performance to Be Measured

Perspective	Effectiveness	Efficiency	Quality	Relationships	Innovation	Financial
Employees	a. 75% of staff pass competency test b. 80% of all employees are on improvement teams	a. 2 hours/order b. 98% of standard	a. Eliminate order checking b. Achieve 99% rating on corporate packaging audit	a. No lost-time accidents b. Reduce turnover 50%	a. 10 Continuous Improvement Teams b. Implement industrial performance tracking	a. $.11 of distribution per dollar shipped b. Pay no detention penalties
Owners	a. 99.2% inventory accuracy b. Allocate 50% of budget savings to continuous improvement	a. Increase throughput 20% b. Respond to all suggestions in 2 weeks	a. Receive Ford A1 rating b. Obtain ISO 9000 certification	a. Participate in local community groups b. Conduct 2 outside tours per quarter	a. Increase market share by 5% b. Establish 10 strategic partnerships	a. 6 inventory turns b. Greater than 25% ROI on all investments
Customers	a. .1% returns b. .4% stockouts	a. Respond to all inquiries in 1 hour or less b. Turn around customer trucks in less than 2 hours	a. .1% errors b. .2% damage in shipment	a. .05% complaints b. 12-hour order lead time	a. Visit 10% of all customers each quarter b. Retain 95% of house accounts	a. Reduce freight claims to .2% of dollars shipped b. No price increases for next year
Community/ Environment	a. .2% damage ratio b. Receive good citizen award from city	a. Respond to all Department of Labor inquiries in 2 weeks or less b. Implement checklists to simplify environmental audits	a. No product contamination b. Eliminate need to distribute products	a. Spend 50% of all disposable dollars with handicapped industries b. Zero lawsuits	a. Recycle all corrugated b. Eliminate birds from warehouse	a. Pay no government fines b. Make product recycling a break-even proposition
Operations	a. 98% fill rate b. 99% delivery on time	a. 82% space utilization b. 95% equipment utilization	a. 99.4% housekeeping rating b. Receive 95 rating on customer service cards	a. Report performance to corporate monthly b. Monthly meetings with MIS on distribution priorities	a. Reduce fork truck damage 70% b. Reduce number of trucking firms used to 6	a. Below budget on expenses b. Energy consumption reduced 10% annually

Figure 3.2 Evidence of Success for the Distribution Improvement Team

| | Performance to Be Measured | | | | | |
Perspective	Effectiveness	Efficiency	Quality	Relationships	Innovation	Financial
Employees	a. Implement gainsharing b. 80% of all employees on improvement teams	a. Run plant at 92% efficiency b. .5% absenteeism	a. Achieve 98% first-pass quality b. Implement shop floor SPQ	a. No lost-time accidents b. Reduce turnover 50%	a. Create functional teams for 80% of all production departments b. Cross-train 80% of staff in 3 functions	a. Increase total compensation 5% per year b. Reduce rework costs by 10%
Owners	a. Grow volume 10% per year b. Allocate 50% of budget savings to continuous improvement	a. Reduce new-product development time to 4 months b. Respond to all suggestions in 2 weeks	a. Be ISO 9000 certified b. Eliminate reinspection prior to ship	a. Reduce warranty claims 10% b. Reduce number of suppliers by 20%	a. Increase market share by 5% b. Conform to ADA by end of third quarter	a. Exceed profit goal b. Greater than 25% ROI on all investments
Customers	a. Achieve 95% on on-time delivery b. Ship 98% of all orders complete	a. Bid all specials in 48 hours or less b. All service calls returned within 1 hour	a. .1% customer returns b. .1% damage in shipment	a. 80% of sales to be repeat orders b. .05% complaints	a. Visit 10% of all customers each quarter b. Conduct 4 customer-training seminars per year	a. No price increases for next year b. Eliminate charges for freight on back orders
Suppliers	a. Do not change 4-week schedule b. Always order in carton quantities	a. EDI 80% of all purchase orders b. Pay all invoices on time	a. Conduct quarterly improvement meetings with top 10 suppliers b. Eliminate incoming inspection	a. Share six-month production plans b. Return all special packaging	a. Visit 10% of all suppliers each quarter b. Participate in new-product design on design for manufacture	a. Increase sales by 10% b. Pay for tooling up-front, and not as portion of part cost
Community/ Environment	a. Receive good citizen award from city b. No layoffs	a. Respond to all Department of Labor inquiries in 2 weeks or less b. Improve discharge water purity to 98%	a. Receive no EPA citations b. Install back-lot drainage system	a. Zero lawsuits b. Spend 50% of all disposable dollars with handicapped industries	a. Obtain three patents per year b. Support local athletic leagues	a. Pay no government fines b. Become self-insured
Operations	a. Forecast error less than 10% b. Implement TPM	a. Reduce cycle time to 48 hours b. Reduce schedule variation to 2%	a. 99.4% housekeeping rating b. Reduce SWCP 10%	a. Report performance to corporate monthly b. Work with product engineering from time of product conception	a. Reduce WIP 10% b. Reduce waste by 10%	a. Below budget on expenses b. Increase ROA 10%

Figure 3.3 Evidence of Success for the Manufacturing Team

from each of your organization's top leaders. The six-step process for developing a Model of Success for your organization is as follows:

Step 1. Decide who should participate in the Model of Success development.

Step 2. Conduct a Model of Success orientation meeting.

Step 3. Complete and compile a Model of Success development questionnaire.

Step 4. Conduct a Model of Success development retreat.

Step 5. Complete and compile a Model of Success refinement questionnaire.

Step 6. Conduct a Model of Success wrap-up meeting.

The first step to take in developing your organization's Model of Success is to decide which of the top leaders in your organization should participate in the development of the Model of Success. This group will be known as The Steering Team, as they will be defining the overall direction of the firm. The Steering Team should consist of the top person and the top person's staff. All significant organizational elements should be represented. The number of people on The Steering Team should be somewhere between 5 and 10. The Steering Team members must have a clear understanding of your business, both good insight and foresight, and a healthy imagination.

The second step in developing your organization's Model of Success is to hold a Model of Success orientation meeting. This two- to three-hour session should be conducted by an outside facilitator, and should cover all the material presented in this chapter and in Chapter 6. This orientation will define

1. The elements of a Model of Success

2. Why your organization needs a Model of Success

3. The use of the Model of Success to drive the process of team-based peak-to-peak performance

The third step is a questionnaire that should be given to the Steering Team a couple of days after the orientation. The Steering Team should be asked to complete this questionnaire and return it to the outside facilitator a few days later. The purposes of this questionnaire are

1. To confirm an understanding of the Model of Success

2. To stimulate the Steering Team to begin to think about their organization's Model of Success

Appendix A contains a Model of Success Development Questionnaire. The first 10 questions of this questionnaire confirm the Steering Team's understanding of the elements of a Model of Success. The second 10 questions stimulate the Steering Team to begin to think about their Model of Success. The outside facilitator should compile the results of the Model of Success development questionnaire. This information will be used in the fourth step.

The fourth step is the Model of Success development retreat. This half-day session for the Steering Team and the outside facilitator should be conducted in an environment where there will be no interruptions. The retreat should begin with the outside facilitator summarizing the results of the first 10 questions of the Model of Success development questionnaire, and ensuring that the Steering Team has an understanding of the elements of the Model of Success. After this brief review, the outside facilitator should work with the Steering Team to define the first draft of the Vision, Mission, Requirements of Success, and Guiding Principles. Appendix A reveals the process of facilitating this retreat.

The fifth step is a questionnaire that should be given to the Steering Team a couple of days after the Model of Success development retreat. The Steering Team should be asked to complete the questionnaire and return it to the outside facilitator a few days later. The twin purposes of this questionnaire are to

1. Refine the Vision, Mission, Requirements of Success, and Guiding Principles

2. Obtain a first draft of the Evidence of Success

Appendix A contains a Model of Success Refinement Questionnaire. The results of this questionnaire should be compiled for the Model of Success wrap-up meeting.

The last step in the definition of the Model of Success is the Model of Success wrap-up meeting. The outside facilitator should present recommendations on all five elements of the Model of Success, based upon the input received on the Model of Success Refinement Questionnaire. This meeting should address all concerns presented in the refinement questionnaire, then try to answer the following questions about the Model of Success:

1. Is it doable? Will our employees understand it, and will they believe it can be accomplished? Is it realistic? Does it uniquely represent our company's future?

2. Is it authentic? Is it an honest attempt at defining a direction, or just a marketing slogan or a public relations gimmick?

3. Is it compelling? Can employees get excited about it? Is it future-oriented, challenging, and aggressive? Is it too ambitious, or not ambitious enough? Will it inspire enthusiasm and encourage commitment?

4. Is it personally enriching? Will employees understand how their lives will be improved by pursuing it? Will employees understand how they will grow while pursuing it? Does it set forth a standard of excellence and reflect high ideals?

5. Is it focused, yet flexible? Will it provide the framework for the unification of all employees' efforts, without restricting the company from pursuing breakthrough opportunities and possibilities?

The result of the Model of Success wrap-up meeting should be unanimous acceptance by the Steering Team of the organization's Model of Success.

THE POWER OF THE VISION/MISSION SET

The power of a Vision/Mission set could easily be demonstrated by recounting the Sam Walton Wal-Mart/Sam's success. But some might say that this was a one-time success story due more to Mr. Walton than to the alignment of the Wal-Mart organization with the leadership-developed Model of Success. Well then, let's look at other success stories that are today borrowing a page from Mr. Walton's book.

Consider the following somewhat generic Vision/Mission set:

Vision:

> To profitably grow our retail chain of specialty superstores by exceeding the expectations of all stockholders, employees, and customers.

Mission:

1. To close traditional stores and replace them with superstores several times larger, with several times more stock-keeping units.

2. To make shopping in our superstores fun.

3. To implement Every Day Low Prices (EDLP).

4. To sell name-brand and premium-quality merchandise, supplied not by competing vendors but by partners.

5. To maintain the convenience and service of our traditional stores.

6. To finance expansion by selling shares of common stock.

7. To expand both the number of stores as well as the sales per store.

8. To expand into new geographical markets, as well as to increase penetration in existing geographical markets.

9. To reduce operating costs through volume purchasing and distribution excellence.

10. To attract and retain highly motivated, well-qualified employees, by providing excellent training, development, incentives, and growth opportunities.

Interestingly, the above Vision/Mission set is not the Vision/Mission set of any one specific retail organization, but rather an approximation of that to be found in several chains, such as

Petco—pet-related products

Pet Depot—pet-related products

Home Depot—home improvement products

HQ—home improvement products

Lowes—home improvement products

Bed, Bath & Beyond—linen and bath products

Linens 'n Things—linen and bath products

Pacific Linens—linen and bath products

Tops—consumer electronics

Staples—office supply

Office Depot—office supply

Baby Superstore—baby items

Gymboree—children's clothing

Yet the success of all of these firms in growth, profit, and consumer satisfaction has been unbelievable. It is clear, in all of these cases, that the definition by leadership of the Vision/Mission set played a key role in the success of their organizations.

3.4 Achieving Model of Success Alignment

A Model of Success can act as a guiding beacon for an organization, as it achieves great performance. A Model of Success can also be a reminder of a company's hypocrisy, and just another failed attempt to bring about change. The difference between the Genesis Enterprise that achieves peak-to-peak performance and the traditional organization that flounders is not the quality of the Model of Success, but the quality of the organization's *alignment* with the Model of Success. There is no greater challenge for the Genesis Leader than to obtain organizational alignment with the Model of Success.

In today's complex organizations, no one is autonomous. All organizational elements and all employees arc interdependent. This interdependence can be an asset if everyone is focused and working together, but a major liability if people are *not* focused and *not* working together. In fact, in an organization that is aligned, change brings about improvements, progress, success, and a sense of accomplishment. By contrast, in an organization that is not aligned, change brings about confusion, demoralization, failure, and a sense of futility. The interdependence of an organization requires that, as change occurs, every person in the organization be aligned. The Model of Success must be instilled into every person in the company, in much the same way as the DNA code infuses the architecture of the whole into every cell of your body. Having every person focused on the Model of Success allows an interdependent organization to work as a powerful whole rather than many conflicting elements. This alignment is powerful, for people will be pulling in the same direction, and pulling harder because they have confidence they are pulling in the right direction.

For a leader to define an organization's direction, he/she must define the Model of Success and then obtain his company's alignment with it. Figure 3.4 reveals the process of pursuing Model of Success alignment. As may be seen, the first step in achieving alignment involves communication. This is not a one-time meeting where the Model of Success is explained, but rather a pervasive, consistent, ongoing, persistent, neverending focus on the Model of Success. Leaders must accept as their primary task, as a cause, a crusade, their role as champion of the Model of Success. Leaders must promote and, yes, even *sell* the Model of Success. Leaders must breathe life into the Model of Success and make it exciting and fun. As will be seen in Part 3, the process of team-based continuous peak-to-peak performance provides a vehicle for the Genesis Leader to communicate the Model of Success to everyone in his/her organization and to provide total focus on the Model of Success.

As may be seen in Fig. 3.4, the communication of the Model of Success will open up three different paths. The most difficult path results in a resistance to the Model of Success. These people, the resisters, don't believe the Model of Success is relevant; due to their lack of trust in Leadership, they cannot be made to understand the Model of Success. The resisters won't comply with the Model of Success, cannot be made to understand it, and will resist all attempts to force compliance with it. Depending upon the historical culture of an organization, the resisters will be anywhere from 15 to 50 percent of the total workforce. These resisters are not bad people. They should not be fired. In fact, they often have valid reasons for their lack of trust in leadership. But persistent communication will not result in the resister becoming aligned. The resisters can be won over only through demonstrated performance. To win over the resisters, the Genesis Leader must not only talk the talk, but walk the walk.

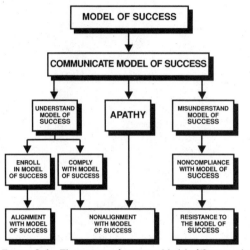

Figure 3.4   The process of pursuing Model of Success alignment

The center path in the process of pursuing Model of Success alignment results is not a *resistance* to the Model of Success but a *nonalignment* with the Model of Success. These nonaligners could be suffering from apathy, which precludes an understanding of the Model of Success, or could be people who understand the Model of Success and comply with it as they don't want to lose their job, but aren't really aligned with it. Typically, the nonaligners have been exposed to many programs (Employee Involvement, Organizational Development, Quality Circles, Total Quality Management, etc.) and look on the Model of Success as being just another passing fad. Depending upon the level of MBF (Management by Fad) in your company, the nonaligners could represent from 20 to 50 percent of your employees. Over time these people have grown numb to management's new programs, and a good bit of time will be required to win them over. But persistent communication *will* awaken these nonaligners, and bring them into alignment with the Model of Success.

The desired path, and the ultimate path, for everyone in a Genesis Enterprise, is the path from communicating to understanding to enrolling to alignment. But remember that alignment is much more than understanding. Alignment is the adoption of the organization's Model of Success as one's own. Alignment means an employee's acceptance of responsibility for making the Model of Success a reality. Alignment cannot be *forced* upon anyone. And alignment doesn't occur to a *group* of people. It is an individual commitment to enroll in the Model of Success. Alignment with the Model of Success will result from the Genesis Leader's persistent, focused communications, and from demonstrated commitment to the Model of Success on the part of all employees. An *aligned* organization will be a *focused* organization, one in which a high level of commitment and loyalty will result in the unified pull of all energies to create peak-to-peak performance. An aligned organization will be a Genesis Enterprise.

3.5   Model of Success Renewal

An organization's Model of Success should seldom change, but should routinely be subject to review. At least annually, the Steering Team should review the Model of Success and compare the company's progress, the changes in the environment and the marketplace, and any shifts in assumptions or paradigms, and either reaffirm or renew the Model of Success. The renewal of the Model of Success typically will involve a change just in a word or a phrase. Only rarely will the renewal be major. On the other hand, if drastic shifts have occurred, there is no better way to send a signal to an organization than to make a significant change in the Model of Success. As the Steering Team reaffirms or renews the Model of Success, this should be communicated throughout the organization, so as to maintain the focus on and the alignment with the Model of Success.

3.6   Conclusion

The most important task of a Genesis Leader is to define an organization's Model of Success and then obtain alignment with it. Remember, the five elements of a Model of Success are

1. *Vision:* A description of where you are headed.
2. *Mission:* How to accomplish the Vision.
3. *Requirements of Success:* The science of your business.
4. *Guiding Principles:* The values we practice as we pursue our Vision.
5. *Evidence of Success:* Measurable results that will demonstrate when our organization is moving toward its Vision.

An organization's Model of Success should be defined by the organization's top leaders. These top leaders shall be known as the Steering Team, and they will not only develop the Model of Success but also be the champions in the pursuit of organizational alignment. To achieve alignment, the Steering Team must present a pervasive, consistent, ongoing, persistent, neverending focus on the Model of Success. This focus must be demonstrated through both communications and actions. The Steering

Team must not only talk the talk, but walk the walk. Lastly, the Steering Team must routinely reaffirm or renew the Model of Success, to ensure that it remains fresh. On the organization's path to becoming a Genesis Enterprise, the Genesis Leader must first transform the organizational culture (Chap. 2), then define the organization's direction (Chap. 3).

References

Belasco, J. A. and R. C. Stayler, *Flight of the Buffalo,* Warner Books, New York, 1993.

Brown, T., "Is Your Company Vision-Driven?" *Industry Week,* May 18, 1992.

Dessler, G., *Winning Commitment,* McGraw-Hill, New York, 1993.

Farnham, A., "State Your Values, Hold the Hot Air," *Fortune,* April 19, 1993.

Fuchsberg, G., "Visionary Missions Becomes Its Own Mission," *The Wall Street Journal,* January 7, 1994.

Johnson, H. T., *Relevance Regained,* The Free Press, New York, 1992.

Kaplan, R. S. and D. P. Norton, "Putting the Balance Scorecard to Work," *Harvard Business Review,* September–October, 1993.

Kirkpatrick, D., "Gerstner's New Vision for IBM," *Fortune,* November 15, 1993.

Kotter, J. P., *A Force for Change,* The Free Press, New York, 1990.

——, *The Leadership Factor,* The Free Press, New York, 1988.

Kouzes, J. M. and B. Z. Posner, *The Leadership Challenge,* Jossey-Bass Publishers, San Francisco, 1991.

Lavin, D., "Robert Eaton Thinks 'Vision' Is Overrated and He's Not Alone," *The Wall Street Journal,* October 4, 1993.

Lee, C., "The Vision Thing," *Training,* February, 1993.

Madden, J. with D. Anderson, *Hey, Wait a Minute, I Wrote a Book,* New York, Ballantine, 1985.

Nanus, B., *Visionary Leadership,* Jossey-Bass Publishers, San Francisco, 1992.

Nelton, S., "Put Your Purpose in Writing," *Nation's Business,* February, 1994.

Neusch, D. R. and A. F. Siebenaler, *The High Performance Enterprise,* Oliver Wight Publications, Essex Junction, Vermont, 1993.

Peters, T., *Liberation Management,* Alfred A. Knopf, New York, 1992.

——, *Thriving on Chaos,* Alfred A. Knopf, New York, 1992.

Pritchett, P. and R. Pound, *High-Velocity Culture Change,* Pritchett Publishing Company, Dallas, Texas, 1993.

Quigley, J. V., *Vision: How Leaders Develop It, Share It, and Sustain It,* McGraw-Hill, New York, 1993.

Sayles, L. R., *The Working Leader,* The Free Press, New York, 1993.

Schaaf, D., "A Vision for All Seasons," *Training,* December 1993.

Tompkins, J. A., "Team-Based Continuous Improvement," *Material Handling Engineering,* March 1993.

Wick, C. W. and L. S. Leon, *The Learning Edge,* McGraw-Hill, New York, 1993.

4

Leaders
Define Motivation

The primary task of a Genesis Leader is to assure peak-to-peak performance. To do this, his or her organization's culture must be based upon peak-to-peak performance, and everyone in the organization must be aligned with the its Model of Success. In this regard, a leader may be thought of as a tour director. The culture is the jungle through which the tour will pass. The Model of Success is the path through the jungle. The alignment with the Model of Success gets all of the stragglers and wanderers onto the path. The remaining task for the tour director is to keep all of his/her people motivated, so that they can overcome all obstacles along their path.

A Genesis Enterprise is characterized by people who exhibit a high level of energy, intensity, passion, and determination to continuously aspire in the direction of their vision. It is not surprising, therefore, that Genesis Leaders exhibit those same characteristics and aspirations, but even more so. Genesis Leaders exhibit these characteristics through:

1. How they think

2. How they communicate

3. How they work

4. How they treat people

4.1 Leaders Define Motivation
by How They Think

As was stated in Chap. 2, "Leadership is not a set of personality traits." However, all Genesis Leaders do have six key mental qualities. These qual-

51

ities represent the essence of a Genesis Leader. These qualities define the inner person of the Genesis Leader, whereas the other three Genesis Leader characteristics (how they communicate, work, and treat people) define his/her outer person. Genesis Leaders will define motivation by exhibiting the following six key mental qualities:

4.1.1   Integrity

Integrity means that the Genesis Leader tells the truth and lives the truth. Integrity means that the Genesis Leader deals in a straightforward, sincere fashion with people and situations, and that they do not compromise on that which they believe to be true. Integrity demands the specification of ethical behavior and the elimination of Mickey Mouse rules and regulations that induce game-playing and cheating. Integrity demands honesty in all dealings, where honesty is measured by the consistency between word and deed, by leaders doing what they say they will do. It is out of this honesty that trust and loyalty spring. Obviously, no organization can be successful without a trust in its leadership, and a loyalty from subordinate to leader and from leader to subordinate. The similarity of the following two quotations from two Genesis Leaders keynotes the essentialness of integrity to a Genesis Leader. First, Margaret Thatcher, the dynamic leader of England, having served more than 11 years as Prime Minister, speaks about her upbringing:

> We were Methodists, and Methodist means *method*. We were taught what was right and wrong in considerable detail. There were certain things you just didn't do, and that was that.

Second, here's Senator Sam J. Ervin, Jr., who, during the nationally televised Watergate hearings, gave clear evidence of his loyalty to the truth when he said

> What's right is right, and what's wrong is wrong, and you can't compromise with integrity.

4.1.2   Credibility

Credibility is related to integrity but is more than integrity, in that it includes being *accountable,* being *genuine,* and being *open.* Credibility is one of the most difficult qualities for a Genesis Leader to maintain, as there exists today a cynicism, a skepticism, and a level of scrutiny that often results in the wrongful loss of credibility. Unfortunately, credibility is earned minute by minute, hour by hour, day by day, and week by week, but may be lost in a moment by a carelessly worded remark, a slip of the tongue, a careless act, or even just the *appearance* of one of these minor transgressions. If Genesis Leaders aren't genuine and open with themselves, they will lose credibility. But even if they *are* genuine and open with themselves, they still stand a real risk of wrongfully losing credibility.

The Genesis Leader's path to credibility, then, is not an easy one. The Genesis Leader must take care in all his/her interactions that they are clear, precise, accurate, and cannot be misunderstood or misrepresented. It is only after a tremendous level of credibility has been established between two people that one's guard may be relaxed. Even then, the Genesis Leader who wishes to maintain a high level of credibility must work hard at being responsive, accountable, sensitive, sincere, and genuine.

4.1.3   Enthusiasm

For many years, managers have been taught that their feelings and emotions should not be brought to work. This is wrong. In fact, as Ralph Waldo Emerson has said, "Nothing great was ever accomplished without enthusiasm." Peak-to-peak performance is most easily achieved when people's feelings and emotions are unleashed. Many managers have believed that any outward display of emotion indicated weakness, that to be enthusiastic about something was to demonstrate a lack of maturity and a loss of professionalism. We have all been in companies where *smiling* was frowned upon! This is all so unfortunate.

The truth is, if you want people to get excited about something, you must first get excited yourself. Genesis Leaders must be excited about, and demonstrate an enthusiasm for, the future. Genesis Leaders must exhibit an energy, have a bounce in their step about what is happening and what will be happening. Have you ever noticed that they call the persons doing cheers on the sidelines cheer*leaders* and not cheer-*managers*? Genesis Leaders must be cheerleaders for their organizations, not in a plastic or phony, but a sincere, genuine manner. It is a fact that enthusiasm is contagious. Even for oneself. If you desire to be enthusiastic, you must simply act enthusiastic. It is as basic as planting apple seeds to get apple trees, planting acorns to get great oaks, and planting enthusiasm to get enthusiasm. Genesis Leaders will be inspirational, and from this inspiration will flow an enthusiasm for peak-to-peak performance, the Model of Success, and the next hour, day, week, month, year, decade...

4.1.4   Optimism

From enthusiasm comes optimism. Optimism is an incurable condition of people who focus on success. Optimism comes from an inner confidence in what you are doing and the course you are pursuing. It is this confidence in oneself that keeps an optimist from getting hung up by minor set-backs, and forever focusing on the path forward. Perhaps the best way to illustrate the power of optimism is to look at a situation in which there was a loss of optimism.

Think about Karl Wallenda, one of the greatest tightrope aerialists of all time. Shortly after Wallenda fell to his death during a performance in Puerto Rico, his wife described Wallenda's loss of confidence. She recalled: "All Karl thought about for three straight months, prior to the Puerto Rico performance, was *falling*. It was the first time he'd ever thought about that, and it seemed to me that he put all his energies into *not falling* rather than walking the tightrope." The great Wallenda simply lost his confidence, and he fell to his death because of it.

By way of contrast, consider Lee Trevino, one of the all-time money winners on both the PGA and the PGA Seniors tours. Prior to a U.S. Open, Lee had consulted a doctor to seek relief from the flu. The doctor told Lee not to play, as his flu might get worse. His reply was, "Might get better … might even win!" He came in second.

Another time, Lee was asked how he thought he would do in the Canadian Open. He responded, "Are you kidding, that's my tournament!" The next week he won his third Canadian Open in four years. Lee Trevino is an optimist. Genesis Leaders are optimists.

4.1.5 Urgency

Genesis Leaders cannot change the past. They can impact the future, but only based upon what they do *today*. What they do *now*! The Genesis Leaders must act with a sense of urgency, so that their organizations will act with a sense of urgency. Genesis Leaders must help their people to understand that peak-to-peak performance is continuous, neverending, and that the time for action is *now*. Genesis Leaders must help their people to get prepared for the next battle, rather than savor the win from the last battle. A Genesis Enterprise truly understands the challenge of time compression, and demonstrates true hustle.

An approach which I adopted more than ten years ago is a salutation I use on most memos. This salutation has now been embossed on a plaque, a T-shirt, and a hat, and has become a sort of personal trademark for me. This salutation summarizes my desire for *action*, my encouragement to do *something*, and my belief that anything that is worth doing is worth doing *now*. My trademark is "Go, Go, Go!"

4.1.6 Determination

Genesis Leaders demonstrate determination by courageously stepping forward; by facing doubts, and uncertainties; by accepting both risk and responsibility; and by moving forward. Genesis Leaders *act.* Genesis Leaders have the courage to pioneer, to step out into the unknown. This is not to say that they never have doubts, uncertainties, or concerns. To the contrary, Genesis Leaders do have these feelings, but they put up a good front. They do not burden others with their concerns, and they push themselves out of the comfort zone and keep on keeping on. The Genesis Leader is brave enough to fail, and has created a work environment where it is okay to fail.

Genesis Leaders are *driven,* and *results-oriented.* They are known for their "take-charge" personality, and because of their determination they are both self-starting and change-oriented. The determination of Genesis Leaders makes them both friendly and firm. Leaders who are too firm bulldoze their people, and don't inspire them to great performance. Leaders who are too friendly do not challenge their people, so that little is accomplished. Genesis Leaders must balance the friendly aspects of being pleasant, personable, likable, and interesting, with the firm aspects of competitiveness, aggressiveness, and high expectations. It is this balance that creates the determination required to pull an organization onward to peak-to-peak performance.

4.2   Leaders Define Motivation by How They Communicate

In Sec. 3.4, communication is spoken of as being the first step toward achieving an organization's alignment with the Model of Success. This communication is not a one-time meeting in which the Model of Success is explained, but a pervasive, consistent, ongoing, persistent, neverending focus on the Model of Success. In fact, Genesis Leaders don't think of communication as something *they* do, but view it from the receiver's end. That is to say, for them communication is not the generation of a message, but rather the *receipt* of the message by the receiver. It is only after a receiver has gotten a message (either correctly or incorrectly) that a message can be said to have been communicated (either good or bad communication, respectively). This receiver-oriented definition of communication, therefore, includes not only what a leader may say, but everything that has an impact on how the receiver may receive the message. While discussing the fact that communication consists of a great deal more than what leaders say, Zaremba, in his book *Management in a New Key: Communication in the Modern Organization,* presents the following examples of organizational communication problems:

1. The inappropriate use of print communication. An overabundance of memos, bulletins, and internal letters.

2. A hyperactive grapevine. An unusually active "informal" communication network, which spreads inaccurate information.

3. A defensive communication climate, which intimidates employees and keeps them from expressing themselves without fear of retribution.

4. A credibility problem within the organization that makes employees wonder about the veracity of the messages they do receive.

5. A weak interoffice mail system that results in correspondence being received late.

6. An ineffective method of notifying employees of how well or how poorly they are performing. This often results in fear, mistrust, and sometimes anger toward the organization.

7. Employee perceptions that no one is concerned with their suggestions and input. This results in employee reluctance to communicate to management regarding important issues that management needs to know about.

8. A heavy and inappropriate reliance on committees and meetings. Meetings are not the panacea for all organizational problems, and sometimes create communication problems because of overuse and/or meeting mismanagement.

9. Informational briefings/presentations that are neither informational nor brief, and are perceived as time-wasters by subordinates.

Zaremba goes on to present the elements necessary for leaders to effectively communicate:

1. Use various methods of sending information in order to facilitate accurate receipt.

2. Cultivate and maintain viable networks that permit the flow of organizational information.

3. Cultivate a supportive organizational climate that is conducive to information-sending and -receiving.

4. Recognize the importance of nonverbal factors in determining communication success.

5. Be capable of making presentations consistent with specific organizational needs.

6. Be capable of interacting with employees on a comfortable, one-to-one level.

7. Intelligently participate in and manage conferences and meetings, consistent with specific organizational needs.

The overall view of communications, then, can be seen as a composite organizational effort and leader effort. In a Genesis Enterprise, the organizational effort will be handled by the Communication Team, whose role is fully described in Chap. 6. Therefore what needs to be discussed *here* is the communication role of the Genesis Leader.

Communication is not just what Genesis Leaders say. Communication also is what Genesis Leaders don't say, how they say what they say, and how they act in general. There is nothing more important to a Genesis Leader's communication ability than an ability to "walk in the other person's moccasins." Empathy is critical to quality communication, but empathy is not just feeling *for* another person, it is feeling *with*. My wife always laughs at me because when I watch a boxing match on television, I "bob and weave." When I watch the movie *Rocky*, it is as if I am in the ring. I feel the punches, I throw the punches, I feel the thrill of victory. This is empathy. It is truly being in the other person's shoes.

Being other person–focused is the key to being successful at receiver-oriented communication. This empathy requires the Genesis Leader to be open and sensitive to others, to realize that all people are unique, and that everyone has the potential to receive the same message differently. A Genesis Leader understands that it is possible for 20 people to hear the same presentation, and for there to be 20 different understandings of what was said. For this reason, a Genesis Leader must communicate in simple words, with conviction and certainty. The objective is to ensure that the receivers get the message the leader is sending. All chances for ambiguity must be eliminated. In this regard, consider Margaret Thatcher's speech to a group of business leaders, in which she stated:

> I came to office with one deliberate intent: to change Britain from a dependent to a self-reliant society; from a give-it-to-me to a do-it-yourself nation; a get-up-and-go instead of sit-back-and-wait Britain.

What clarity, what empathy, what effective communication! You may agree or disagree with Mrs. Thatcher, but clearly you received her message, you understood her.

In a similar way, independent of one's political views, the greatest communicator of the twentieth century was Ronald Reagan. President Reagan has the special talent of helping the listener to receive the president's message by telling stories. The late Speaker of the United States House of Representatives Tip O'Neil said of President Reagan:

> He's always got a disarming story. I don't know where he gets them, but he's always got them. He calls up: "Tip, you and I are political enemies only until six o'clock. It's four o'clock, now, can we pretend it's six o'clock?" How can you dislike a guy like that?

President Reagan had a mastery of his voice and your feelings. He could make his voice quiver and sometimes even break while telling an emotional story, with the result of a tear forming in the corner of the eye of the thousands of people listening. In addition to his ability to tell a story, Reagan was a master at the simplicity of communication. In the book

Superachievers, Ronald Reagan's mastery of simple communications was presented as follows:

1. *Simple language.*   He stays clear of complex words or phrases. His audience does not need a dictionary to understand his thoughts. Like a good sales representative, he knows that life is too short to waste time with complicated language.

2. *Simple mini-memos.*   As governor of California, he developed a highly successful system for handing down decisions. After hearing out his subordinate's detailed recommendations, he would draft a concise one-page, four-paragraph summary of a problem with clear recommendations on how to solve it. His style initially drew criticism but got better results than that of the previous governor.

3. *Simple persuasion techniques.*   In his presidential campaign, he scored points with highly persuasive statements such as, "Recession is when your neighbor loses his job. Depression is when you lose yours. And recovery is when Jimmy Carter loses his." Some of his simple but profound one-lines have created tremendous impact. For example, "How can we love our country and not love our countrymen?" Or, concerning the Panama Canal, "We built it, we paid for it, it's ours, and we are going to keep it."

4. *Simple life philosophies.*   Son of a shoe salesman, Ronald Reagan exudes an air of simple virtues. Haynes Johnson, a *Washington Post* writer, commented in a front-page editorial, "He lacks the arrogance or insecurities of some presidents. The presidency does not own him: he's not uptight in the job. Those who have known him for years say he has changed hardly at all since entering the White House."

In conjunction with this simplicity of communication, consider the following conversation between President Woodrow Wilson and a reporter:

REPORTER: How long would it take you to prepare for a simple ten-minute speech?

WILSON: Two weeks.

REPORTER: How long for an hour speech?

WILSON: One week.

REPORTER: How long for a two-hour speech?

WILSON: I'm ready now.

In addition to effective communication being clear and simple, effective communication requires an endless repeating of the same message. In fact, an indication that a Genesis Leader's message is beginning to be received is when the Genesis Leader is tired of presenting the same message. He or she must continue to present the same message over and over again via several different communication mediums. It is this frequent, consistent repetition that will result in the message being received.

ABRAHAM LINCOLN: GENESIS COMMUNICATOR SUPREME

Although President Reagan was the greatest communicator of the twentieth century, probably the greatest communicator of all time was Abraham Lincoln. In the book, *Lincoln on Leadership,* the author Donald Phillips dedicates the last unit of the book to communications. The three chapters in this unit are

1. Master the Art of Public Speaking
2. Influence People Through Conversation and Story Telling
3. Preach a Vision and Continually Reaffirm It

Included in "The Lincoln Principles" at the end of these chapters are the following thoughts, which are certainly critical for today's Genesis Leader:

- Be your organization's best speaker.
- Use humor and body language.
- Prepare thoroughly for every presentation.
- A speech is not done, nor an article complete, until it has been delivered/published.
- Reinforce what you say in writing.
- Be pleasant in all dealings.
- Speak in simple terms. Be friendly.
- A good laugh is good for you.
- A good story will often influence people and soften disagreements.
- Loyalty flows from private conversations.
- Everywhere you go, at every conceivable opportunity, reaffirm, reassert, and remind everyone of your vision.
- Do not force your vision on others; persuade them to your way of thinking.
- Live your vision in your own personal leadership style.
- When implementing change, call on the past, relate to the present, and use both the past and present as a link to the future.

Certainly, Abraham Lincoln was a Genesis Leader.

4.3   Leaders Define Motivation
by How They Work

Genesis Leaders have the same work ethic as other professionals who excel. It matters not if you are talking about a basketball player, a movie star, a politician, a salesperson, or whatever. This work ethic feeds upon itself and results in the peak performers doing better and better until, for some reason, there is a change in the work ethic. Reasons for change in the work ethic could be an injury, loss of a loved one, contentment, burnout, failure to grow, etc. Figure 4.1 illustrates the model of how peak performers evolve.

A difficult issue for some people, with respect to Fig. 4.1, is attempting to define the starting point. In fact, what exists for many people in Fig. 4.1 is a kind of chicken-and-egg problem. You see, people enjoy their work because they get good results, but they get good results because they work hard and smart, but they work hard and smart because they have high energy, but they have high energy because they enjoy their work. So these people cannot really begin by enjoying their work, because enjoying their work is a result of the good results obtained by their working hard and smart. So they must start by working hard and smart. But they can't really start working hard and smart, because working hard and smart is a result of the high energy that results from enjoying their work….Get the picture?

Nevertheless, for other people there is a normal starting point. The normal starting point for these people is high energy. This high energy comes

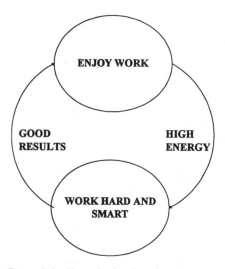

Figure 4.1   The cycle of peak performance

not from an enjoyment of one's work but rather from being a self-starting, motivated person. It is from this externally generated high energy that people begin to work hard and smart, and from which the cycle begins. Thus, for a Genesis Leader, the high energy required to jump-start the Peak Performance Cycle comes not from his or her work, but rather from how he/she *thinks* (Sec. 4.1). To build upon how the Genesis Leader thinks, the two topics that must be addressed are the topics Work Hard and Smart, and Enjoy Work.

4.3.1 Work Hard and Smart

If all that one does is work hard, one will not be successful. Interestingly, if all that one does is work smart, one also will not be successful. Mike Ditka, the Hall of Fame football player and Super Bowl champion coach of the Chicago Bears, puts it like this:

> Know the value and definition of hard work. You work hard not just by sweating, but by applying your physical and mental capacities to perform a job thoroughly and properly. Brains always beat brawn. Work hard, but work smart.

Working hard and smart is important for a Genesis Leader because it sets the pace for an organization. The Genesis Leader is a role model for the organization, and as such sets the standard for both hard work and smart work. Genesis Leaders need to be aware of the fact that people are watching them. Where Genesis Leaders choose to spend their time will become the organization's focus. Because Genesis Leaders are the role models, they must maintain a high level of visibility and consistent communications (Sec. 4.2).

Visibility is critical, as being a Genesis Leader is not a spectator sport. Genesis Leaders do not sit in the stands and watch. But neither do Genesis Leaders go down onto the field of play, substituting for their players. The Genesis Leader is the coach. The Genesis Leader teaches the game, sets the pace, and calls the plays. The Genesis Leader is highly visible, as it is his/her lead that is followed.

This is one of the key attributes of the tremendous success of Wal-Mart. A key portion of Sam Walton's success was his tremendous visibility throughout his organization. Of course, the Genesis Leader knows that being on the front line isn't easy. Being highly visible also makes you highly vulnerable. Genesis Leaders accept this challenge as they know they must be out in front, dealing with real problems where the organization can watch them perform, and learn from them. Guidelines for the Genesis Leader—ones that may differ from what has traditionally been thought of as hard and smart working tips—include the following:

1. *Make the right decisions.* Making the right decision means making the right *decision* at the right *time,* and communicating the decision to the right *people.* Always focus on all *three* rights to make right decisions.

2. *Don't become a time-management nut.* Defining one's day in 30-minute increments, and working only on high-priority items, is an obsolete concept of hard work. Interruptions are an important part of a Genesis Leader's day, and provide the leader with the much-needed picture of what is really happening.

3. *Pay attention to the right details.* One can get buried in details. Deal only in those details relevant to the decision you need to make. Delegate to others the handling of those details relevant to their level of decision making.

4. *Go the extra mile.* Exceed expectation in everything you do. Really listen to people. Ask questions and questions. Be friendly, be real. Provide higher quality and greater responsiveness than people thought possible. Impress everyone you touch. Treat every interaction and assignment as if your credibility were at stake—it probably is.

5. *Think loose.* Realize that change is inevitable. Accept change. Anticipate change. Don't let change control you. Know when to cut your losses. Don't be afraid to admit a mistake; learn from it and move on.

4.3.2 Enjoy Work

There is a philosophy that says, "If people are happy, they will do their job better." I don't agree with this philosophy. In fact, I believe the opposite to be true: When people do their job well, they are happy. Happiness flows from the satisfaction and the recognition of a job well done. There are four things that a Genesis Leader should do to personally enjoy work, and to ensure employee satisfaction and recognition of a job well done:

1. *Grow as a person.* The topic of organizational learning will be covered in Chap. 8. The issue here is not organizational learning but individual learning, individual growth. The growth of the Genesis Leader is important to an organization for three reasons. First, he/she derives personal satisfaction from learning, and thus enjoys work. Second, the Genesis Leader's learning sets the pace for the rest of the organization's learning, and, third, when the Genesis Leader recognizes this, it ignites new ideas and thinking throughout the organization. A Genesis Leader's learning may occur in any of the following areas:

   a. Enhanced understanding of a company's operations, industry, competition and/or customers.

b. Learning from a mistake that was made.

c. Enhanced understanding of the future of his/her business by learning about other companies or industries and/or the economy in general.

d. Increased awareness and/or skills in dealing with people, communicating, growing, measuring, etc.

e. Enhanced education in some business-related or business-unrelated aspect. This could include anything from reading a good book to taking a college course in marketing to learning how to fly an airplane.

2. *Be a realist.*   The Genesis Leader must be realistic. Realism is a form of intellectual honesty, and demands that we see things as they truly are. Realism on the part of the Genesis Leader is critical to employees achieving satisfaction, as they don't have to deal with or attempt to overcome mental games or self-delusion on the part of the leader. The Genesis Leader, by being realistic, not only sets realistic expectations that can be met, but also encourages others to be realistic. This will result in job satisfaction both for the Genesis Leader and for the organization.

3. *Be natural.*   There can be little job satisfaction or enjoyment when the leader is a phony. Genesis Leaders must be themselves, be accessible, and be predictable. For this to occur, the Genesis Leader must get to know his/her employees and the employees must get to know the Genesis Leader. A Genesis Leader will gain commitment and respect from his/her employees by spending time with them, listening to them, showing compassion, caring.

4. *Have fun.*   A Genesis Leader must be committed to having fun. To do this, the Genesis Leader must do two things: first, be positive; second, don't be negative. To be positive one must:

a. *Celebrate success.*   Have a party. Don't be so serious. Loosen up. Buy pizza for the company. Clap.

b. *Say "thank you."*   Show genuine appreciation for the work people have done. Nothing is a substitute for sincere, public praise for a job well done.

c. *Laugh.*   Maintain your sense of humor. Find some humor in yourself and in your mistakes. Unleash the child within.

To not be negative, the Genesis Leader must learn to deal with

a. *Criticism.*   Leaders will be criticized and be the recipient of cheap shots. The Genesis Leader must understand that such slander comes with the territory.

b. *Disappointment.*   People will let you down. They will miss deadlines, perform poorly, and fail to communicate.

The Genesis Leader will determine the relevance of criticism and disappointment. There is no question that these will occur, the only question is how will the Genesis Leader respond? If the he or she responds to criticism with a counterattack, or responds to disappointment with an outburst, there is little likelihood that people will enjoy their work.

There are two courses of action that a Genesis Leader can take to respond to criticism. The first is to write a letter responding to the criticism. This letter should totally set the record straight, should allow you to totally vent your anger—and should never be mailed. Throw this letter away after it is written and take no further action. Second, if the criticism will really have an impact on the performance of the organization, you need to respond. But don't respond to the criticism; instead, write a memo presenting the truth and explaining the facts of the situation. Present this memo in a positive manner via a "for your information" format.

Similarly, there are two courses of action a Genesis Leader can take to address a disappointment. The preferred approach is a chat. This chat should not focus on punishment but rather on gaining a better understanding of expectations, roadblocks, and barriers. The focus of the chat should be, "What can the Genesis Leader do to help the person meet future expectations?" If the chat hasn't been effective, the second course of action is a more formal interaction which, although it won't be an enjoyable discussion, shouldn't be personal and should focus not on the individual but rather on the individual's performance. In this discussion, a formal, time-phased path for corrective action should be established. Both courses of action dealing with disappointment should be ended on a positive note, with the anticipation of positive results in the future.

4.4 Leaders Define Motivation by How They Treat People

The Golden Rule states "Do unto others as you would have them do unto you." Another translation of Luke 6:31 says "Treat others as you want them to treat you." It would seem clear, then, that if Genesis Leaders treat people in the same way as they want people to treat them, all will be fine. However, it isn't that easy. Although most commonly interpreted that way, the Golden Rule doesn't say that you should treat others the same way you like to be treated. The Golden Rule says that since you want others to treat you like you like to be treated, you should treat others as *they* would like to be treated. Or more simply, treat others as they would like to be treated. This is the definition of how a Genesis Leader treats people; how they want to be treated.

Treating people how they want to be treated has something to do with compassion, politeness, courteousness, trust, dignity, respect, and fairness. Obviously, these topics could easily fill this entire book. Since our purpose isn't to produce a treatise on business manners, we will not address the many, many aspects of business etiquette and the many, many challenges of dealing with people. Instead, the following principles will serve as basic guidelines for a Genesis Leader treatment of people:

1. *Like yourself.* A Genesis Leader must have a positive self-image before he/she can have a positive image of others.

2. *Accept others.* Accept people as they are, not as you would like them to be. Accept differences in people, and love diversity.

3. *Respect others.* Every person is unique and no matter if friend or stranger, merits your appreciation, honor, and respect.

4. *Trust others.* Demonstrating your trust in other people not only makes those people trustworthy, it also encourages them to trust you.

5. *Think "we."* A Genesis Leader will not succeed if he/she thinks "I." Great performance is the result not of an "I" but a "we" mentality.

6. *Be real.* Genesis Leaders are real people and, like all people, have feelings, concerns, and interests. Genesis Leaders should socialize, participate in small talk, be seen, and be involved.

7. *Say "thank you."* Truly appreciate people helping you. A Genesis Leader will say thank you many, many times every day.

8. *Anger slowly, or not at all.* A Genesis Leader may or may not have a temper. However, if a Genesis Leader does have a temper, it will only very rarely be seen.

9. *Encourage others.* Know when to give someone a pat on the back and a pep talk. The Genesis Leader will be available when people need his/her support.

10. *Be a nice person.* Genesis Leaders are liked by many. They are gentle, kind, and considerate.

4.5 Conclusion

It is the Genesis Leader's job to assure motivation within an organization, so that the Genesis Enterprise can overcome the obstacles along its path. Genesis Leaders define motivation for their organizations through

1. How they think

2. How they communicate

3. How they work

4. How they treat people

The inner qualities of a Genesis Leader are defined by how the Genesis Leader thinks. The six mental qualities of the Genesis Leader that define how he or she thinks are

1. Integrity
2. Credibility
3. Enthusiasm
4. Optimism
5. Urgency
6. Determination

The outer qualities of the Genesis Leader that define motivation are how the Genesis Leader communicates, works, and treats people. To be a good communicator, the Genesis Leader must

1. Define communications from a receiver orientation.
2. Be aware that communications consist of much more than what leaders say.
3. Realize that effective communication requires considerable effort.
4. Realize that empathy is critical to quality communications.
5. Realize that quality communication requires clarity, simplicity, and the ability to tell stories.

The starting point for a Genesis Leader is high energy. Genesis Leaders have high energy because they are self-starters who are motivated to do well. This high energy feeds hard and smart work, which in turn nets good results. These good results contribute to Genesis Leaders enjoying their work, which contributes to their high energy. This self-perpetuating cycle allows Genesis Leaders to achieve peak-to-peak performance. Genesis Leaders work hard and smart by

1. Making the right decisions
2. Not becoming a time management nut
3. Paying attention to the right details
4. Going the extra mile
5. Thinking loose

The four keys to Genesis Leaders' enjoyment of work are

1. Personal growth
2. Realism

3. Naturalness

4. A sense of fun

Genesis Leaders define motivation by treating people how they want to be treated. This requires that they

1. Like themselves

2. Accept others

3. Respect others

4. Trust others

5. Think about "we"

6. Are real

7. Say "thank you"

8. Anger slowly or not at all

9. Encourage others

10. Are nice people

The primary task of the Genesis Leader is to assure peak-to-peak performance. This chapter has defined how the Genesis Leader defines the motivation for the organization, so as to pursue peak-to-peak performance.

References

"A Master Class in Radical Change," *Fortune,* December 13, 1993.

Belasco, J. A. and R. C. Stayer, *Flight of the Buffalo,* Warner Books, New York, 1993.

Bennis, W. and B. Nanus, *Leaders: The Strategies for Taking Change,* Harper and Row, New York, 1985.

Brown, T., "Joel Barker: New Thoughts on Paradigms," *Industry Week,* May 18, 1982.

Deutschman, A., "The CEO's Secret of Managing Time," *Fortune,* June 1, 1992.

Dock, J. D., "Managing Change: The Art of Balancing," *Harvard Business Review,* November–December 1993.

Falvey, J., "Selling to the Sales Force," *Sales and Marketing Management,* April 1992.

Fleschner, M. K., II, "Mike Ditka: Winning with Teamwork The Bear's Way," *Personal Selling Power,* April 1992.

Gschwandtner, G., "Margaret Thatcher Leads You to Success," *Personal Selling Power,* October 1993.

——, G., *Superachievers,* Prentice-Hall, New York, 1984.

——, "General Alexander Haig: A Four-Star Success Story," *Personal Selling Power,* April 1991.

Huey, J., "Sam Walton in His Own Words," *Fortune,* July 29, 1992.

Kotter, J. P., *A Force for Change,* The Free Press, New York, 1990.

Kouzes, J. M. and B. Z. Posner, *The Leadership Challenge,* Jossey-Bass, San Francisco, 1987.

Lebow, R. *A Journey into the Heroic Environment,* Prima Publishing, Rocklin, California, 1992.

Maynard, B., "Winning Organizations in the 90s," *TeleProfessional,* April 1993.

Neusch, D. R. and A. F. Siebenaler, *The High Performance Enterprise,* Oliver Wight Publications, Essex Junction, Vermont, 1993.

Phillips, D. J., *Lincoln on Leadership,* Warner Books, New York, 1992.

Tompkins, J. A., "Project Leadership," *Industrial Product-Bulletin,* January 1990.

——, "Team-Based Continuous Improvement: How to Make the Pace of Change Work for You and Your Company," *Material Handling Engineering,* February 1993.

——, *Winning Manufacturing: The How-to Book of Successful Manufacturing,* IIE, Norcross, Georgia, 1989.

Waitley, D., *10 Seeds of Greatness,* Fleming H. Revell Company, Old Tappan, New Jersey, 1983.

Wick, C. W. and L. S. Leon, *The Learning Edge,* McGraw-Hill, New York, 1993.

Zaremba, A. J., *Management in a New Key: Communication in the Modern Organization,* IIE, Norcross, Georgia, 1989.

5

Shifting from Management to Leadership

The science and practice of management is just a babe when compared to the history of leadership. Nevertheless, as organizational complexity has grown over the last 50 years, the focus of attention has been on management, not leadership. Although many have gotten into a management-versus-leadership battle, I will not fall prey to such a discussion here. The clear fact is, just as a good basketball team must have both a good offense and defense, so too must a good organization have both good management and good leadership. The problem, then, lies not in management versus leadership, but rather in the out-of-balance situation most organizations find themselves in today. Most of them have an abundance of management and a shortage of leadership. To create the required balance, a shift from management to leadership is required. Thus, this chapter is not a management-bashing chapter, but rather a chapter about *shifting*. To become a Genesis Enterprise, it is imperative that this management-to-leadership transformation occur. Therefore, the management discussion that follows is presented not to editorialize about management, but rather to illuminate the topic of leadership by exploring the shift from management.

To begin the exploration of the shift from management to leadership, and to understand why this shift is mandatory today, one only needs to reflect on how the words *management* and *leadership* are most often used. *Management* is most often used as a noun, and is defined as *the group of people who achieve orderly results by controlling schedules and budgets*. To the contrary, the word *leadership* is most often used as a verb, and refers to *the process of creating change to obtain results*. It is, then, by reflecting upon our present business climate that we may understand why this shift from management to leadership is needed today. In stable business times when businesses are evolving to the future, it is certainly appropriate for management to exert its controlling influence over an organization. To the contrary, in dynamic business times such as the present, it is absolutely critical that a shift to leadership occur, to bring about the required level of changes to adapt to the marketplace. There is no question that today the business climate is dynamic, and that what is needed is a shift from management to leadership.

RETHINK THIS...

Although many managers aren't willing to face the necessity for the shift to leadership, their action betrays their true understanding of this necessity. Think about this: What is the hottest topic in business circles today? What are people talking about? What are conferences being called? What is on the cover of all the business magazines?

Is the hottest topic controlling budgets? No, I think not. Is the hottest topic controlling schedules? No, that's not it. The hottest topic is *resomething*. What is resomething? Well, it is about creating change to obtain results. Think about the following:

Realign	Reform	Reshape
Rebirth	Refresh	Retrench
Rebuild	Reimagine	Restructure
Recondition	Reinvent	Rethink
Recreate	Remake	Retransform
Redesign	Renew	Revamp
Rediscover	Renewal	Revival
Reengineer	Reposition	Revolutionize

In fact, a sure bet to success in bookselling these days is to resomething. Why? Because management knows that in these dynamic times, we must create change to obtain results. They know we must redo management. Although they may have a difficult time facing reality, they know they must shift from management to leadership. Or is it a *re*shift from management to leadership...?

5.1 The Genesis Enterprise Requires Strong Management and Strong Leadership

The most common management-bashing theme of the last 10 years has been the short-term orientation of management. This has led many to the conclusion that we need to manage differently. To the contrary, management by its very nature has a short-term orientation. We don't need a new way to manage. What we need is a better balance between management and leadership. To understand the balance between management and leadership, it is useful to look at the following four possible combinations of weak and strong management and leadership:

Type 1. Weak management and weak leadership

Type 2. Strong management and weak leadership

Type 3. Weak management and strong leadership

Type 4. Strong management and strong leadership

A Type 1 organization, with weak management and weak leadership, is not long for this world. The organization will not know where they are (weak management) and will not know where they are going (weak leadership). There will be no focus on either the present or the future. In fact, there will be no focus at all, as people are simply going through the motions without any awareness of or concern about what is happening. These organizations are living *in* the past, *off* their past. They will continue to exist only as long as their past will allow. Left to their own, these firms will die a sad and lonely death. Other alternatives include a management and/or leadership transformation, or an acquisition.

An effective management transformation will result in a Type 2 organization, an effective leadership transformation in a Type 3 organization, and an effective management and leadership transformation in a Type 4 organization. Acquisitions have the full range of possibilities, from remaining a Type 1 organization and dying a sad and lonely death to being transformed into a Type 2, 3, or 4 organization. A Type 1 organization will either be transformed or it will die.

A Type 2 organization, with strong management and weak leadership, will have on hand an abundance of reports that document the organization's present performance. Unfortunately, there will be no focus or direction for the future. Risk will be minimized, control will be maximized, and decisions will be top-down and taken only after all alternatives have been analyzed and then a predictable path forward defined. Innovation will not occur, and changes in the marketplace will be viewed more as problems that need to be fixed rather than opportunities for growth and improvement. Type 2 organizations are the most common today, and it is these organizations that most need this book and that most need a shift from management to leadership to become a Genesis Enterprise.

In today's world of professional managers and MBAs, there are no large Type 3 organizations. The only Type 3 organizations found in business are small entrepreneurial companies. These Type 3 organizations, which have strong leadership but weak management, have a focus on the long term of their firm but little understanding of or focus on today's performance. A gambler mentality is prevalent, with little structure or assessment of risk. Decisions are made without a true understanding of the implications, and as growth occurs the organization spins out of control. Deadlines, promises, and budgets are not adhered to, and frustration and chaos loom. Type 3 organizations don't need a shift from management to leadership but rather must achieve the proper management/leadership balance by adding professional management to their organization. Type 3 organizations need to become Genesis Enterprises; Parts 1–6 of this book are applicable, but Part 2 should be read again with a focus on the idea that Managers Must Manage.

Type 4 organizations, which have both strong management and strong leadership, are the prototype of the Genesis Enterprise. It is the goal of this book to convert the Type 2 organizations to Type 4 organizations, by shifting from management to leadership. This shift will create a balance between strong management and strong leadership that will result in the organization achieving peak-to-peak performance.

The SUCCEED/FAIL, FAIL/SUCCEED cycle, explained in Chap. 1, may be viewed as a management/leadership cycle. Often when a new firm is created, it is created with an entrepreneurship that is strong on leadership but weak on management (Type 3). The founder realizes the firm's management shortcomings and brings in professional managers to run the company. The professional managers install budgets, policies, and procedures, and the company does very well.

However, as time progresses, the bureaucracy that once was needed to create order has begun to stifle innovation. The company loses its edge and its profitability, and upper management is fired. A new leader is brought in, who innovates and encourages change. New products are created that win in the marketplace, and the company expands. Unfortunately, insufficient management controls are in place, so mistakes are made.

The leader is dismissed, and professional managers are hired to regain control. Budgets, policies, and procedures are reinstalled, and now, with the new product line, success returns. The company does well. However, as time progresses, the bureaucracy that was needed to create order is now, once again, stifling innovation. The company again loses its edge, etc. This recurring cycle often exists because an organization doesn't grasp the need to balance management and leadership.

5.2 The Challenge of Shifting
from Management to Leadership

Professional managers have worked hard to become good managers. They have gone to school, held a variety of jobs, and read many books. They take great pride in being in charge, in being the person who makes decisions. The attitude often set forth is "The buck stops here." These managers enjoy the "burden" of management, and have tied their ego to their being the decision-maker, the problem-solver, and the top manager. The suggestion that these managers shift from management to leadership is not well received, for these managers enjoy and understand management but are uncertain about leadership.

The greatest challenge, then, to shifting from management to leadership in a firm, is that the managers don't want to be moved out of their comfort zone. They are comfortable being managers. This is so sad, because in most firms where we have strong management and weak leadership (Type 2), there exist more rewards for leadership than for management. We have more managers than we need, but because of the management comfort zone, many managers will shortchange themselves and their organization by continuing to manage and failing to lead. It is in these situations that managers need to listen to Pogo when he says, "We have met the enemy and he is us." It is the failure of these managers to shift to leadership that is restricting the growth and success of their organizations. This is the greatest challenge in creating a Genesis Enterprise. We must get management to shift to leadership, to create the balance of strong management and strong leadership.

5.3 Shifting: How Leaders
See Themselves

It was from the perspective of the managers and leaders that, at the beginning of this chapter, *management* was defined as a noun and *leadership* as a verb. Management is defined by who you *are*, whereas leadership is defined by what you *do*. A simple way to determine if a person is a manager or a leader is to ask what he/she does for a living. If you were to ask the head of a human resources department this question, a *manager* would respond by saying, "I am the Manager of Human Resources." If you asked this same question of the head of a human resources department who was a *leader*, the response you would get is "I work throughout the company to be sure we have the right people doing the right jobs with the right skills and training while being fairly compensated." You see, managers define their job by who they *are*, whereas leaders define their job by what they *do*.

Managers see themselves as the boss for whom people work. For this reason, managers think of themselves as being accountable. Conversely, leaders see themselves as working *for* their people, and therefore make their people accountable for their *own* actions. It is managers' short-term, narrow focus that keeps their eye on the bottom line. To the contrary, leaders have a broader, long-term focus that keeps their eye on the horizon. Managers like the role of manager, and leaders like the role of leader. Thus, for an organization to achieve the proper balance between management and leadership, individual managers must personally shift from management to leadership.

KEEPING HIS EYE ON THE HORIZON

What would you call a company that has a 75 percent market share in a fast-growing market but wants to increase market share? The same company has a 58 percent gross profit margin, with net earnings that make it the most profitable company of its size in the world. At the same time, the company doubles in size roughly every two years, and is basing its future on beating AT&T, IBM, Matsushita, Motorola, Philips, Sega, and Sony. What would you call such a company?

One label is "hyperaggressive," another is "greedy," another is "competitively paranoid." It matters not what label is used, what you are labeling is the very, very successful Intel. At its helm, the leader with his eye on the horizon is the "Mad Hungarian," Andy Grove. At a time when his firm was faced with a greater competition than ever before (from a product developed jointly by IBM, Motorola, and Apple Computer), how did this leader respond? By investing $1.1 billion in research and development and $2.4 billion in capital investment, while developing not only the product after next but also the product after, the product after, the product after, and pursuing a whole new market, consumer electronics.

How does Mr. Grove respond when asked about the rising competition? He says, "We needed a little threat, a good target. The juice is flowing." When asked if they would be doing what they were doing without the threat poised on the horizon, he responds, "Truthfully, no. We are making gutsier moves investment-wise, pricing-wise, every way, because we've got a competitive threat. The next result is we'll get to advance to the next level of competition."

Now, *that* is leadership that keeps its eyes on the horizon and sees all that it can see.

5.4 Shifting: How Leaders Are Seen by Others

When asked to differentiate between managers and leaders, most people focus on one of three topics.

First, leaders demand accountability for performance. Whereas a manager may demand hard work, conformance to rules, and predictability, leaders are interested in results. Leaders are less interested in the *presentation* and more in the *innovation,* less in the *style* and more in the *creativity,* and less in *how* something was done and more in *what* was done. This manager/leader dichotomy of course flows directly from the manager's focus on *control* and the leader's focus on *change.*

Second, managers believe in structure, in following a chain of command and in a logical, orderly decision process. Leaders don't believe in structure, and in fact often don't even have organizational charts. Leaders obviously don't follow a chain of command, because they don't believe in a chain of command. Leaders feel no hesitation in talking to anyone and everyone in the organization. Although leaders desire a reasonable level of analysis, they understand that many opportunities were missed by the organization because it waited for just one more analysis prior to making a decision. The leader often will make a decision and boldly move forward in spite of a risk of failure. A manager will want to get one more analysis, one more task force, one more meeting, one more opinion....

Third, a good manager is most often described by people as being very intelligent, a good decision-maker, a good problem-solver, a quick study, a person who asks difficult questions, a person with a good analytical mind, etc. A good leader most often is defined as an inspirational person, a good listener, a person with a passion for the business he/she is in, a caring person, an enthusiastic person, a person of integrity, etc. Note how the good-manager descriptions all refer to how the manager controls decisions, whereas the leader descriptions all refer to how the leader relates to people.

Managers are clearly viewed by others as managers, and leaders are clearly viewed as leaders. Thus, for an organization to achieve the proper balance between management and leadership, individual managers must shift their relationship with people within the company from a relationship based on *control* to a relationship based on *change.*

5.5 Shifting: What Leaders Do

What leadership does is what has been defined in Chaps. 2, 3, and 4 of this book. Leadership is responsible for defining culture, organizational direction, alignment, and motivation. Interestingly, management has tasks that directly relate to each of the leadership tasks but are totally different.

Both management and leadership share the responsibility for shaping an organization's culture. The dinosaur culture presented in Chap. 2 is the culture of management, whereas the crocodile culture is the culture of leadership. The manager's attitude toward change is *static consistency,* whereas the leader's attitude toward change is *dynamic consistency.*

Whereas a leader is responsible for defining an organization's Model of Success (Chap. 3), the manager's equivalent task is one of planning and budgeting. Whereas the leader's role here is that of looking at the long-term big picture and defining the organization's overall direction, the manager's role is that of defining short-term specifics and allocating resources. Similarly, whereas a leader is tasked with obtaining organizational alignment with the Model of Success (Chap. 3), the manager's job is that of organizing and staffing. The leader makes sure people do the right things, whereas the manager makes sure people do things right. Finally, whereas the leader is responsible for defining motivation (Chap. 4), managers are responsible for controlling people's performance. Whereas leaders encourage results, mangers monitor results.

In each of these cases, it is management that is seeking *control* while leadership is seeking *growth,* management that *administrates* and leadership that *innovates,* management that relies on *systems and controls* and leadership that relies on *people and trust,* and management that asks *how and when* and leadership that asks *what and why.*

5.6 Conclusion

Genesis Enterprises must have both good management and good leadership. Today, most organizations have an abundance of management and a shortage of leadership. To create the required balance, a shift from management to leadership is required. Table 5.1 summarizes the required shifts from management to leadership as defined in this chapter.

Getting managers to shift to leadership is not easy. You are asking them to step out of their comfort zone. It is therefore the responsibility of Genesis Leaders to help others to become Genesis Leaders. In fact, accepting the responsibility for growing other Genesis Leaders is a sure sign of a person being a Genesis Leader.

Table 5.1   The Required Shifts to Create the Required
Management/Leadership Balance of the Genesis Enterprise

Management	Leadership
Control	Change
Short-term	Long-term
Know where they are	Know where they are going
Who you are	What you do
Boss of people	Servant of people
Accountable for results, and people accountable for conformance	Hold people accountable for results
Narrow focus	Broad focus
Focus on bottom line	Focus on the horizon
Presentation, style, and *how* things are done	Innovation, creativity, *what* was done
Structure, chain of command	Flexibility, openness, and progress
Orderly decision process	
Described by how they control decisions	Described by how they relate to people
Dinosaur culture	Crocodile culture
Statically consistent on change	Dynamically consistent on change
Planning and budgeting	Define Model of Success
Organizing and staffing	Obtain organizational alignment
People doing it right	People doing the right things
Controlling performance	Defining motivation
Administrates	Innovates
Relies on systems and controls	Relies on people and trust
Asks how and when	Asks what and why

References

Belasco, J. A. and R. C. Stayer, *Flight of the Buffalo,* Warner Books, New York, 1993.

Dumaine, B., "The New Non-Manager Managers," *Fortune,* February 22, 1993.

Huey, J., "The New Post-Heroic Leadership," *Fortune,* February 21, 1994.

——, "The Leadership Industry," *Fortune,* February 21, 1994.

Kirkpatrick, D., "Intel Goes for Broke," *Fortune,* May 16, 1994.

Kotter, J. P., *A Force for Change: How Leadership Differs from Management,* The Free Press, New York, 1990.

——, *Corporate Culture and Performance,* The Free Press, New York, 1988.

——, *The Leadership Factor,* The Free Press, New York, 1988.

Kouzes, J. M. and B. Z. Posner, *The Leadership Challenge,* Jossey-Bass Publishers, San Francisco, 1991.

Nanus, B., *Visionary Leadership,* Jossey-Bass Publishers, San Francisco, 1992.

Pell, A. R., "Effective Leadership Means Empowerment," *The Wholesaler,* December 1993.

Tapscott, D. and A. Caston, *Paradigm Shift,* McGraw-Hill, New York, 1993.

PART 3

The Evolution of Teams

Experts, consultants, union leaders, executives, professors, machine operators, and many others are agreeing with what is being said daily in newspapers, magazines, books, conferences, and seminars: "Successful organizations will be team-based organizations." The simple fact is that the allure of teams is irresistible. The benefits of teams are real, and demand the attention of leaders. Team-based organizations will

1. Respond quicker to change and more effectively to opportunities

2. Deliver better quality and customer service

3. Reduce costs and increase profits

4. Have improved communications, morale, and employee satisfaction

5. Outperform non-team-based organizations

It would be easy to fill the next 20 pages with surveys which prove that teams are the only viable approach to becoming a Genesis Enterprise. At the same time, many organizations are not being successful with teams. Several case studies exist which demonstrate the failure of teams. In fact, I believe more organizations will fail with teams in the next five years than will be successful. If teams are so right, how can this be the case? The answer lies in a true understanding of teams (Chap. 6), a true understanding of empowerment (Chap. 7), and a true understanding of the process of shifting from individuals to teams (Chap. 8). There is a major difference between the companies that "do teams" and the companies that adopt teams as the way they do business. Part 3 provides a unique and an in-depth understanding of how to really make teams work for your organization.

6

Understanding Teams

Possibly the biggest challenge in creating a successful team-based organization is overcoming all the existing paradigms of teams. Everyone is familiar with teams and has their own personal understanding of teams. Unfortunately, rarely do two people have the same understanding. The reason for this is that there are several different types of teams, several different levels of teams, several different phases of team evolution, and several different roles to be played on teams. This chapter will clarify these differences and lay the foundation for the next two chapters, in which the process of creating a team-based organization is presented.

6.1 Team Definition

In Chap. 3, the question "What is good leadership?" was left unanswered. It is in the context of understanding teams that the difficulty in answering the "good leadership" question may be further understood. Any attempt to list the traits of a good leader results in frustration, as many of these traits are mutually exclusive. For example,

- A leader must be very intelligent, but also able to relate to people.
- A leader must be forceful, but also sensitive.
- A leader must be dynamic, but also patient.
- A leader must be an excellent speaker, but also an excellent listener.
- A leader must be decisive, but also reflective.

The simple fact is that no individual can combine all of these qualities. This is why we need teams. Certainly a team, as a totality, can possess all of these qualities. It is by combining all of these qualities that a team will be able to outperform not only any individual, but also the sum of the individuals on the team. This combining of the parts so as to have a whole that is greater than the sum of the parts is called *synergy*.

Synergy occurs wherever $1 + 1 = 6$. It is the synergy concept that is at the core of the definition of teams. A team is a small number of people who use synergy to work together for a common end. It is through this definition and an understanding of synergy that one can understand why leaders need followers as much as followers need leaders. It is, in fact, the synergistic work of followers that makes leaders, not the leaders who make the followers.

To be certain that all is understood, note that committees, task forces, and groups are not teams. A whole company is not a team. The daily recognition of the value of teamwork (although very desirable) does not make a team. A team is a small number of people who use synergy to work together for a common end. Therefore, to determine if a team exists, we must be able to answer the following three team-definition questions positively:

1. Are there a small number of people involved?

2. Do the people use synergy to work together?

3. Do the people have a common end?

Now, given this understanding of teams, we can evaluate certain groups to see if they are true teams. Is a choir a team? Yes, a choir consists of a small number of people. Yes, the members of the choir combine their voices via synergy (harmony). And yes, the choir has a common end of making beautiful music. So a choir is a team.

Does a church congregation singing a song on a Sunday morning qualify as a team? No, it is not a small number of people. What is a small number? It depends upon the circumstances; maybe 10, 20, or even 100. However, a church congregation of 600 is not a small number.

How about a baseball team? Yes, a baseball team consists of a small number of people. Yes, the members of the baseball team all want to win the game. A key question, however, is does a baseball team use synergy to work together? Well, some teams, yes, and some, no. On some baseball teams, each individual on defense plays only his/her position and there is no support, teaming together, or synergy. Similarly, on some baseball teams each individual on offense thinks only of himself/herself and there is no synergism on hits and runs, squeeze plays, hitting away from the runners, sacrifice flies, advancing the runner, etc. In these cases, baseball would not be a team sport. On other baseball teams, where on both offense and defense the players use synergy so as to play together, baseball is definitely a team sport.

How about a swimming team? Is a swimming team a team? Yes, a swimming team consists of a small number of people who all want to win the swim meet. But except for the relays, there is no use of synergy to work together and so, no, a swimming team is not a true team.

Now that we understand the definition of teams, it is important to understand the process whereby an organization becomes a team-based organization. There is a major difference between organizations that "do teams" and organizations that become team-based organizations. Doing teams is just another "flavor of the month" program. A wide variety of team programs have come and gone over the last 30 years. These programs (such as participative management, job enlargement, job enrichment, organizational development, quality circles, T groups, quality of life, employee involvement, etc.) have little to do with a company becoming a team-based organization. In fact these programs drive organizations *away* from becoming team-based organizations, because of their lack of long-term success.

Although a Genesis Enterprise may have "done teams" somewhere in its past, it now knows it will never break through to peak-to-peak performance via a team *program*. The key to becoming a team-based organization is the *process* of becoming a team-based organization. The difference between team success and failure is the understanding that team *programs* don't work, but that a properly designed team *process* can be made to work. The team process presented in this book has been developed by Tompkins Associates over a 15-year period while working in hundreds of organizations. This process works, and will lead a firm to become a Genesis Enterprise. The essence of the team-based process defined herein is not a program that you do, but rather a definition of how your company functions. For this reason, the Genesis Enterprise process defined in this book should be taken as a whole. Adapt to your situation, but don't skip portions of the process, or you too will be another failed team case study. In fact, as you might guess, I am often told of case studies of failed team programs and processes. One hundred percent of the time, these failures can be tracked to one or more omissions from the Genesis Enterprise process as defined herein.

6.2 Different Types of Teams

As a starting point for the process of becoming a team-based organization, it is important that you understand the five different types of teams that must exist in the Genesis Enterprise:

1. Steering Team
2. Leadership Team

3. Communication Team

4. Design Team

5. Work Team

Each of these teams is very different from the others, and with the possible exception of combining the Steering Team and Leadership Team in smaller organizations (less than 150 people), they all must be a portion of the process for an organization to become a team-based organization. Each of the next five subsections of this chapter defines one of these team-based organizational teams. These five subsections are summarized in Table 6.1.

6.2.1 Steering Team

In most organizations the Steering Team already exists and, for the most part, already functions like a team. The Steering Team should consist of the top executive and this executive's key staff. The Steering Team should be a small team of somewhere between 5 and 10 members. The Steering Team has the following two tasks:

1. *Steering organization.* It is the job of the Steering Team to establish the Model of Success and to be the initial communicator of the Model of Success. Steering Team members should individually and collectively demonstrate a focus on the Model of Success. The Steering Team must consistently and persistently work toward Model of Success alignment as discussed in Sec. 3.4.

2. *Steering process.* Through the definition, guidance, and motivation of the Leadership Team, the Steering Team should guide the overall team-based process.

It is important that the Steering Team demonstrate their commitment to the process of becoming a team-based organization by following the process. Therefore, even though the same group of people today may have a name Executive Committee, Management Committee, Board, Policy Committee, etc., have a regular meeting time, and have an ongoing modus operandi, it is important that the Steering Team change to conform with the Genesis Enterprise process. This team should be called the Steering Team, should have a regular scheduled meeting for just Steering Team business, and conform to the rules, procedures, and methods of the Genesis Enterprise process.

6.2.2 Leadership Team

The Leadership Team is to provide the leadership for the transformation to a team-based organization. To do this, the Leadership Team must work

Table 6.1 The Types of Teams in a Team-Based Organization

Type	Objective	Number of members	Frequency of meetings	Other
Steering Team	To establish, communicate, and maintain focus on the Model of Success, and to guide and support the Leadership Team.	5 to 10	Weekly until Model of Success and Leadership Team have been established. Then monthly.	Team should consist of top executive and key direct reports representing a broad organizational cross-section. Team leader should be top executive.
Leadership Team	To work toward Model of Success alignment; to define, charter, orient, encourage, motivate, support, and accept accountability for teams; and to assure performance.	8 to 16	Twice weekly for first few weeks. Then weekly.	This team is the workhorse of the team-based process. The people on this team will be required to spend several hours each week on the team process.
Communication Team	To ensure that everyone in the organization has a clear understanding of the Model of Success, the status of teams, and the organization's status.	10 to 20	Weekly, with monthly Communication Forums.	This team is a critical one in assuring alignment and motivation. Information and understanding are power, and this team's job is to speed information and understanding throughout the organization.
Design Team	To design or redesign the company by using a blue-sky, clean-sheet, green-field process of innovation and creativity to bring about significant performance improvements.	Varies depending upon Design Team scope. Could be 3 or 4, or 10 to 20.	Varies depending upon Design Team scope, from three times daily to monthly	This team is the place where the concurrent engineering and reengineering efforts within a company reside. An important element in becoming a Genesis Enterprise through breakthrough thinking.
Work Team	To bring the process of continuous improvement to life. To unleash the power of the people in the organization.	6 to 9	Weekly	Need to understand the differences between Cross-functional Work Teams and Functional Work Teams. Cross-functional Work Teams work *across* an organization for cultural transformation. Functional Work Teams work *down* an organization for performance improvement.

toward Model of Success alignment, must define, charter, orient, encourage, motivate, support, and accept accountability for teams, and must ensure peak-to-peak performance. The Leadership Team is to function as the workhorse of the Genesis Enterprise process. The Leadership Team should consist of 8 to 16 well-respected people, involved in all aspects of the company. If it is a union shop, it would be fine to include a couple of people from the union organization. The leader of the Leadership Team should be a well-organized, action-based person who has a broad-based perspective, a strong belief in the team process, and good communication skills. The Leadership Team should meet weekly, and should proactively help each team to overcome its difficulties. The Leadership Team should follow this process:

1. Conduct orientation.
2. Define priorities.
3. Charter teams (to be discussed in Chap. 7).
4. Provide team orientation.
5. Encourage, motivate, and support teams.
6. Ensure team progress.
7. Monitor and report results.
8. Grow process.
9. Return to Step 3.

PROCESS STUCK ON THE WRONG
DEFINITION OF THE LEADERSHIP TEAM

A family-owned manufacturing company of about 500 people had an Executive Team of 7 (to include 3 family members) who made most decisions about how the company functioned. The next level of the organization consisted of 8 department heads, who in theory had a lot of autonomy in running their operation. A decision was made to combine the Steering Team into a single Leadership Team. A Leadership Team of 15 was created, a Model of Success developed, a Communication Team and four Work Teams chartered, and the process sat flat. There was not a Leadership Team. What they had was a Leadership Group that consisted of the Executive Team (that really *was* a team) and 8 other guys who did not feel comfortable dealing with the Executive Team.

After six months of frustration, the nonfunctioning 15-member Leadership Team was split into a 7-member Steering Team and an 8-member Leadership Team. Acting as a liaison between the Steering

Team and the Leadership Team was a very thoughtful, clever-thinking non-family-member from the Steering Team. Guess what? The Steering Team started steering, and after a while the Leadership Team started leading the process. Today a successful, growing, profitable company has truly become a Genesis Enterprise. Oh, the glory of a Genesis Enterprise, when things are done well!

6.2.3 Communication Team

Most organizations have two things in common:

1. Poor communications
2. Leadership that cannot understand why poor communications exist

Leadership is troubled, as they have worked hard establishing and then using a formal communication system. This formal communication system is top-down. Typically, bottom-up and horizontal communications don't work. Worse yet, many studies have shown that somewhere between 10 to 30 percent of all communications are lost as they travel through each level of an organization. That is to say, only 75 percent of what the president says, the vice president understands; that only 50 percent of what the president says, the director of operations understands; that only 25 percent of what the president says, the supervisor understands; and that the worker rarely understands what the president said.

Some leaders attempt to minimize this loss by communicating in writing. This helps, but not much. The thing not realized by the president is that his/her vocabulary, language, and assumptions differ from the workers' to such a large degree that similar losses in written communication often occur.

The fact is, information and the understanding of information is power. Information and understanding of information are to an organization's Genesis Enterprise process what gasoline is to an automobile. This is even more critical during times of organizational transformation, because if the people don't have the information, the informal communications system will generate information that most likely will be detrimental to the process. Or, going back to the analogy, when the automobile lacks gas, people in the throes of chaos put water in the gas tank.

It is clear that for an organization to become a Genesis Enterprise organization, a top-to-bottom, bottom-to-top, and side-to-side communications network must be established and used. The responsibility of ensuring that these communications take place is the Communication Team's.

It is the Communication Team's responsibility to ensure that everyone in the organization has a clear understanding of the Model of Success, the status of teams, and the organization's status. The Communication Team often consists of 10 to 20 members and meets on a regular weekly basis. Tools used by Communication Teams vary, but tools that have worked well include

1. *Newsletters.* Most organizations have some form of regularly produced newsletter. If one does not exist, the thought of developing a newsletter just for Genesis Enterprise communications should be considered. Each newsletter should include the organization's Model of Success, updates on all teams, and recognition of all team activities.

2. *Model of Success.* The Communication Team should have the Model of Success attractively printed and framed. These framed Models of Success should be hung throughout the company, and extra printed copies should be produced for individuals to hang in locations they deem appropriate. All team meeting rooms should have a framed Model of Success on the wall.

3. *Bulletin boards.* The Communication Team should review all company bulletin boards. Appropriate Genesis Enterprise information should be placed on the bulletin boards and maintained in a timely fashion.

4. *Events.* The Communication Team should evaluate special events for all employees. These special events should not be baseball games or picnics (although another team may wish to sponsor these types of events), but should be plant visits, videotapes, or guest speakers that will focus attention on the Model of Success, the Genesis Enterprise process, and/or the organization's performance.

5. *Word-of-mouth.* The members of the Communication Team should come from a broad cross section of the organization. The members of the Communication Team should be posted and well known. Everyone in the organization should be encouraged to talk with the Communication Team members. While maintaining a policy of total amnesty for the sources of all communications, the Communication Team members should work to achieve the Communication Team objectives on a one-on-one basis.

6. *Surveys.* From time to time the Communication Team may wish to proactively seek inputs from the organization. These surveys should be done anonymously and should provide a forum for both structured tabular responses as well as unstructured open responses.

7. *Communication Forum.* All Genesis Enterprises should have a regularly scheduled monthly Communication Forum. These forums are critically important to ensuring organizational alignment, understanding, and celebration. A major shortfall in organizations today is the lack of opportunities to celebrate our organizational success, to provide feedback, to rekindle the "family" spirit, and to say "thank you." The Com-

munication Forum is the opportunity for all this to occur. The Communication Forum is the paramount regular event where an organization's transformation can be put on display.

The agenda for the Communication Forum should consist of a review of the Model of Success and the Team Rules (to be presented in Chap. 8) and the team presentations. Each team presentation should be done by a team reporter, who should spend three to four minutes reviewing the success, progress, issues, strengths, and even weaknesses of their team. The people to attend the Communication Forum should be the Steering Team, the Leadership Team, the Communication Team, and one representative of each team. The Communication Forums should be fun, lively, and action-packed. After each presentation, people should be encouraged to ask questions. Questions should be answered in such a way as to ensure full understanding.

To encourage Communication Forum interaction, the Communication Team may wish to create a Question Box. The purpose of this box is to obtain anonymous questions that will be asked at the Communication Forum. These questions should be asked of the appropriate party at the Communication Forum by a member of the Communication Team, while indicating that they came from the Question Box. Every effort should be made to make the Communication Forum a true celebration, and a place to recognize and thank teams for their efforts.

8. *Visual Management System.*   It is extremely important that the Communication Team work on organizational alignment, team information, team recognition, and performance visibility. A tool that can help in all these regards is a Visual Management System (VMS). Figure 6.1 is an illustration of a VMS. A VMS is a large board that could quite easily be $20' \times 8'$ and consume an entire wall. The four key elements of a VMS are

   a. *Model of Success*—to maintain organization focus and alignment
   b. *Team listing*—to inform everyone what is being worked on
   c. *Approved projects*—to recognize team progress and success
   d. *Visual measurement system (Vms)*—to act as a scoreboard to document and add visibility to the organizational performance and the organization's Evidence of Success

A notebook version of the VMS can be provided to remote locations or to people who travel. Typically this notebook version is updated monthly. The Model of Success typically is done on the VMS in a permanent fashion. The Team Listings and Approved Projects should be done in such a way so that they can be easily updated. The Vms portion of the VMS should be updated at least weekly, and perhaps even hourly. The Communication Team should accept responsibility for managing these updates. The questions to be answered to design the VMS are

Figure 6.1   Visual Management System (VMS)

    a. What organizational and team Evidence of Success should be regularly and frequently reported on, and what decisions or actions need to be taken?

    b. What information is required to measure the Evidence of Success, make the decisions, or take the actions? (See Sec. 3.2.)

    c. What data is needed to get the information?

    d. How do we obtain data?

    e. How/who should convert data into information?

    f. How do we portray information, and how do we design VMS?

    g. Where do we locate the VMS, and how many should we have?

    h. What will it cost to construct the boards?

    i. What should be the implementation plan?

    j. Do we have approval from the Leadership Team to proceed?

    k. Once a VMS has been implemented, how/who should train employees on it?

    l. How/who should audit VMS acceptance, refinement?

    m. How/who should upgrade and improve the VMS so that it can respond to everyone's needs?

    n. Who should educate new employees on VMS, and how?

    o. How can the Communication Team maintain the organization's interest in VMS?

    The positive impacts that result from the visibility and recognition of, and the performance feedback on, VMS should not be underestimated. In many organizations where there has been little sharing of performance data, the implementation of a VMS will have major cultural and motivational impacts. Information is power, and the purpose of VMS is to transmit information, so it isn't surprising that the VMS transmits power.

UNDERSTANDING THE FEELINGS OF
A COMMUNICATION TEAM

It would be easy to write 20 different stories here under the same headline. Let me tell you one that brought tears to the eyes of many in the room as it unfolded. The third presentation at a Communication Forum was a presentation by a thoughtful, deep individual who was a reporter for the Training Team. The Training Team was a Cross-functional Work Team with a focus on providing the necessary training to all employees. At this particular Communication Forum, the Training Team reporter defined a literacy outreach that would allow employees who had reading problems to learn how to read. The reporter explained how people could either sign up for training at the company, or if they preferred anonymity, they could sign up directly with a local community college. The Training Team reporter indicated that there was some concern about whether people would be willing to step forward with their reading problems.

Two reporters later, a reporter from a Functional Work Team gave an excellent presentation on his team's progress. As this young man began to leave the front of the room, he paused and said he had one more thing to say. He said "he was proud to work at a company that cared about their employees to the extent that the company would provide training on reading." This young man then made the bold statement in front of the entire company's leadership and management that "he could not read and he would sign up for the course and he hoped by stepping forward that others would do likewise as this was important if the company was to achieve its vision." As I wiped a tear from my eye, I looked at the president of the company sitting next to me. He, too, had a wet eye. We all clapped. The young man sat down. We wiped our eyes again and the next reporter took the floor. These are the feelings that evolve in a Genesis Enterprise Communication Forum.

6.2.4   Design Team

Within a Genesis Enterprise, the process of peak-to-peak performance must be a focus, but so too must the process of design and redesign. The expression "If it ain't broke, break it" certainly is critical to a Genesis

Enterprise, but so too is the expression "If it's broken, fix it." Design Teams have to do with the process of design and redesign, and the expression "If it's broken, fix it." Possibly the two most popular buzzwords of the early 1990's were *reengineering* and *concurrent engineering*. A true measure of the level of chaos created by a fad is the number of synonyms that are invented to say the same thing. Reengineering was also referred to as *work reengineering, work-systems redesign, business process redesign, rearchitecting, case management,* and *new industrial engineering*. Concurrent engineering was also referred to as *simultaneous engineering, design for manufacturability, mechatronics, winning manufacturing product development,* and *Taguchi methods*. The role of reengineering was *the design or redesign of organizational structures, systems, and procedures to improve performance*. Similarly, the role of concurrent engineering was *the design or redesign of products and manufacturing facilities to improve performance*. The role of a Design Team is the combination of the roles of reengineering and concurrent engineering: *to design or redesign organizational structures, systems, procedures, products, and facilities to improve performance*. Although all of these design or redesign efforts are different, it is absolutely critical that within a Genesis Enterprise these efforts not be segregated from the overall Genesis process, but be fully integrated and a portion of creating peak-to-peak performance.

The functions performed by Design Teams have not been done well over the last 20 years. It is my belief that this is why the topics of reengineering and concurrent engineering were such a fertile ground for buzzwords and their accompanying chaos. In a November–December 1993 *Harvard Business Review* article, the authors state:

> In all too many companies, reengineering has been not only a great success but also a great failure. After months, even years, of careful redesign, these companies achieve dramatic improvements in individual processes only to watch overall results decline.

And then in the Bible of reengineering, *Reengineering the Corporation,* Hammer and Champy state:

> Our unscientific estimate is that as many as 50 percent to 70 percent of the organizations that undertake a reengineering effort do not achieve the dramatic results they intended.

Similarly with concurrent engineering, Jean Owen in a *Manufacturing Engineering* article states:

> All this sounds great, but don't forget the land mines. The path to successful concurrent engineering is strewn with them, according to Dr. Daniel R. Tobin. Most of them are cultural, not technological. Seduced by promises of huge savings, many companies hired consultants, made

massive investments in technology, tore down the walls between departments, developed multifunctional teams, bought the software and hardware to make it all happen, and found the return on investment pretty mediocre.

Similarly, from a *Business Week* article entitled "Flops":

If companies can improve their effectiveness at launching new products, they could double their bottom line. It's one of the few areas left with the greatest potential for improvement.

The approach to increasing your company's design or redesign batting average is to be certain that design teams are chartered within the overall process of creating peak-to-peak performance, and to properly define the breadth and depth of the Design Teams within their charter.

Design Teams chartered with too narrow a breadth will not be successful, as they will only be looking at a portion of the total. At best, a suboptimization will take place. At worst, not only will improvement not occur, but overall performance will drop, as the changes made to the portion of the total, although improving this portion, are detrimental to the broad picture. Design Teams should be chartered with a broad focus. This broad focus should relate to the creation of value in the ultimate company performance as viewed by the customer. Within the Design Team's charter, it should be clearly stated what performance improvements are expected to result from the Design Team. Once again, these performance improvements must be performance improvements as viewed by the customer.

Design Team charters that restrict the Design Teams will not allow them to penetrate to the core elements of the organization, to address the real opportunities so as to bring about peak-to-peak performance. For this reason, Design Teams should be chartered to allow an in-depth pursuit of the core issues impacting design. Design Teams should be chartered to

1. Leave the paradigms of the past behind
2. Develop their recommendations independent of present practice
3. Establish a clean-sheet, blue-sky, green-field design for both today and tomorrow.
4. Be innovative and creative.

As few restrictions as may be shall be placed on Design Teams.

Table 6.2 presents several Design Team failures which resulted from charters that suffered from breadth and depth problems. The number of people involved in a Design Team can vary from 3 to 4 for the design of a process to 10 to 50 for the design of an automobile. Also, the frequency of meetings can vary from three times a day for the design of a product to monthly for the redesign of an entire organization. It is only

Table 6.2 Design Team Failures

Charter said	Results obtained, and why
Improve company communications by redesigning receptionist position.	No results obtained. Charter too narrow.
Improve company communications, but don't change phone systems, mail systems, or bulletin board.	No results obtained. Charter too restrictive, lack of depth of opportunities to pursue.
Improve how company does business.	No results obtained. Charter too broad and too deep. No focus or real leadership direction.
Reduce inventories, but don't change inventory management systems or inventory needs of the shop.	No results obtained. Charter too restrictive, lack of depth of opportunities to pursue.

through a well-developed and thoughtful charter that a Design Team can be successful. The failures of reengineering efforts and concurrent engineering efforts have less to do with the process of reengineering and concurrent engineering and more to do with the chartering of these teams. Keys to chartering a Design Team include the following:

1. The Design Team is a portion of the process of creating peak-to-peak performance, and will conform to the Model of Success and the overall team process.

2. The Design Teams will have intimate contact with the Leadership Team.

3. The Design Teams will work with the Communication Team to achieve awareness and understanding throughout the organization.

4. The charter will include specific performance-improvement expectations.

5. The Design Teams should have a broad focus that relates to the ultimate company performance as viewed by the customer.

6. The Design Teams should be chartered to allow an in-depth pursuit of the core issues.

7. The Design Team's charter should not limit or restrict the Design Team's pursuit of performance improvement, but rather encourage and stimulate the Design Team to achieve peak-to-peak performance.

8. Design Teams should be encouraged to look outside of their company's boundaries to pursue problems, challenges, and opportunities.

9. Design Teams should be made aware of the fact that they will be involved, and may be responsible for the implementation of their designs.

10. Design Teams should be encouraged to test new designs to whatever level possible, to refine the design and minimize problems during implementation.

AT&T SUCCESS WITH
DESIGN TEAMS BRINGS MAJOR SUCCESS

Since the mid 1980s, AT&T had experienced lackluster performance from their Global Business Communications System business. This $4 billion business unit was not making progress, and by 1989 had hit a wall. Several Design Teams were created to redesign the business's core processes. The Design Teams found a present system that did not work. There was no integration or accountability for how the business telephone systems sold by AT&T were eventually installed. In fact, the process from sale to installation required 16 hand-offs. Profits and customer service were unacceptable.

After a nine-month assessment, the Design Teams recommended and received a green light to redesign the process with the goals in mind of minimizing the time between sales and installation, minimizing hand-offs, and working as an integrated company to increase both customer service and profitability. After a full year of redesign to include several trials, the team rolled out its new process in April 1991. The results have been amazing, with profits reaching record highs, customer willingness to repurchase climbing from 53 to 82 percent, adjustments for dissatisfied customers dropped from 4 to .6 percent, and an 88 percent customer service rating of Excellent.

6.2.5   Work Teams

Work teams in Genesis Enterprises are the place where the process of creating peak-to-peak performance resides. The purpose of work teams is to improve operations a little each day by unleashing the power of the people. The most shocking fact for Genesis Leaders to note is that for work teams to produce many, many $100, $500, $1000, $2000, $5000, $10,000, and $50,000 improvements, no new thoughts need to be generated. In organizations that have yet to become Genesis Enterprises, there are literally thousands of ideas in the minds of workers that would significantly improve operations. In fact, it is not unusual for there to be over $100,000 in savings documented in the first few weeks after the team process has been initiated, savings that come forth simply because people are testing the sincerity of leadership to adopt the worker's ideas. Of course, the Genesis Leader wants to know why these ideas didn't come forth prior to pursuing the peak-to-peak performance process. Listen to the answers:

1. "I told this to my supervisor four years ago and he told me to go back to work. So I went back to work."

2. "I was told there was no money in the budget to do these types of things."

3. "The only people in this organization who are allowed to have good ideas wear neckties and have an office up front. If one of the smart guys doesn't think of it first, it will never get done."

4. "They don't listen to us. For years we have told them how to do it, but they will not or cannot listen."

5. "I was told to go back to work. If they wanted my two cents they would ask."

6. "The guys up front don't respect us. They think just because they went to college, they're smarter than we are."

7. "God gave me a good brain and a good pair of hands. At this company, they are only interested in my hands."

8. "Six years ago John Smith told them how to improve his job and he got fired. You want me to speak up now?"

9. "I told my supervisor how to do the job in half the time. He took my idea, and he and his wife got a free dinner. He didn't ever say thanks. That was the last time I'll ever tell management my ideas."

10. "Why share your ideas? They don't listen to us. The guys set me straight 10 years ago. My job now, I get my 8 and I hit the gate."

Work teams differ from all other types of teams, in that while only one Steering Team, Leadership Team, and Communication Team exist in an organization, many work teams exist in a Genesis Enterprise. Work teams differ from design teams, in that work teams focus on incremental improvement whereas design teams focus on innovation. Table 6.3 documents this work team versus design team dichotomy.

Table 6.3 Work Teams versus Design Teams

Perspective	Work team	Design team
Focus	Incremental improvement	Innovation
Time Frame	Ongoing, long-term	Quick hit, short-term
Impact	Undramatic, ongoing	Dramatic, big splash
Pace	Small steps	Big steps
Improvements	Gradual and constant	Abrupt and volatile
Mode	Maintain and improvement	Scrap and start new
Timing	Continuous and incremental	Intermittent and nonincremental
Charter	How to improve	How to reinvent

There are two different types of work teams:

1. *Cross-Functional Work Team.* A team addressing a specific improvement opportunity (topic), with representatives from across the company.
2. *Functional Work Team.* A team addressing a specific geographical area (department), with representatives only from that area.

Cross-functional Work Teams have the largest impact on cultural transformation, but functional work teams have the largest impact on improved performance. For this reason, at the outset of the transformation from individuals to teams, it is normal for three or four cross-functional teams to be chartered, and only after these teams have started to work as teams should the functional teams be created.

One point of clarification is needed. Several different companies have seen tremendous results flowing from Cross-Functional Work Teams, and thus they disagree with the statement about cross-functional teams having a primary focus of cultural transformation. Typically what is happening in these cases is that although the organization thought it was chartering a Cross-Functional Work Team, what they really chartered was a Design Team. Certainly, Design Teams offer opportunities for tremendous results, and it is the lack of clarity between a Design Team charter and a Cross-Functional Work Team charter that creates this confusion. Remember, Design Teams focus on innovation, Work Teams focus on incremental improvements.

Work teams typically consist of between 6 and 9 members and meet on a weekly basis. The scope of the work-team charter should be consistent with the knowledge of the members on the team, and of sufficient focus to allow the team to achieve real performance improvements. When problems occur with the scope of the charter, consideration should be given to forming either a Strategy Team or Linked Work Teams.

Strategy Teams, as shown in Fig. 6.2, become a parent to several work teams for purposes of integrating the interrelated elements of a particular peak-to-peak performance opportunity. Strategy Teams should meet weekly and should have at least one representative from each of its Strategy Team offspring work teams. The charter for each offspring work team should fully reflect the relevant aspects of the Strategy Team's opportunity, evidence of success, constraints, and expectations. Strategy Teams should not only support and integrate their offspring work teams but should also set the overall strategic direction for the opportunity being addressed.

Linked Work Teams, as shown in Fig. 6.3, allow for the interrelationship of two or three work teams, while the Leadership Team still provides the overall guidance and direction of the teams to be linked. If it is necessary

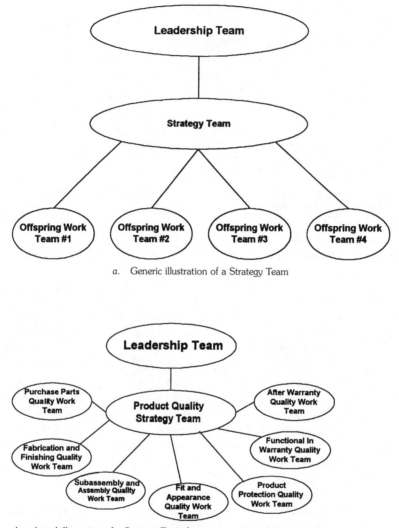

a.   Generic illustration of a Strategy Team

b.   Actual illustration of a Strategy Team for a consumer appliance company

Figure 6.2   Strategy Team's relationship to Leadership Team and Offspring Work Teams: a. a generic illustration; b. an actual illustration for a Product Quality Strategy Team for a consumer appliance company

for more than three work teams to be linked, the Strategy Team approach should be utilized, as this will allow for more positive, efficient, and effective communication. The charter for each linked work team should indicate the linkage between teams and the relationships required to properly achieve the desired performance improvements. Linkage between work teams should be done either through team leaders, team liaisons, or both.

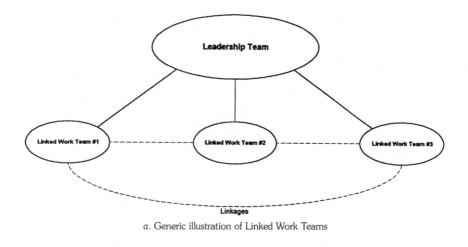

a. Generic illustration of Linked Work Teams

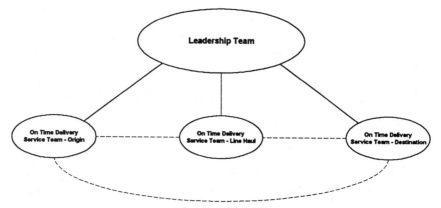

b. Actual illustration of Linked Work Teams for a trucking company

Figure 6.3 Linked Work Teams: a. a generic illustration; b. an actual illustration for a trucking company

---

CHRYSLER SCORES SUCCESS WITH NEON

The Japanese media have called the Chrysler Neon "the Japan killer." The United States press touts Neon as the first U.S. vehicle "with a real chance to challenge the Japanese dominance in the subcompact market." What makes this car so unique? Consider a few quotes from a June 1994 *Training* magazine article:

- Massive worker involvement has been Neon's hallmark. Production workers participated in the design of the vehicle and in decisions about the ergonomics of the production line. Early worker-involvement attempts at the Neon Belvidere plant date to at least

1987, when the plant was still building the Omni, but the pace really picked up in 1989 when worker teams were organized to suggest cost-cutting methods The full-involvement rollout came with Neon in 1992.

- Candor at the Belvidere plant is startling. Employees up to and including plant manager John Felice expound freely on Neon's flaws and what's being done about them. "The defects I'm talking about, the customer will never see," said Felice, "we find it, we eliminate it, we prevent it from happening again."

- The production workers were not at first eager to be involved with the design process. "There was not trust there," says union local president Rielly. "Our people honestly felt that no matter what they said, the engineers were going to do whatever they wanted. Once our people found out that what they said mattered and the engineers were going to accept it, it was 'Hey, if you've got something to say—say it.'"

6.3 Levels of Teams

Just as there are different types of teams, so too there are also different levels of teams. Not understanding these levels of teams can bring on the total failure of the team-based process. The six levels of teams are

1. Traditional Group

2. Natural Group

3. Suggestion Team

4. Improvement Team

5. Semi-Autonomous Team

6. Self-Managing Team

Each of these levels has a progressive increase in autonomy, from Traditional Groups and Natural Groups that have no autonomy to Self-Managing Teams that have much autonomy.

The first two levels of teams are not teams but rather groups. Groups differ from teams in that groups rely on the sum of the "individual bests" and not the synergy of the team. Groups do not collectively pursue performance improvement, but rather use the group to share information and opinions and to make *ad hoc* agreements to help one another. Groups do not have charters and have no predefined process, objectives, or evidence of success. The only commitment individuals have to a group is to attend the next meeting. After that meeting, a commitment may or not be made to attend the next meeting or to "send someone in their place." It is acceptable to send others in your place to a group meeting, as they can fill you in on the information and opinions presented and little will be missed. Since there is no synergy and no commitment, nothing is lost. To the contrary, it is never possible to send someone in your place to a team meeting. Team members must personally attend team meetings, as it is through the complementary, common commitment that the team will obtain synergy and, therefore, significant process improvement.

Traditional Groups are people who come together from time to time to discuss topics. Sometimes the topics to be discussed are defined and sometimes they are not defined. Rarely will there be an agenda or minutes. Traditional groups consist of individuals who decide whether they wish to participate in the group based upon how much help they think the group will provide them with in accomplishing their objectives. Traditional Groups are useful to the point that individuals share information. Traditional Groups can be an asset to an organization or can be a total waste of time. There are no real processes, rules, or roles defined, so whether or not Traditional Groups will be worthwhile cannot be predicted or duplicated. Traditional Groups have meetings, and every now and then something good happens; other than this, not much can be said about them. But then again, not much *needs* to be said, as we all have been part of many Traditional Groups.

Natural Groups are not teams but may at some point in the future become teams and although they still rely on the sum of the "individual best" they can be structured so that although they are not a team, they do respect the value of teamwork. Although Natural Groups do not have a charter, rules, agendas, and minutes, typically they do have the "natural" group leader, the supervisor. Natural Groups often meet on a regular schedule (such as for 10 minutes, first thing each day, for 30 minutes at the beginning of the shift on Tuesday and Thursday, or whatever), and do have a topic of discussion predefined. Often the topic of discussion is quality and schedule attainment. Also it would not be unusual for human resource issues, safety, product damage, and general business affairs to be discussed in a Natural Group.

It also is quite possible that from the Natural Group will come a requirement for creating a team. In these cases the "natural" leader, the supervisor, would go to the Leadership Team and ask to be chartered, or perhaps the Natural Group would write its own charter and submit it to the Leadership Team for acceptance. The effort put into the formation of a Natural Group by the Leadership Team is either none or minimal. Not surprisingly, therefore, the results achieved often are none or minimal.

It is interesting, however, to watch, as an organization's culture is transformed from individual to team, how the Natural Groups fight to become and perform like a team. It is, in fact, this Natural Group evolution to teams that often results in the formation of the majority of an organization's Functional Work Teams. The Leadership Team should encourage the existence of Natural Groups, should provide a few hours of "Natural Group" leader training (see Sec. 6.5 and Sec. 8.4), and should monitor the Natural Group's progress and be ready to promote it to a team at the appropriate time.

A Suggestion Team is a real team with limited autonomy. The output from a Suggestion Team is a recommendation to pursue a specific path. Interestingly, although Suggestion Teams most often are called Suggestion Teams at the outset, they really are not yet teams, any more than a group of players is really a football team at the first day of practice. Nevertheless, a Suggestion Team will act like a team and be treated like a team, and will be expected to become a true team. A Suggestion Team will follow an accepted charter, will follow team rules, roles, development patterns, and meeting guidelines. A Suggestion Team's charter will clearly limit the Suggestion Team to making recommendations.

This is not a trust thing, this is an evolutionary thing. No more than would you expect a 2-year-old to get a job, or an 8-year-old to paint the house, or a 16-year-old to work full-time, or a 22-year-old to be the president of a major company. This is not a trust thing, it is a development thing. A Suggestion Team at the outset is not even a team; leadership certainly would not be wise to allow this team to make major decisions. The Leadership Team is not restricting the Suggestion Team by making it a Suggestion Team at the outset any more than a parent is restricting a 2-year-old by not allowing the child to play in the street. At the same time, just as parents should work to allow their children to grow, so too should a Leadership Team work to allow its Suggestion Teams to grow. Once a Suggestion Team has evolved by making several good suggestions and is truly functioning as a team, it should be promoted to an Improvement Team.

An Improvement Team is the logical next step for a Suggestion Team. At the appropriate time, the Leadership Team should officially upgrade the charters of Suggestion Teams to Improvement Teams. The autonomy of an Improvement Team involves the team having the authority and responsibility to solve certain types of problems unto themselves. An Improvement Team can implement changes given the constraints placed upon them in the area of capital expenditure, impacts on other areas, and whatever other constraints may be relevant. It is clear that the upgrade of the Improvement Team charter must be done well and clearly so that there are no surprises down the road. It must be made clear to the Improvement Team that the charter is not meant as a ceiling on their activities but rather as a defining document, so that other teams are not caught off-guard by something being implemented that impacts them while they are not being informed.

The fifth level of teams is a Semi-Autonomous Team, it being an adjusting point between an Improvement Team and a Self-Managing Team. In some cases this level of team is skipped, and in other cases this is an important point of adjustment. When a Semi-Autonomous Team is created it is clear who has the greatest level of adjustment: the supervisor. It is not clear who has the second greatest level of adjustment: the Semi-Autonomous Team, the Leadership Team, or the Steering Team. Care must be taken here to help the supervisor through this adjustment. More information is presented on this topic in Sec. 8.4. A Semi-Autonomous Team is a team responsible for planning, solving problems, implementing improvements, and participating in making decisions and setting goals. Once again, it is critical that the Leadership Team do a good job of upgrading the team's charter, and clearly communicate these upgrades to the Semi-Autonomous Team.

The ultimate team is the Self-Managing Team, which, within certain guidelines, runs a portion of its business. Typically, only Functional Work Teams evolve to become Self-Managing Work Teams, and it almost always takes a team at least a year to reach this level. A Self-Managing Team is just what its name indicates, a team that manages its own affairs, with the only constraints being those defined in their charter. In fact, other than having a contact person (maybe a leader, maybe not), participating in the Communication Forum, and communicating its actions to the appropriate parties, a Self-Managing Team can decide on its own rules, roles, procedures, schedule, etc. Some Self-Managing Teams may do everything but plan overtime; some may not want to be involved with hiring/firing, or want to do employee evaluations, etc. This team is truly self-managed.

Now, a major, big-time, don't-make-this-mistake warning is in order. Self-Managing Teams are your objective, a true sign of the evolution from individuals to teams, a true indication of creating peak-to-peak performance, and a key to the success of your organization. To the contrary, self-directing teams are a huge mistake, a true sign that a company is lost, a true indication of failure, a sure sign of a company's demise.

Why am I so hung up on the small difference between Self-Managing and Self-Directing? Because Self-Managing Teams build a company up and Self-Directing Teams tear a company down. Think of the meaning of Self-Directing Teams: teams directing where the company is headed. There is no Model of Success, no Steering Team, and no Leadership Team. These teams decide their own direction and off they go.

It sounds silly. Well, sure, it *is* silly, but behind a confused, misunderstood interpretation of empowerment, this is exactly what many companies have done, and they have created chaos. Allow me to delay the discussion of empowerment until Chap. 7, but let me be clear here that the use of the term *empowerment* in conjunction with the use of the term *Self-Directing Work Teams* is big-time dangerous. As in *stay away, do not touch, nada, run,* etc. Get the picture? We do not want self-direction. We want leadership direction and self-management. This is the true indication of a team-based organization, and I assure you that major success will abound. Self-managing teams are what the Genesis Enterprises will achieve.

6.4   Team Development

I may be the only person alive who did not know intuitively that you never win a team to the team-based process. Just as an evangelist cannot convert a congregation to Christianity, so too a team-based consultant cannot singlehandedly change an organization into a team-based organization. I had to learn that one does not convert masses but individuals. Thus, the challenge of becoming a team-based organization is not winning teams to the process but winning individuals to the process. Figure 6.4 demonstrates the process of winning individuals to teams, and the team development phases that correspond to each level of individual acceptance.

In Fig. 6.4, each person is represented as having a mental team switch which can be either in the Yes or No position. Yes means that the individual has been converted to teams, and No means that they have not been converted to teams. Phase I in Fig. 6.4 begins with 100 percent of the people not being with teams. This is normal. Teams are unknown, new, and a change, so people in exhibiting their natural tendencies will not be for teams. Relatively quickly, however, several people will throw their switch. They may not truly believe in teams, but they are aware of the need for change, so they convert to believing in teams. These are the easiest converts but not necessarily the strongest.

As Phase II is approached, there exists a majority of people who do not support teams and a minority that do. With leadership persistence, the Phase II transformation takes place and at the end of Phase II there are more people who have been converted to teams than not. As we enter Phase III, team acceptance grows in relatively short order. Phases III and IV are complete, and we find ourselves with 5 percent not accepting teams and 95 percent who do accept teams. This is as good as it gets. You will never achieve 100 percent acceptance, and should not be overly concerned with attempting to achieve 100 percent. The last 5 percent are hard, and you should continue without their support. Phase V is an interesting phase. It is during this phase, even though the switches say Yes, that there is a fall-off in results. This phase is actually a time to alter the charter and recycle to Phase I. Interestingly, Phase V is not well understood in the team development literature, even though we have experienced this phase with every team we have ever established. The team literature does an excellent job defining Phases I through IV. It is based upon these definitions and our personal experiences that the next five subsections define the five phases.

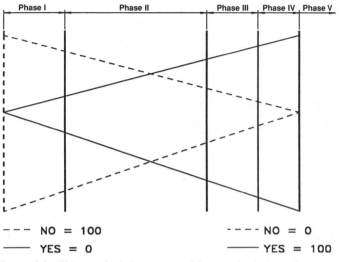

Phase I | Phase II | Phase III | Phase IV | Phase V

$--$ NO = 100

$--$ NO = 0

— YES = 0

— YES = 100

Figure 6.4 Winning individuals to teams and the team development phases

6.4.1 Phase I—Forming

The first phase finds the team member asking the questions "Why am I here?" "What is expected?" "What is going to happen?" "How do I fit in?" People feel a mixture of anxiety and anticipation. The level of uncertainty is great, so many have decided not to speak but just to watch and listen. This watch-and-listen routine can result in the team going into a stall. The team leader needs to encourage and, if necessary, to force participation. You cannot have a team where only the leader speaks. Things that will get people involved have to do with their pride in being chosen for the team and their attempts to understand their role. The few who accept teams at this phase are excited about teams, and will immediately table several good ideas that have been known on the floor for years. These ideas are what bring the quick-hitting results mentioned in Sec. 6.2.4. It is critical that these ideas be fully pursued by the Leadership Team, and it is in fact these ideas that drive the process to Phase II.

6.4.2 Phase II—Storming

The second phase finds the team willing to vocalize their anxiety. The few that have accepted teams can't believe that the other people don't understand and see the need for teams. The many who haven't accepted teams can't believe that the few who have accepted teams could be so gullible. People are comfortable with their traditional role of taking orders and doing their jobs, and aren't at all sure they now want to "do management's job just because they can't!" Arguing, power struggles, frustration, anger, and politics are growing. People are asking, "How can I get out of this?" "Why do I have to waste my time on this?" "Where is all this going?" This is an opportunity for the team leader not to suppress the conflict but to manage it as an opportunity for growth, awareness, understanding, and acceptance of the team process. Although this "storming" may feel awkward, the fact is this is a very positive and important part of the evolution to becoming a Genesis Enterprise. This proves out by the end of Phase II, when there are more people who accept teams than those who do not accept teams.

6.4.3   Phase III—Norming

Because of the conflict in Phase II, there comes to pass an awareness and an understanding of the team purpose and the team charter. The team now has more people who accept teams, so there begins to be a spirit of "we" rather than "me." This sense of trust, cooperation, and respect results in others accepting teams. Team members have various levels of trust at this phase, with some believing in teams but having a hard time throwing out their paradigms of the past. For this reason, often in the Norming phase, the ideas that are not pursued are not the best ideas team members have. They will be the trial balloon ideas. To assure continued progress and moving from Phase III to Phase IV, the Leadership Team must pursue its ideas to their full extent.

6.4.4   Phase IV—Performing

It is during Phase IV that a team truly begins to function like a team. You can feel the excitement, the synergy. Ninety-five percent of all team members accept and are committed to teams. The team produces good work, and does it well. There exists team confidence, loyalty, and pride in the results achieved. Team members still argue, but this is all now seen as part and parcel of the evolutionary team process. Conflict and arguments are fine; they represent an opportunity for team members to grow and to investigate other perspectives. Questions being asked by team members include: "What new issues should we address?" "How can we be more effective?" "Are we continuously improving?"

6.4.5   Phase V—Maturation

Phase V is a phase that people who write books for a living do not understand. They believe in Forming/Storming/Norming/Performing, and then you live happily ever after. To the contrary, folks who actually do this Genesis Enterprise stuff for a living have had the shock of their lives when they found themselves in the fifth phase of a four-phase process. Although the books all say Forming/Storming/Norming/Performing, believe me there is always a Phase V, Maturation. Maybe the reason Phase V is omitted is that it is not a wonderful phase. The maturity of the team that was evoked by Phases I, II, III, and IV results in the team getting tired, losing its edge, falling into "groupthink." Groupthink sets in when teams members all begin to think alike; there is no diversity of opinion, and no one wishes to dissent from his or her "wonderful team." This leads to over-confidence (false confidence), which in turn results in faulty decision making and the accompanying fall-off of performance. In addition, as a team matures, the remaining problems to tackle become more difficult. This further adds to burnout, and to a tendency to fall back on the old way of "letting others do the thinking, I just want to do my job." It is at this point that one of four changes has to be made by the Leadership Team:

1. If the team has completed its charter and performance is beyond the Leadership Team's expectations, it is time to disband the team, to thank the team members, to recognize their accomplishments, and to move on to the next opportunity.

2. If the team has completed its charter and performance is not beyond the Leadership Team's expectations, it is time to alter the charter and to put the team back to work. The charter alteration could be an upgrade in team level, an increase in scope, or an addition of another opportunity.

3. If the team has not completed its charter but Maturation is upon it, it is time to do a team-member upgrade. This involves sending one, two, or several volunteering team members to a conference, seminar, plant visits and/or visits to customers or other locations or your organization. This outside look often will recharge a team and lead to more performance improvement.

4. If the team has not completed its charter but Maturation is upon it and no one volunteers for a team-member upgrade, it is time to do an oil change. An oil change is a random rotation of team members. This should not be done as a reward or punishment. Typically, with a seven-member team, two members would be rotated at an oil change.

Interestingly, no matter whether the charter is altered, team members are upgraded, or team members are oil-changed, when any one of these things occurs, the team will return to Phase I. Now it is very likely that the team will move through the phases much more quickly the second, third, fourth, etc. time, but never forget that you will return to Phase I, then II, then III, and IV, and yes, you will return to Phase V again. This is how creating peak-to-peak performance should happen. This is the process of team development and of the Genesis Enterprise.

6.5   Team Roles

Unfortunately, much like the four phases of team development that I did not understand as being the *five* phases of team development until I had gone through the four phases several times, there has been an evolution in the understanding of the roles played on teams that has occurred over the last 15 years. It is now clear that for a team to successfully evolve and perform these six team roles must be filled:

1. Team Sponsor
2. Team Liaison
3. Team Leader
4. Team Reporter
5. Team Recorder
6. Team Member

The next six subsections define these roles.

6.5.1   Team Sponsor

A team sponsor is the person who defines the need for a team. This person sells the opportunity of the team to the Leadership Team, and sometimes writes the first draft of the charter. The team sponsor may move on to become the team leader, liaison, or member, or may not be further involved after the team has been chartered. The team sponsor often will gather some initial statistics and define the potential for improvements. Sponsors can be company presidents, new employees, and even people outside of the company.

At a company picnic a few years ago, a production foreman's 16-year-old daughter asked why the company was so obviously divided between office workers, production workers, and management. The production foreman asked her daughter what she meant, and the daughter pointed to several things at the picnic (where people sat, who ate first, how people interacted, etc.) that indicated where everyone fit in the pecking order. In this case, the 16-year-old daughter became the team sponsor of a company culture team that was very instrumental in bringing the company peak-to-peak performance success.

Sponsors come from different educational levels, backgrounds, and experiences. The Leadership Team should encourage team sponsors to come forward. The Leadership Team should create easy, nonthreatening ways for potential sponsors to share their thoughts. Of course, the easiest method of learning from team sponsors is to listen. To go to the floor, to be amongst the people, and to listen. About half of all successful team sponsors are people who you would never guess would be such. This tells us that the need for teams is as well understood at the top of the company as it is at the bottom. All people associated with an organization should be encouraged to put forth their ideas and to be a team sponsor.

6.5.2 Team Liaison

A clear indication of whether an organization is pursuing self-managing teams or self-directed teams is the existence of a team liaison. Organizations pursuing self-management will have team liaisons, whereas organizations pursuing self-direction will not have team liaisons. A team liaison provides direction for a team as it pursues its charter. A team liaison is a person from the Leadership Team assigned to the team to ensure that it is following the Genesis Enterprise process and that progress against the charter is being made. (An alternative reporting arrangement exists when a Strategy Team exists, in that in this circumstance there will be a team liaison from the Strategy Team to the Leadership Team, and several different team liaisons from the Strategy Team to each of the Offspring Work Teams.) The team liaison, however, is not a member of the team, and thus should be involved only in support of the team leader, in assuring team focus on its charter, and in responding to questions from the team. The team liaison has the authority and the responsibility to speak for the Leadership Team (Strategy Team). Each question asked of the team liaison by the team can receive one of four responses:

1. I don't understand the question. Please clarify by helping me to understand...

2. Yes. The team may go forward.

3. No. This should not be pursued for the following reasons...

4. I don't feel comfortable responding to that, but I'll take it to the Leadership Team (Strategy Team), get their response, and be back to you in a week.

Of course, the team liaison needs to be fully accountable to the Leadership Team (Strategy Team) for all responses provided to the team. The team liaison shall act as the communication conduit between the Leadership Team (Strategy Team) and the team. The team liaison should report to the Leadership Team (Strategy Team) at each Leadership Team (Strategy Team) meeting, and accept responsibility for working with the team leader to achieve team success. Especially early on, the team liaison should meet with the team leader after each meeting, and help the team leader to help the team make progress. The specific responsibilities of the team liaison are to

1. Support the team leader
   a. In ensuring that the team meets on a regular schedule
   b. In addressing any team member attendance problem
   c. In ensuring that a recorder is assigned at the beginning of each meeting to take legible/understandable minutes; and that minutes are submitted for typing/copying in a timely manner
   d. In having the team adhere to the team rules
   e. In focusing the team on the Model of Success
   f. In creating a climate of trust and openness
   g. In evolving the team, growing the team, assessing team progress, upgrading team members, and "changing the oil"
   h. In managing team conflict by proactively inquiring into other's viewpoints
   i. In identifying team training opportunities

2. Attend team meetings.

3. Once a team achieves self-managing status and regular weekly meetings are not held, to check with the team leader on a weekly basis to ensure team evolution on performance and peak-to-peak performance.

4. Participate in team meetings on an as-needed basis. To be aware of the fact that the team liaison is not the team leader nor a team member but an observer, facilitator, and resource. To be an active listener by listening well, fostering an environment for listening well, and being a cheerleader as appropriate.

5. Report to the Leadership Team on the team's successes, problems, evolution, and status.

6. To provide the team with input on how to best structure their recommendations to assure Leadership Team understanding. To help the team develop quality recommendations. To communicate recommendations from the team to the Leadership Team, and to communicate back approval, rejection and/or feedback.

7. To follow up on all Leadership Team–approved projects, and to provide regular status updates to the Leadership Team.

8. To emphasize the Model of Success and to assure team alignment with the Model of Success.

6.5.3 Team Leader

The team leader role in a Genesis Enterprise is critical. The team leader must be action-oriented, sensitive to others, and a good communicator. Good team leaders instinctively know that the reason for the team's existence is to improve performance through the synergistic interactions among team members. Unlike group leaders, whose task is to optimize the contributions of the group members, the Team Leader's task is to obtain real team performance that exceeds the sum of the contribution of the team members. Team leaders ensure quality communication and participation, run meetings, provide focus on the Model of Success and the team charter, build commitment, grow team members, manage team boundaries, and accept responsibility for team growth and progress. In addition, a team leader is also a team member, and so the team leader does real work, participates in decisions, and has opinions just like all other team members.

It is the team leader being a team member, however, that can cause difficulties on a team. The team leader must understand when it is best for him/her to be involved, and when it is best to let another team member step forward. Some team leaders want to do too much themselves, and some too little. It is critical that the team leader carry his/her own weight, but do so while projecting an attitude that he/she does *not* have all the answers and that his/her input is just one of many. The team leader should not be making team decisions, and should clearly project the attitude that the team will *not* be successful without the synergistic interplay of the entire team. This team-leader path is a narrow one, and one that must be walked carefully, but differently, with each team. No two team leaders will ever have identical teams, so no two team leaders should ever act the same. An aid that has been useful in helping team leaders to understand their role is the comparison between Supervisory Leadership, Group Leadership, and Team Leadership. Table 6.4 presents these roles. Since team leaders have more experience practicing Supervisory Leadership and Group Leadership rather than Team Leadership, it is normal for team leaders to err on the side of too much involvement, control, guidance, and direction, rather than too little. The team leader must focus his/her energy on this delicate balance, with help from the team liaison.

Team leaders shall be selected by the Leadership Team (Strategy Team) and should have a "no-fault" option of declining the team-leader role. The team leader should not pick the team members; this too should be done by the Leadership Team. There is no such thing as "co-team leaders." Each team can only have one team leader. The Leadership Team should keep the following ideas in mind when selecting a team leader:

1. The team leader must believe that people are the company's greatest asset.
2. The growth of people is natural.
3. Team growth is neverending.
4. The team leader is a facilitator, coach, and counselor.
5. Team-based continuous improvement is a process, not a program.

Table 6.4   Role Comparison Between Supervisory Leadership, Group Leadership, and Team Leadership

Approach to	Supervisory leadership	Group leadership	Team leadership
Change	React to change	Encourage change	Work with team to create change
People	Direct people	Involve people	Grow people and obtain synergy
Diversity	Minimize diversity	Allow diversity	Build upon diversity as team asset
Decisions	Explain decisions	Get input for decisions	Facilitate and support team decisions
Development	Train people	Develop people	Develop people and team
Coordination	Manage one-on-one	Coordinate group effort	Build trust and team identity
Conflict	Minimize conflict	Ignore conflict	Use conflict as opportunity to learn

6. Mistakes are okay, a part of learning.
   a. Be open, honest, and worthy of trust.
   b. Accept change, and realize that change is natural.
   c. Promote teamwork.
   d. Be open to new ideas.

The specific responsibilities of the team leader are to

1. *Listen to team members.*   The team leader must set the example by actively listening to team members. The team leader must involve the entire team in the discussion; draw quiet team members into the discussion; be certain only one person speaks at a time, that no one is interrupted, and that no one talks all the time.

2. *Create a climate of trust and openness.*   There must exist a climate of trust both within the team and between the team leader and the team members. It is only by developing this trust that team members will be open, and feel safe enough to say what they really think.

3. *Eliminate fear.*   Under the circumstances fear is a natural emotion, as the team-process asks team members to change their role within the company. This takes time, and the team leader, by creating a climate of trust and openness, must work to help team members overcome their fear. Team leaders must be patient if this is to evolve over time.

4. *Value diversity.* By encouraging active participation by all team members, the team leader is encouraging team members to present their views. It is very important that different views be encouraged, dissected, and understood. Differences of opinion should be openly and straightforwardly confronted. It is team diversity that is the heart-beat of team synergism.

5. *Focus on Model of Success, team charter, and team results.* A key role of the team leader is to be sure the team is making progress on its charter while maintaining focus on the Model of Success. The team leader should have several meeting planning horizons for team results, and help the team to make progress on this horizon. Time is of the essence, and team leaders must be accountable for effective time utilization if there is to be real performance improvement.

6. *Share information.* A supervisory leadership role has always been to hoard information, and to share it only on a "need-to-know basis." This is not a part of a Genesis Enterprise. The only way team members will actively participate in teams is if they feel they understand what is happening. If they feel information is being withheld from them or isn't to be trusted, there is little chance that team members will support the process of creating peak-to-peak performance.

7. *Lead effective meetings.* Section 8.1 will focus on how team leaders should lead effective meetings. For now, let it simply be said that it is the responsibility of the team leader to keep the team energized, structured, functioning in accordance with the team rules, disciplined in their problem-solving methodology, performing assignments between team meetings, and clearly moving forward.

8. *Break down barriers.* It is the team leader's job to identify and destroy any and all barriers to team success. These barriers may be cultural or political, or involve individuals who don't support the team process. There will be some supervisors who don't want their people to attend meetings. There will be some managers who will talk against the process. The team leader, with the support of the team liaison, must take action to break down these and other barriers.

9. *Grow the team.* The team leader must grow both the team members and the team collectively. The team leader must help the team to learn from mistakes, to go outside the team for information as necessary, and to encourage learning both through understanding other team members and individual and team self-assessment.

10. *Encourage creativity, risk-taking, and the creation of peak-to-peak performance.* The team leader, with the help of the team liaison, must help the team members to think creatively, and outside of their present situation. The problem-solving and decision-making skills of the team

should be enhanced, as should the team's ability to reach a conclusion. The team leader must encourage team members to support the decisions of the team and to actively support the implementation of these decisions.

AN OVEREXTENDED SUPERVISOR
BECOMES A SUPER TEAM LEADER

Bob had a bad case of ulcers, and was doing well neither from an effectiveness nor a physical perspective. Bob's department had quality, schedule, and budget problems. The Vice President of Manufacturing had two chats with Bob about early retirement. Bob didn't want to leave, but he knew he wasn't pulling his weight.

Then the company became team-based, and Bob became an extremely effective team leader. Within eight months, Bob had provided the leadership for his department to become a self-managed team with amazing quality, schedule, and budget turnarounds. In eight months, the company's poorest supervisor had become its best team leader. Looking back, it became clear that no supervisor could have been effective prior to the installation of the team-based process. There was simply no way one person could deal with the materials, scheduling, engineering, machine utilization, training, setup, and other day-to-day challenges. There were 18 to 24 hours of work to be done in the 8-hour day. Simply amazing, what happens when you create a realistic environment for a person to perform in. Perhaps even more amazing, last month's checkup showed that Bob's ulcers no longer existed. Simply amazing, the power of a team-based organization!

6.5.4   Team Reporter

The role of the team reporter may appear to be that of a spokesperson for the team at the monthly Communication Forum. This certainly is one aspect of the team reporter task, but not the entire task. Being the team reporter should be a month-to-month assignment. Next month's team reporter should be selected at the first team meeting after each month's Communication Forum. In this way, although the assignment is to make a presentation at the Communication Forum, the team reporter acts as team progress champion for the next month. You see, the reporter doesn't want to have to stand up in front of the Communication Forum and say, "My team has met four times since the last Communication Forum, and we are actively looking into three projects, but we have no results to report."

The team reporter wants to be able to report on how well the team is performing. Thus, the hidden portion of the reporter's task is to act as a motivator for closure, for progress, and for action, so that when he or she stands up at the Communications Forum they will have several significant things to say, to demonstrate their team's progress and the real peak-to-peak performance improvements coming from their team.

6.5.5 Team Recorder

Team recorders are assigned at the beginning of each meeting, and the role should be rotated among all of the team members except the team leader. The apparent role of the team recorder is to take the minutes of team meetings. These minutes should be a record of the meeting (date, time, location, attendees, topics discussed, decisions made, assignments, and call for next meeting) and should provide to both team members and non-team members an understanding of what happened at the team meetings. Team members should look upon these minutes as being a thread of consistency from team meeting to team meeting.

A second, also important, role of the team recorder is that he or she functions as an equalizer and a hook of involvement for all team members. Within the team meetings there are no titles, bosses, pecking order. All team members are equal. The equal assignment of recorders around the room is an illustration of this equalization. It is very helpful for a worker to see the president of the company being assigned the task of team recorder, just as he or she was in prior weeks. The recorder task also provides for the involvement of all team members. Being responsible for writing the team minutes requires the recorder to pay attention and to truly listen to all team members. This practice will facilitate the team's overall ability to listen to one another.

An important mistake to avoid is to have the team recorder be responsible for producing the minutes. It works much better if, after a team meeting, the recorder gives the team minutes to the team leader. This allows the team leader to help the recorder not only with production and distribution but also with those issues of spelling, grammar, and accuracy that may cause some embarrassment to the team members. To some, the recorder's role is not going to seem an important one, and these people are going to want to assign a permanent recorder who always does the minutes. This is a mistake, and will slow down the evolution of the team and the growth of team identity. Trust me—use a revolving recorder.

6.5.6 Team Members

In Chap. 2 and then again in Sec. 6.1 of this chapter, the "What is good leadership?" question was discussed. A similar question, in that it too cannot be answered, is, "What are the characteristics of the members of an ideal team?" Although there has been extensive research on this topic, there are no magic formulas to ensure team success. In the most in-depth analysis yet conducted of what constitutes the ideal team, Dr. R. Meredith Belbin spent over nine years of research in the composition of teams.

The result of this work indicates that an ideal team consists of the people described in Table 6.5. Of course, the challenge in trying to configure such a team is that in the real world there are only a certain number of people who have the technical understanding and involvement with the scope of the team to be positive contributors. Therefore, what we must do is learn from Dr. Belbin's work that what we want on a team is *diversity*. This diversity of team membership should include diversity in talent, personality, age, background, experience, education, sex, race, and all other member features. Perhaps just as interesting a result from Dr. Belbin's work about the diversity that is required to have a successful team, is the corollary that what results in the poorest team is a "pure team." In other words, a team that consists of all the same type of people will not be a successful team. The reason this is so interesting is that many organizations, in an effort to ensure successful teams, go through an extensive testing process to be sure that all team members meet the organization team profile. This effort to ensure successful teams actually does just the opposite: it assures team failure. In fact, if during the selection of team members someone says, "Don't place Bob on a team; he's just a troublemaker," I have just decided I want Bob on the team. You *want* troublemakers, you *want* diversity. Select team members in such a way as to maximize diversity and you will select successful teams.

Team members should be nominated to serve on teams and should be required to attend a team orientation session, but should be given a "no-fault" opportunity to decline to serve on the team. At the orientation, the potential team member should be given an overview of the team process, should participate in a review of the team charter, and should be told that the definition of a team member is *a person who has agreed to be committed to the team, to work with the team, and to work toward team success.* If, after the team orientation, the person decides not to be a team member, this is fine. The Leadership Team should replace the people not wishing to serve and should hold a second team orientation. It is in fact the allowing of people to have a "no-fault" opportunity to decline to serve on a team that causes most people to want to serve on a team. Having a few decline to serve on teams early in the process of implementing teams is good, since it allows everyone to see that no one is being forced into "doing teams."

Team members should understand that their role has the following requirements:

Table 6.5 Members of an Ideal Team

Type	Typical features	Positive qualities	Allowable weaknesses
Company worker	Conservative, dutiful, predictable	Organizing ability, practical common sense, hard-working, self-disciplined.	Lack of flexibility, unresponsiveness to unproved ideas.
Chairman	Calm, self-confident controlled	A capacity for treating and welcoming all potential contributors on their merits and without prejudice. A strong sense of objectives.	No more than ordinary, in terms of intellect or creative ability.
Shaper	Highly strung, outgoing, dynamic	Drive, and a readiness to challenge inertia, ineffectiveness, complacency, or self-deception.	Proneness to provocation, irritation, and impatience.
Plant	Individualistic, serious-minded, unorthodox	Genius, imagination, intellect, knowledge.	Up in the clouds, inclined to disregard practical details or protocol.
Resource investigator	Extroverted, enthusiastic, curious, communicative	A capacity for contacting people and exploring anything new. An ability to respond to challenge.	Liable to lose interest once the initial fascination has passed.
Monitor-evaluator	Sober, unemotional, prudent	Judgment, discretion, hard-headedness.	Lacks inspiration or the ability to motivate others.
Team worker	Socially oriented, rather mild, sensitive	An ability to respond to people and to situations and to promote team spirit.	Indecisiveness at moments of crisis.
Completer-finisher	Painstaking, orderly, conscientious, anxious	A capacity for follow-through. Perfectionism.	A tendency to worry about small things. A reluctance to "let go."

1. To be aligned with the Model of Success and to understand the impact of the Model of Success on them

2. To support and have ownership of the team charter, and to accept responsibility for the level of team empowerment specified in the charter

3. To honestly advocate from their own perspective while actively listening to the positions of others, and to be flexible in weighting the positions of others in making decisions

4. To respect diversity and to learn from others

5. To trust the team leader and other team members

6. To participate in the meetings by communicating openly and honestly

7. To be focused on creating peak-to-peak performance for both the task at hand and the team

8. To support the team leader

9. To use their talents and energy to work for the team's success

10. To do assignments on time and to the best of their ability

11. To exercise self-restraint in an effort to allow other team members to contribute and to grow

12. To sacrifice for the benefit of the team

13. To support all decisions made by the team

14. To be accountable for the implementation of all team recommendations

15. To accept full ownership of team-recommended improvements

6.6   Team Progression

There are two team progression philosophies. The first is what I call the train, train, train approach to becoming a team-based organization. This philosophy advocates having everyone in the company attend a large amount of team training. This training may require each person to attend 40, 100, 150, or as high as 200 hours of communication, team management, problem solving, listening, etc., etc., etc. training. Needless to say, this training is very expensive and can easily take six months or longer to complete. All the while, the company continues to operate "business as usual."

Even though this training often has excellent content, it is rarely well received by the workers. They are not interested in learning things that at the time seem irrelevant. Further, only a small amount of this learning sticks, because there is no place to apply the lessons learned as there are no teams until the training is complete. The reports of progress from the train, train, train philosophy describe not improvement in operations but rather the number of hours of training provided. Eventually the training ends and some team efforts are pursued. Unfortunately, since the emphasis was on training and not on the process of becoming a team-based organization, rarely are these teams successful. Typically, management concludes the effort and moves on to a new program with a feeling of satisfaction, for its team is now ready to face the challenges of tomorrow because the people in the organization are now much better trained to work as teams to do their jobs.

Blah, blah, blah! This is not a team-based process. This is training for training's sake, and has nothing to do with becoming a Genesis Enterprise.

The second team progression philosophy is called *the process-based approach* to becoming a team-based organization. This approach advocates doing teams. What is done is to create a team! Then create another team. Will mistakes be made? Sure. That's great! Mistakes are opportunities to learn and should be embraced as jewels of learning. Will training be required? Sure. How to do it? How about Just-In-Time training? You develop the training in advance, but then you present the training when a team indicates that it needs training, Just-In-Time. Team leaders and team liaisons should look for opportunities to train. The philosophy of Just-In-Time training says that when a team uncovers a need for training, the team should receive training to allow it to discover new knowledge, which should then be (Just-In-Time) applied by putting the new knowledge into practice (Recovering). This Uncover, Discover, Recover process of Just-In-Time training truly allows for both individual and team member growth, as well as for team collective growth and for the performance improvements that result from putting the new knowledge into practice.

The team progression that should be followed to pursue a process-based approach to becoming a team-based organization is as follows:

1. Team charter is drawn up by the Leadership Team.

2. Team orientation takes place.

3. Team reviews charter.

4. Team accepts/refines charter.

5. Team creates team ownership of charter.

6. Team pursues process as defined on team charter.

7. Leadership Team reviews progress of existing teams and takes appropriate action. When time is right, Leadership Team recycles to Step 1.

6.7 Characteristics of Successful Teams

Successful teams are not necessarily teams where morale is high and people are happy. Morale and happiness are individual characteristics, not team characteristics. Just as successful teams may consist of both happy and sad people, so too may unsuccessful teams consist of both happy and sad people. What is important in defining a successful team is not the individuals on the team but the team as a whole. The 10 characteristics that define a successful team are the following.

1. *The team has a collective and expanding understanding of the Model of Success and the team charter.* The team members have struggled and from time to time continue to struggle, with the meaning of the Model of Success and the content of the team charter. This struggling is good, as it builds team commitment. The team members share a common vision of where the team is headed, and realize that their success can be achieved only through the entire team working together as one.

2. *Team commitment and confidence is growing.* There is an ongoing increase of trust, respect, and support. Individual commitment and confidence flow from the pride in the growth of the team's commitment and confidence. There evolves a sense of team excellence and a conviction that mediocrity will not be accepted. Conflict is viewed as an opportunity to learn, and there is no win/lose attitude but rather an attitude of mutual discovery and support of the team's growth in understanding.

3. *There exists a feeling of interdependency.* As individuals acquire new skills and talents, these are viewed not as individual assets but as team assets. Each team member feels that he or she is important to the team and that he/she can and will influence the team. The team will listen equally to all team members and is stronger as a whole than they are as individuals. All team members have a sense of belonging.

4. *The team feels good about its opportunity to make presentations at the Communication Forum and, as a team, takes pride in the credit and recognition the team receives from these presentations.* The team works hard to document performance improvement results and to present these at the Communication Forum.

5. *The team is action/progress-oriented and is achieving significant peak-to-peak performance improvement results.* The team pulls together to each do their part to achieve team results. The team members are prepared for team meetings, and responsive to the needs of other team members.

6. *There exists clear, honest, open, and effective communication.* Team members openly express themselves, and feel free to ask questions with the confidence that other team members will respond with candid answers. There are no hidden agendas, no politics, and everything is above-board. Team members answer not only the questions asked but also in the spirit of the questions asked. Team members avoid the practice of providing narrow responses that require other team members to play "20 questions" to obtain a real understanding. The team has a common language that allows all team members to gain the same understanding of what team members are saying. The team members share common access to all information relevant to the team. Team members are anxious to share information, as information is viewed as being the key to each team member's contribution to the team.

7. *All team members value and appreciate team diversity, as explained in Sec. 6.5.6.*

8. *The team members have a shared perspective of how their team functions.* There is a shared understanding of the team-based process, the team roles, and how the team will achieve success.

9. *The team members believe in and conduct self-assessments to improve their performance and their ability to accomplish more.* The team members believe that the team should continuously improve. It is in this spirit that the team members ask of themselves, "How well are we functioning as a team?" "What barriers are preventing us from being more successful?" and "What can we do to achieve more?"

10. *Team members have a common and shared view of how the team is progressing.* Team members have shared Evidence of Success and have the same view on Evidence of Success status. They feel comfortable with the team's progress, but are anxious for greater results. They are optimistic about continued success and how this success will be measured.

6.8   Conclusion

One of the greatest challenges in creating a successful team-based organization is overcoming all the existing paradigms of teams. This chapter has presented the foundation upon which the transformation from individuals to teams may be based. This transformation from individuals to teams is a core element in becoming a Genesis Enterprise. A team is defined as *a small number of people who use synergy to work together for a common end.* In a Genesis Enterprise, there will exist five different types of teams:

1. Steering Team

2. Leadership Team

3. Communication Team

4. Design Team

5. Work Team

The six different levels of teams are

1. Traditional group

2. Natural group

3. Suggestion team

4. Improvement team

5. Semi-autonomous team

6. Self-managing team

To understand team development, one must understand that teams do not accept the process of creating peak-to-peak performance but that individuals accept this responsibility. As the team members accept their responsibility for creating peak-to-peak performance, the teams evolve through the five phases:

Phase I   Forming

Phase II   Storming

Phase III   Norming

Phase IV   Performing

Phase V   Maturation

For a team to successfully evolve and perform, the six team roles should be

1. Team sponsor

2. Team liaison

3. Team leader

4. Team reporter

5. Team recorder

6. Team member

Although many companies have adopted an approach of train, train, train to try to become a team-based organization, this program is doomed to failure. To the contrary, it is a process-based approach to becoming a team-based organization that works. Quite simply, to become a team-based organization, the organization must create, grow, and evolve teams. Successful teams are teams in which:

1. The focus is on the Model of Success and the team charter
2. Team commitment and confidence is growing
3. Team members exhibit a feeling of interdependency
4. The team feels good about Communication Forum presentations
5. The team is action-oriented and is achieving significant progress
6. There exists clear, honest, open, and effective communication
7. Team members value team diversity
8. Team members have a shared perspective on how their team functions
9. The team members believe in continuously improving their team
10. Team members have a common and shared view of how the team is progressing

References

Belbin, R. M., *Management Teams: Why They Succeed or Fail,* Butterworth Heinemann, London, England, 1981.

Caggiano, C., "The Profit-Promoting Daily Scorecard," *Inc.,* March 1994.

Carson, N., "The Trouble with Teams," *Training,* August 1992.

Davenport, T. H. and N. Nohric, "Case Management and the Integration of Labor," *Sloan Management Review,* Winter 1994.

Drucker, P.F., "There's More Than One Kind of Team," *Wall Street Journal,* February 11, 1992.

Gordon, J., "Work Teams: How Far Have They Come?" *Training,* October 1992.

Hall, G., J. Rosenthal, and J. Wade, "How to Make Reengineering Really Work," *Harvard Business Review,* November–December 1993.

Hammer, M. and J. Champy, "Reengineering the Corporation," *Harper Business,* New York, 1993.

Heguet, M., "Worker Involvement Lights Up Neon," *Training,* June 1994.

Johnson, H. T., *Relevance Regained: From Top-Down Control to Bottom-Up Empowerment,* The Free Press, New York, 1992.

Kaeter, M., "Reporting Mature Work Teams," *Teams,* April 1994.

Kaplan, R. S. and D. P. Norton, "Putting the Balanced Scorecard to Work," *Harvard Business Review,* September–October 1993.

Katzenbach, I. R. and D. K. Smith, *The Wisdom of Teams,* Harvard Business School Press, Boston, 1993.

Kleiner, B. M., "Managing Communication Successfully in Your Management System," *Industrial Management,* September–October, 1993.

Kouzes, J. M. and B. Z. Posner, *The Leadership Challenge,* Jossey-Bass, San Francisco, 1991.

Maguire, B., "Integrate Performance Measures to Focus Every Employee on What Matters," *Institute of Industrial Engineering Conference Procedures*, IIE, Norcross, GA, 1994.

Meyer, C., "How the Right Measures Help Team Excel," *Harvard Business Review*, May–June 1994.

Moran, L. and K. Hurson, "Mastering the New Role of Team Leadership," *48th Annual Quality Congress Proceedings*, ASQC, Milwaukee, WI 1994.

Navarre, L., "Wolfpack: Reengineering an Organization for Global Competition," *Industrial Institute Annual Conference*, Norcross, GA, 1994.

Neusch, D. R. and A. F. Siebenaler, *The High Performance Enterprise*, Oliver Wight Publications, Essex Junction, VT, 1993.

Niles, J. L. and N. J. Salz, "Why Teams Poop Out," *48th Annual Quality Congress Proceedings*, ASQC, Milwaukee, WI, 1994.

Ott, J. S., *The Organization Culture Perspective*, Brooks/Cole Publishing Company, Pacific Grove, CA, 1989.

Owen, J. V., "Concurrent Engineering," *Manufacturing Engineering*, November 1992.

Paulser, K. M., "Total Employee Involvement—Why Are You Waiting?" *Industrial Engineering*, February 1994.

Peters, T., *Thriving on Chaos*, Alfred A. Klopf, New York, 1987.

Power, C., K. Kerwin, R. Grover, K. Alexander and R. D. Hof, "Flops: Too Many New Products Fail. Here's Why and How to Do Better," *Business Week*, August 16, 1993.

Pritchett, P. and R. Pound, *High-Velocity Culture Change*, Pritchett Publishing Company, Dallas, TX, 1993.

Provost, L. and S. Leddich, "How to Take Multiple Measures to Get a Complete Picture of Organizational Performance," *National Productivity Review*, Autumn 1993.

Sayles, L. R., *The Working Leader*, The Free Press, New York, 1993.

Tapscott, D. and A. Caston, *Paradigm Shift*, McGraw-Hill, New York, 1993.

Templin, N., "Auto Plants, Hiring Again, Are Demanding Higher-Skilled Labor," *Wall Street Journal*, March 11, 1994.

VanAken, E. M. and D. S. Sink, "Addressing Problems and Implementation Issues of Self-Managing Teams," *International Industrial Engineering Conference Proceedings*, Norcross, GA, 1992.

Wellirs, R. and J. Workler, "The Philadelphia Story," *Training*, March 1994.

Zarembra, A. J., *Management in a New Key*, Industrial Engineering and Management Press, Norcross, GA, 1989.

Zemke, R., "Rethinking the Rush to Team Up," *Training*, November 1993.

7

Understanding Empowerment

Chapter 6 demonstrated that despite the fact that everyone is familiar with teams, we are inconsistent and imprecise in what we think about them. There is a lot more to teams than many have thought. This chapter will provide exactly the same type of revelation.

Probably one of the hottest terms of the 1990s was *empowerment.* As a buzzword, empowerment came to the forefront almost overnight, was thought to have magical powers, and then just as quickly as it came upon us, it got a bad reputation and was dismissed as a mistake.

In one Gallup Survey probing the empowerment subject, 66 percent of the respondents said that employees had been encouraged to get involved with decision making, but only 14 percent felt that employees were authorized to make the kind of decisions that management was talking about. In another survey, 96 percent of the companies indicated that they believed in teamwork and empowerment, but only 24 percent had a commitment to providing a process for this to occur. Interestingly, although smaller firms have reported greater success with empowerment, the 24 percent of all companies is not uniform across all *sizes* of companies. Only 13 percent of the companies in the 0-to-99 employee range, 25 percent of the companies in the 100-to-499 employee range, and 36 percent of the companies having over 500 employees have a commitment to providing a process for empowerment to take place.

Another interesting split in the understanding of empowerment existed based upon the level of the person in the company. Fifty percent of all executives believed that their company understood how to empower, but only 9 percent of the managers and supervisors felt their company understood empowerment. Why this lack of clarity? Why this misunderstanding? Why all the empowerment mistakes? Just as in Chap. 6, it has to do with understanding. It has to do with the definition of terms, and with everyone using the terms in a consistent manner. This chapter will do for empowerment what Chap. 6 did for teams.

7.1   The "E" Word

So, what happened to the empowerment train, after it got such a grand send-off from the train station? The concept of pushing decision-making authority down to the appropriate level in an organization seems so logical. How could empowerment get hit so badly that some are afraid even to use the term—hence the concept of "the E word"? Here are some E-word stories:

- Empowerment is based upon sharing power. So what happens is, the new "power" people start wielding authority with the same disregard for teamwork as the old people, and chaos prevails.

- Empowerment is based upon being accountable for your own performance, so good "performance" people make decisions that, although contrary to the good of the whole, will allow them to look good.

- Empowerment is natural for mature adults. In fact, empowerment will occur almost magically. "Zap, and it is done."

- Empowerment allows the workers to make their own decisions, so all the middle managers are no longer needed. Empowerment is the key to delayering and downsizing an organization. Lower cost, happier people, and better performance. "It doesn't get any better than this."

These E-word misunderstandings all lead to problems. In fact, these E-word misunderstandings of empowerment are so prevalent that before I define empowerment, it is important that I say what empowerment is *not*:

1. Empowerment is not abandonment.
2. Empowerment is not letting people do their own thing.
3. Empowerment is not letting people or teams define their own direction.
4. Empowerment is not a style of management or leadership.
5. Empowerment is not a concept or philosophy.
6. Empowerment is not the expansion of authority for employees to make more decisions.

So what *is* empowerment? First, it is critical to understand that empowerment is a *process*. Empowerment is not something that *has been* done, empowerment is something that *is being* done. Leaders do not grant, give, install, or bestow empowerment. Empowerment is something leaders cultivate, grow, and harvest. Empowerment is not giving power or redistributing power but the building, developing, and increasing of power through a synergistic process of cooperation, sharing, and working together. Individuals cannot grow power through synergy; only teams can do this. Synergy, by definition, is what teams do, and so empowerment cannot be an individual thing but must be a team thing. Hence, my definition of empowerment:

> Empowerment is the leadership process of building, developing, and increasing the power of an organization to perform through the synergistic evolution of teams.

Please read that definition a few times. Please really understand that definition of empowerment. Please be sure that when you use the word *empowerment,* the people to whom you are communicating understand this definition. A key characteristic of a Genesis Enterprise will be the universal understanding of this definition of empowerment. Genesis Enterprises will understand that

- Empowerment is a leadership process.
- Empowerment is building, developing, and increasing the power of an organization to perform.
- Empowerment is the synergistic evolution of teams.

GUERRILLA AND RENEGADE TEAMS: LOST IN SPACE

Unbelievable. In an article entitled "Guerrilla Teams: Friend or Foe," a Guerrilla or Renegade Team is defined as a team that springs up in the middle of a traditional organization where senior management does not support a team process. The article explains that although the team will likely be "quashed" and even if it enjoys some initial success it will most often be "too worn down by the struggle to continue," that there are some friendly tips on how to keep Guerrilla Teams "alive and well."

Give me a break! This type of stuff is so shallow and lacking in understanding of leadership, teams, and empowerment that it's almost funny. The thing that makes it *not* so funny is that the article appeared in the magazine *Training,* which is an excellent magazine for materials on leadership, teams, and empowerment.

Let me not just pick on this one article. I have a whole file of articles and yes, even a whole shelf of books that don't have a clue what they're talking about. My intention here is not to throw stones, but rather to send out a word of caution about what you read and what you believe.

Please help others to understand the truth about leadership, teams, and empowerment. We don't need to have our companies making detours via Guerrilla or Renegade Teams, or whatever fad is coming next, and getting lost in space.

7.2 Leadership's Empowerment Role

In the Genesis Enterprise, leadership has the responsibility for empowering, and teams the responsibility for performance. Leaders cannot succeed without teams, and teams cannot succeed without leadership. This is why Part 2 of this book deals with leadership and Part 3 with teams. This is as it must be. Genesis Enterprises must have strong leadership who accept accountability for empowering teams, and strong teams who accept accountability for performance. The following 10 factors define the role of leadership in the process of empowerment:

1. *Leadership must define organizational direction and ensure alignment.* The Steering Team as defined in Chaps. 2 and 6 must define an organization's Model of Success and obtain the organization's alignment with the Model of Success.

2. *Leadership must define the team process.* The Steering Team must define the team process, just as the rules of play must be defined for a baseball game. The Steering Team must define the topics defined in Chap. 6 with regard to
   - Types of teams
   - Levels of teams
   - Team development
   - Team roles

   The Steering Team also must address the mechanism by which teams succeed, as presented in Chap. 8.

3. *Leadership must define the flows of information within an organization.* The information flows in a Genesis Enterprise will be different from the information flows in a traditional organization. In a traditional organization, there exists a hierarchical information flow from the work level up through a Management Information System (MIS) to a Financial Information System (FIS) and an Executive Information System (EIS). Unfortunately, the MIS/FIS/EIS have nothing to do with leadership, little to do with the management of performance, and even less to do with team performance. For this reason, the information systems in a Genesis Enterprise must be significantly altered

from the information systems that existed in the traditional organization. The MIS/FIS/EIS systems must be replaced with the following:

- Leadership Information System (LIS): Customer Satisfaction, Financial Results, and Market Position Information
- Performance Information System (PIS): Operational Scoreboard, Business Trends, and Customer Service
- Team Information Systems (TIS): Peak-to-Peak Performance, Operational Improvements, and Results versus Goals

With this reconfigured flow of information, the Steering Team, Leadership Team, and Communications Team will utilize the LIS, PIS, and TIS to do their jobs. Design teams will focus on the PIS, and work teams will utilize both the PIS and the TIS. Genesis Leaders know that information is power. The process of empowerment demands that leadership provide the information that allows teams to accept accountability for their team performance. Genesis Enterprises will thrive on the availability and abundance of truly relevant information.

4. *Leadership must define the thrust of teams.* It is the task of the Leadership Team to define teams. This thrust must define why a team exists, what issues are to be considered, and what are the Evidences of Success for the team. The team thrust should define the subject of a team's endeavors and serve as the guiding light for the team's evolution.

5. *Leadership must define the time frame for performance improvement.* The Leadership Team must set specific, time-based goals for the team. These goals act as a guide for a team by defining the time frame in which results are expected. The Leadership Team must exhibit care that the goals established relate to measurable enhancements to the Evidence of Success, and not to the specific improvements that will result in the improved performance.

6. *Leadership must define team participants.* The Leadership Team must define the team leader, team liaison, and team members. It is the responsibility of the team liaison to bring the team leader on board with the team, and to support the team leader bringing the team members on the team. The Leadership Team must also define how much time should be spent by the team leader and members on the team activities.

7. *Leadership must define constraints.* The Leadership Team must define the scope of teams, things that the team cannot change, and the authority within which the team must function. Specific budgetary issues should be addressed, so that there exists no question as to what a team can and cannot do.

8. *Leadership must define the evolution of team authority.* In Chap. 6, the evolution of a team from a Suggestion Team to an Improvement Team to a Semi-Autonomous Team to a Self-Managed Team was presented. The Leadership Team must define an overall plan for the evolution of the empowerment process for a team. This plan should be specific, in that it should define specific tasks but be flexible in time frame. The time frame should then be defined by the Leadership Team as a team evolves. Table 7.1 presents an example of how a Leadership Team may define the evolution of a team authority.

9. *Leadership must define the team support structure.* The Leadership Team must be sure that the team has available the necessary resources required to perform its task. These resources may include access to information, people, computers, clerical support, etc. These resources should be described as specifically as possible, and should be communicated not just to the team but also to the people impacted by this allocation of these resources.

10. *Leadership must define the deliverables expected from the teams.* The Leadership Team must set forth the specific deliverables expected from the team, for the team to ensure its interconnectedness with the rest of the organization/process. These deliverables should include minutes, presentations, reports, and recommendations.

Table 7.1 The Empowerment Evolution for the Assembly Team

Type of team	Authority	Time frame (effective date)
Group	None	1994
Natural work group	Provide inputs on housekeeping, safety, damage materials, and quality	Early 1995
Suggestion team	As above, plus make performance improvement suggestions to Leadership Team on productivity and quality improvements	Mid-1995
Improvement team	As above, plus implement inventory accuracy, attendance, quality, and production reporting challenges	Mid-to-late 1995
Semi-autonomous team	As above, plus schedule changeovers, overtime, holidays and vacations, budgeting, capacity planning, and interface with purchasing and sales	Late 1995 to early 1996
Self-managed team	As above, plus customer interface, partnership evolution, team management, team member selection and appraisal, and product design	Some time in 1996

A review of these 10 factors indicates that the first 3 factors are tasks that must be done by the Steering Team. These tasks (define direction and assure alignment, team process, and information flows) are all foundation tasks upon which the evolving Genesis Enterprise will be built. The last 7 factors are all Leadership Team tasks that are a part of the ongoing Team Chartering process. A key aspect of the Genesis Enterprise will be this chartering process. It is this chartering process that allows the Leadership Team to pursue the empowerment of teams.

LEADERSHIP MUST UTILIZE BRAINPOWER

Intellectual capital is the most valuable asset of your company. Your company's competitive edge in the marketplace is the sum of everything everybody in your company knows. A key here is realizing that what is meant by "everybody" is *everybody*. Not just the research people, the engineers, the "knowledge workers," but *everybody*. The Genesis Leader understands that "everybody" means every employee, and thus accepts the responsibility for empowerment of the entire organization. It is in fact the empowerment of an organization's brainpower that results in the greatest use of its intellectual capital. It does little good in an organization to have wise people sitting around being wise. It is by empowering the wise people that the Genesis Leader, through the synergy of teams, can maximize return on investment of intellectual capital.

7.3 Chartering Teams

The seven steps of the process of chartering teams are as follows:

Step 1 Leadership team defines thrust for new team.

Step 2 Sponsor drafts charter.

Step 3 Leadership team reviews charter.

Step 4 Leadership team approves charter.

Step 5 Team reviews charter.

Step 6 Team accepts charter.

Step 7 Team evolves through the charter.

Step 1 involves the Leadership Team deciding what teams should be created. At the outset of the process of creating a team-based organization, the early teams should be cross-functional work teams, as it is cross-functional teams that provide the greatest opportunity for the organization's cultural transformation. Surprisingly, the Leadership Team process of selecting the first priorities is not straightforward. This, in fact, is more a reflection of the Leadership Team being a new team and going through the Norming/Storming stages than of the Leadership Team's true difference of opinion. Nevertheless, if this hurdle is not overcome, the evolution of the organization can get bogged down in the defining of these early teams.

For this reason, a Requirement of Success survey should be developed and used to define the thrust of these first teams. After the first teams have been chartered and are operational, additional cross-functional and functional work teams should be created by the Leadership Team in accordance with the potential for performance improvement.

Step 2 of the chartering process involves the selection by the Leadership Team of the person best qualified to write the team charter, and then this person preparing a draft of the charter. The person who prepares the first draft of the charter may or may not be a member of the Leadership Team. The person who prepares the charter is referred to as the Team Sponsor. Often, if the Team Sponsor is a member of the Leadership Team, this sponsor will also become the Team Liaison. If the Team Sponsor is not a member of the Leadership Team, then a different Team Liaison will have to be selected. The form that should be used by the Team Sponsor to draft the team charter is the charter form that will be used throughout the chartering process. A blank team charter form is given in Fig. 7.1. Appendix B presents several examples of team charters.

Step 3 of the process of chartering teams is the review by the Leadership Team of the preliminary charter. Typically, the Team Sponsor will present the preliminary charter. The Team Liaison will record team comments and revise the charter accordingly for Step 4, Leadership Team approval of the team charter. The Team Liaison will then meet with the Team Leader to discuss the charter and, if the Team Leader has not been a Team Leader previously, to help the Leader understand not only the charter but also the role of the Team Leader. The Team Leader will receive a Team Leader orientation and, given the Team Leader's acceptance of this role, the Team Liaison will then work with the Team Leader to have a Team Orientation. All Team Members will be invited to the Team Orientation.

At this meeting the Team Leader, Team Liaison, and Team Members will all be oriented into the team-based process and review the Team Charter (Step 5). At this point, the Team Leader and Team Liaison will work together to help the Team Members understand the Team Charter.

After Step 5, individuals will be given an opportunity to decline the opportunity to serve on the team. If people decline to serve, the Team Liaison shall go back to the Leadership Team to obtain approval for potential new members. The Team Liaison and/or Team Leader shall repeat Step 5 for any new members. Once the Team Membership has been solidified, then the Team should meet again (Step 6) to accept its charter.

Charter for the _____ Team
Team Sponsor: _____
Date: _____

      Leadership Team Preliminary _____
      Leadership Team Final _____

_____ Team Review _____
_____ Team Acceptance _____

1. *Opportunity*: (What is the reason this team exists?)

2. *Process*: (What are the steps to be followed, and what are the questions to be answered by this team?)

3. *Evidence of success*: (What results are expected, in what time frames, for this team to be successful?)

4. *Resources*: (Who are team members, team leaders, and team liaison; who will support the team if needed; how much time should be spent both in meetings and outside of meetings; and what additional resources are available to the team?)

5. *Constraints*: (What authority does the team have; what is the overall time frame for the evolution of the empowerment process; what things cannot be changed; what items are outside the scope of the team; and what budget does the team have?)

6. *Expectations*: (What are the outputs from the team, when are they expected to be complete, and to whom should they be given?)

Figure 7.1   Team Charter form

The Team Liaison shall have the following three choices in dealing with changes to the Team charter that are made by the Team:

1. For items considered to be refinements and not major changes in the Charter: to accept the refinements as they are defined.

2. For items considered to be major that change the thrust of the Charter: to either reject the changes as they are defined or place the changes on hold, discuss with the Leadership Team, and return to the next meeting with a clear direction.

3. For items about which the Team Liaison is uncertain: to place such items on hold, discuss with the Leadership Team, and return to the next team meeting with a clear direction.

Once the team has accepted its charter (Step 6), then the Team Charter may be published and distributed. The team is off and running. The team understands not only its level of authority, but also the empowerment path forward as the team evolves through their charter (Step 7).

BOUNDARYLESS, SPEED, AND STRETCH

In the annual report letter released in March of 1994, Jack Welch, CEO of General Electric, defined the following three operating principles that will be key to General Electric's "Building a work force with an absolutely infinite capacity to improve everything."

> *Boundaryless.* "Piercing the walls of 100-year-old fiefdoms and empires called finance, engineering, manufacturing, marketing, and gathering teams from all those functions in one room, with one shared coffee pot, one shared vision, and one consuming passion: to design the world's best jet engine, or ultrasound machine, or refrigeration."

> *Speed.* "Speed means that new products are coming out with drumbeat rapidity." Speed also means focusing GE's efforts on "the speed of our order-to-remittance cycle (from time of order to when we get paid) as well as allowing us to shift the center of gravity of the company rapidly toward the high-growth areas of the world."

> *Stretch.* "Stretch is a concept that would have produced smirks, if not laughter, in the GE of three or four years ago, because it essentially means using dreams to set business target—with no real idea of how to get there."

Mr. Welch states that he is looking for "leaders at every level who can energize, excite, and coach rather than enervate, depress, and control. In some cases, this means parting company with some impressive people who won't block for others or play as a part of a team." What an endorsement for the use of boundaryless and speed-based teams that respond to stretch charters to pull an organization towards peak-to-peak performance. No doubt about it, Jack Welch is a Genesis Leader.

7.4 Conclusion

Empowerment has been widely misunderstood. In fact, the lack of understanding of empowerment has led many, many organizations to the conclusion that team-based organizations simply don't work. To the contrary, the Genesis Enterprise will be a team-based organization in which empowerment will be understood to be the leadership process of building, developing, and increasing the power of an organization to perform through the synergistic evolution of teams.

In the Genesis Enterprise, leadership has the responsibility for empowering, and teams the responsibility for performance. The Steering Team has the organizational responsibility for laying the foundation for teams. The Leadership Team has the organizational responsibility for chartering teams. This chartering process defines the empowerment of teams, and it is the framework within which a Genesis Enterprise will create peak-to-peak performance.

References

Belasco, J. A. and R. C. Stayer, *Flight of the Buffalo*, Warner Books, New York, 1993.

Geber, B., "Guerrilla Teams: Friend or Foe?" *Training*, June 1994.

Holpp, L., "Applied Empowerment," *Training*, February 1994.

Hyatt, J. C., "GE Chairman's Annual Letter Notes Strides by 'Stretch' of the Imagination," *The Wall Street Journal*, March 7, 1994.

Kouzes, J. M. and B. Z. Posner, *The Leadership Challenge*, Jossey-Bass Publishers, San Francisco, 1991.

Landes, L., "The Myth and Misdirection of Employee Empowerment," *Training*, March 1994.

Parsons, N. E., "Employee Empowerment: A Tactical Approach," *Quality*, February 1994.

Stewart, T. A., "Brainpower," *Fortune*, June 3, 1991.

Tompkins, J. A., "Team-Based Continuous Improvement," *Job Shop Technology*, March 1993.

——, "Team-Based Continuous Improvement: How to Make the Pace of Change Work for You and Your Company," *Material Handling Engineering*, January, February, March, and April 1993.

——, "Teams," *Industrial Product Bulletin*, October and November 1992, January, February, and March 1993.

Vogt, J. F., and K. L. Murrell, *Empowerment in Organizations*, Pfeiffer & Company, San Diego, California, 1990.

8

Shifting from Individuals to Teams

Genesis Enterprises will shift the emphasis from "I" to "we." Genesis Enterprises will not "think individuals" but will focus on teams. Genesis Enterprises will be team-based organizations where strong leadership will grow successful teams. Genesis Leaders will define a peak-to-peak performance culture, provide organizational direction, and assure organizational motivation, while becoming a team-based organization.

A major roadblock to the success of a Genesis Leader is a basic lack of understanding of how to create the shift from individual to team. As described in Sec. 6.6, there are two fundamental approaches to creating this shift: the process-based or results-driven process, versus the training-based or activity-centered process. The trap that is laid, and the mistake that is often made, result from some "commonsense" philosophy which in reality is, alas, nonsense. Consider the following traps:

> Continuous improvement requires a commitment to learning. How, after all, can an organization improve without first learning something new?
> DAVID A. GARVIN
> *Harvard Business Review*

> Quality takes a long time to learn and I wish we had accepted that earlier. It would have saved us a lot of anxiety and frustration....People spend what seem like huge amounts of time reading about quality or going to training courses, only to realize they don't know much and their company hasn't really started quality management....One of the surprises is the length of time it takes to actually begin; in our case it took two years.
> PATRICIA A. GALAGAN
> *Nations Business*

Pure common sense, you say? Well, doesn't it follow that

1. To become a team-based organization, a company must practice continuous improvement.
2. Continuous improvement requires continuous learning.
3. Continuous learning requires training.
4. Therefore, the approach to become a team-based organization is training, and so what we must do is pursue a training-based process.

This commonsense approach leads to

1. The retention of a consulting firm to do training
2. A classroom training program that makes every school teacher smile
3. Huge expenditures on training that result in little true performance improvement
4. Success stories that read
   - "318 people have completed all 90 hours of the XXX program.
   - 250 people have completed the 60-hour XX program.
   - 79 people have completed the 40-hour X program.
   - Positive morale.
   - Good feedback on training.
   - No performance improvements.
   - No results."

This is not common sense; this is nonsense. This does not work, and although there are many, many consultants out there providing a train, train, train program, and although these programs may *feel* good, they simply don't produce results. Let me be clear: The training-based or activity-based or activity-centered process to become a team-based organization is *wrong,* will not *work,* and cannot be *made* to work. The problem lies in a total misunderstanding of the learning process. Learning, as it is needed by your organization today, has little to do with training as practiced by organizations today.

Think about learning. If you close your eyes and think about learning, most of us see a mental picture of ourselves sitting in a classroom. A teacher is at the front of the room, actively involved in the process of teaching. You passively listen. The teacher is responsible for the learning process. This "formal education" picture is clear in our minds, as we have all spent many years participating in this learning process. Thus, it is not so strange that, when asked to think about learning, we pull out our old mental image and once again envision a classroom.

Unfortunately, this thinking about learning is wrong, is obsolete, and is the culprit that leads many organizations astray in their pursuit of becoming a team-based organization. Why does classroom training most often fail to fulfill the learning needs of the organization? Here are the Top 10 reasons:

1. *Training is not done Just-In-Time.* The proper philosophy of learning is Uncover–Discover–Recover. Uncover the need for knowledge. Discover new knowledge, and Recover by putting new knowledge into action. Classroom training typically only addresses the Discover element. Because classroom training is not Just-In-Time, the leading responses to it are:
   a. "They talked about a lot of things I will never need to know." (Failure to Uncover the need for new knowledge.)
   b. "I'm not sure what I learned has application to what I do." (Failure to Recover by putting knowledge to work.)

2. *Training is not a part of the process of creating peak-to-peak performance.* Training is seen as this month's program, not as part of an overall process. Teachers teach their program, but don't tie their program into the organization's Model of Success or to what is happening in the organization today.

3. *Training is inflexible.* There is an assumption that one size fits all, when in fact it is clear the needs vary from "extra-small" to "extra-extra large." Generic training is provided, independent of need. In fact, what is key is not what is learned, but what programs have been attended.

4. *Training is sabotaged.* Managers and supervisors don't support training. They see training as a waste of time, and so they undercut its effectiveness and often make fun of and openly criticize the training.

5. *Training burnout occurs very quickly.* Especially for people in Operations, the thought of sitting in a classroom for four or more hours a day is unbearable. Independent of the effectiveness of the teacher, many people turn off well before the teacher does.

6. *Training is not built into the schedule.* When people return from training, all of their work is still there, waiting for them. They resent the training, as it takes time away from their "real job."

7. *Training accountability doesn't exist.* There is no or little training follow-up, and no or little measurement of the effectiveness of training. Students logically conclude, "If there isn't any follow-up, how important can this training be?"

8. *Training is of individuals, not of teams.* Training is given to individuals, but not to the people around the individual, and so there exists little desire to get involved with what was learned. Even worse, sometimes there exists resentment from the people who didn't go to the training toward the ones who did.

9. *Training isn't viewed as an organizational priority.* Although all the right words were said, when decisions had to be made on attending or not attending training, often the decision is taken not to attend the training. Urgent problems take precedence over training, and thus a lack of training continuity exists.

10. *Training objectives are not focused.* Poorly focused training objectives result in trying to do too much in too short a time frame. This time compression leads to a lecture-only format, which is counterproductive to real learning.

The formal-educational mental picture has little to do with organizational learning, successful teams, peak-to-peak performance, and becoming a Genesis Enterprise. This formal-educational mental picture must be replaced by a process-based or results-driven process of learning that will support the shift in an organization from individual to teams. This process-based approach to organizational learning may be called "learning-by-doing," "action learning," or "team-based learning." The purpose of this chapter is to build upon the Chap. 6 foundation of teams and the Chap. 7 foundation of empowerment, to create the needed shift from individual to teams within an organization. The five sections of this chapter define the following five keys to successfully evolving a team-based organization:

1. Having successful team meetings

2. Organizing for team-based success

3. Avoiding team failures

4. Achieving team-based success

5. Becoming a learning organization

8.1 Having Successful Team Meetings

The Team Development process of forming/storming/norming/performing/maturation, defined in Sec. 6.4, presents the progression from a group to team. Although none of us either likes meetings or needs more meetings, we must be aware of the fact that for this progression to occur, there must be team meetings. In fact, team meetings are the place where teams become teams. It is only after several meetings that teams become teams and the shift from individuals to teams occurs in an organization. It is from this perspective that the importance of successful team meetings may best be understood. Consider:

1. Genesis Enterprises will have undergone a shift from individuals to teams.

2. To shift from individuals to teams, an organization must consist of several successful teams.

3. For teams to become successful, they must conduct successful team meetings.

Therefore, to become a Genesis Enterprise, an organization must conduct successful team meetings. The following are some guidelines for an organization to conduct successful team meetings.

1. *First impressions.* Especially early in the evolution of a Genesis Enterprise, the first impressions received by the Team Members will have a big impact on how they support the team and the process. These first impressions will include how they are invited to the team orientation, the team orientation, the first meeting after the orientation, etc. Every effort should be made to help Team Members at the outset to be comfortable with the process and to break down barriers. Team Liaisons and Leaders must work extra hard early in the process, to minimize Team Member surprises, hassles, and awkwardness.

2. *Team meeting etiquette.* All Team Members must understand and adhere to the following:
   a. As explained in Chap. 6, Team Members may not send "someone in their place" to team meetings but personally attend.
   b. Team Members all must be punctual, and team meetings should start and stop on schedule.
   c. No telephone calls or interruptions shall be allowed during team meetings. Beepers will be turned off.
   d. Within the team, there are no bosses, supervisors, or rankings. All Team Members are equal.
   e. Team Members will not seek to win an argument. Team Members should balance advocacy and inquiry and should speak candidly, openly, and clearly, and listen actively.

3. *Team roles are followed.* In Sec. 6.5, the roles of Team Sponsor, Team Liaison, Team Leader, Team Reporter, Team Recorder, and Team Member are all defined. It is important that all of these roles be filled and that there be clarity as to who is filling each role. Many teams have had unsuccessful team meetings because they failed to identify or fulfill one of the team roles.

4. *Team rules.* There are six team rules that we have found to be necessary to support successful team meetings. These rules facilitate trust, openness, and participation. They should be hung on the wall

in the team meeting rooms, and should be reviewed at the outset of each team meeting. The team rules are

a. Total honesty
b. Total amnesty
c. Listen to others
d. Stay focused
e. Manage time
f. Be prepared

The Team Leader should be certain the Team Members have the following understandings of the rules:

a. *Total honesty.* Team Members are encouraged to say what they think. No politics, no game-playing and no adversarial relationships. Everyone is encouraged to express his/her views and to contribute his/her beliefs to the team.

b. *Total amnesty.* There will be no repercussions back to individuals for things said at team meetings. Individual views and beliefs will not be quoted in the team minutes. This rule is not meant to create a veil of secrecy but rather to encourage total honesty without fear of negative reactions.

c. *Listen to others.* Team Members are encouraged to actively listen to others. Team Members must be aggressive in trying to understand what others are saying. To do this well, Team Members must listen both for facts and feelings, make eye contact, minimize listening distractions, and paraphrase back to the speaker what the listener heard so as to assure purity of communication.

d. *Stay focused.* Team meetings should stay on the agenda topics. All comments should contribute to the discussion at hand. Side talk should be minimized.

e. *Manage time.* Team meetings should run as scheduled. Most of the time, team meetings should be 60 minutes or less. Once a team has gotten used to dealing with a 60-minute time-frame meeting, efficiency and effectiveness will improve.

f. *Be prepared.* At the end of each team meeting, assignments will be made. Team Members are responsible to complete these assignments on schedule. Not completing assignments in a timely manner should not be accepted. Team Leaders and Team Liaisons, as appropriate, should support Team Members completing assignments on schedule.

5. *Action orientation.* Team meetings must bear fruit. The Team Leader and Team Liaison should plot a team's progression and should share the timing and path forward in accordance with the team charter with the Team Members. There should always exist a sense of urgency and direction to the team meetings. For team meetings to be

successful, the majority of the Team Members must believe that the team meetings are worthwhile and action-oriented.

6. *Team meeting agenda/team meeting minutes.* All team meetings must follow a written agenda and should result in an orderly progression of thought on the "agendized" topics. A typical team agenda should be
   a. Assign recorder.
   b. Review meeting rules.
   c. Review Model of Success.
   d. Review last meeting.
   e. Pursue objectives.
   f. Review assignments.

   The first four items should take 2 to 5 minutes. The last item should take 2 to 5 minutes. Thus, the majority of the meeting time should be spent pursuing the meeting objectives. After the meeting, the Team Recorder should give the Team Leader the meeting minutes. These minutes should record decisions, actions items, and assignments. The Team Leader should review the minutes, have them prepared and distributed.

7. *Meeting focus.* Team meeting focus must flow from the team charter. The Team Leader should frequently refer to the Model of Success and the team charter so as to provide the context and purpose of all team deliberations. The Team Leader should help the Team Members stay on target and progressively lead the team to achieving results.

8. *Communications.* Team communications should be natural and spontaneous. All barriers to effective communication must be eliminated. The Team Leader should work to achieve an overall balance in team participation. The entire team should work together to ensure that all that is said is both heard and understood.

9. *Thought-provoking.* A normal day doesn't include much time for most people to think. The day-to-day harried, rushed pressures of the moment prevent many of us from having the opportunity to sit back and think. Successful team meetings should not only be a time to think but also a time when our thinking is stimulated by the thoughts of others. Team meetings are the place where the synergy of teams occurs. The Team Leader must create an environment where ideas flow and Team Members are stimulated to think outside of the box.

10. *Team meeting assessment.* If a team is not having successful team meetings, it is important for the Team Leader and/or Team Liaison to take action to improve performance. A good method of highlighting the difficulties of a team is the utilization of a Team Assessor. A Team Assessor is a Team Member who is assigned the role of assessor.

The assessor should be a meeting observer and should use one of the following three formats to help the team improve team meeting performance.

a. *Freelance.* The Team Assessor should take notes during the meeting and then spend a couple of minutes just prior to the meeting's conclusion providing the team with feedback on how the team performed. Both positive and negative aspects of the meeting should be discussed by the Team Assessor and the team.

b. *A-B-C-D.* All team meeting deliberations may be defined as

    A = Administrative—routine housekeeping team issues

    B = Building the Business—working toward the Model of Success, the team charter, and team success

    C = Crisis—urgent, firefighting, hot activities that demand immediate attention

    D = Dumb—things that don't contribute to the topic at hand or to the team moving forward

In this case, the Team Assessor would keep track of the time in the meeting spent on each of the A-B-C-D categories. The meeting review checklist presented in Fig. 8.1 might be helpful to the Team Assessor in evaluating the team meetings. At the end of the meeting, the Team Assessor would report on what percent of the meeting time was spent on A-B-C and D discussions. It would not be surprising to see a new team report its activities as

    A = 30%
    B = 10%
    C = 30%
    D = 30%

Similarly, it would not be unusual to see a performing team receive an assessor's report that says

    A = 5%
    B = 90%
    C = 5%
    D = 0%

c. *Team meeting assessment form.* At the end of the meeting, the Team Assessor would report to the team areas of strength, areas of weakness, and a total score. Teams would complete every week the form given in Fig. 8.2 to help the Team Assessor determine the team's perspective on the quality of team meetings. On a monthly basis, problem areas and team progress should be discussed.

PROCESS	EXCELLENT	GOOD	AVERAGE	OPPORTUNITY
1. All members present and on-time.				
2. Meeting started on time.				
3. Agenda prepared for start of meeting.				
4. Model of Success and Team Rules reviewed.				
5. Everyone abided by Team Rules.				
6. All members were prepared to meet.				
7. Member assignments completed prior to meeting.				
8. Every Team Member participated.				
9. Team followed agenda and stayed focused.				
10. Team Members given assignments.				
11. Meeting finished on time.				

USE-OF-TIME CRITIQUE	MINUTES	% TIME
A — Administrative Issues		
B — Business Improvement		
C — Crisis Issues		
D — Dumb Issues		

ADDITIONAL COMMENTS

ASSESSOR:	MEETING DATE:

Figure 8.1   Meeting review checklist

Instructions: Circle the number that best rates your team's meetings. Scale: 0 = Never 1 = Seldom 2 = Usually 3 = Frequently 4 = Always					
1. Everyone understands purpose of meeting.	0	1	2	3	4
2. Everyone is involved in decision making.	0	1	2	3	4
3. Everyone is committed to team decisions.	0	1	2	3	4
4. Everyone participates. No one dominates.	0	1	2	3	4
5. The entire team attends.	0	1	2	3	4
6. Team meets on a regular basis.	0	1	2	3	4
7. Meeting begins on time.	0	1	2	3	4
8. Meeting ends on time.	0	1	2	3	4
9. Model of Success is reviewed.	0	1	2	3	4
10. Recorder is selected.	0	1	2	3	4
11. Team rules are reviewed.	0	1	2	3	4
12. Everyone abides by team rules.	0	1	2	3	4
13. Team Members are prepared for meeting.	0	1	2	3	4
14. Every Team Member participates.	0	1	2	3	4
15. Team Leader keeps discussion on track.	0	1	2	3	4
16. Team Members are given assignments.	0	1	2	3	4
17. Atmosphere is relaxed, comfortable, and informal.	0	1	2	3	4
18. Minutes of meeting are distributed promptly.	0	1	2	3	4
Column Total					
Grand Total					

Figure 8.2 Team meeting assessment

8.2 Organizing for Team-Based Success

Figure 8.3 illustrates the traditional hierarchical, pyramidal organizational structure that has resulted in silos of organizational awareness. Information only flows *down* vertical silos, and the majority of the people in an organization don't have a clue as to what is happening. The hierarchical, pyramidal organization is now widely seen as being ineffective, and must be augmented by the flatter, more integrated, responsive, customer-driven, team-based organizational structure as given in Fig. 8.4.

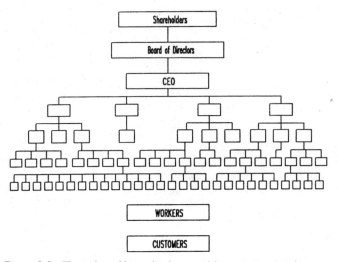

Figure 8.3   The traditional hierarchical, pyramidal organizational structure

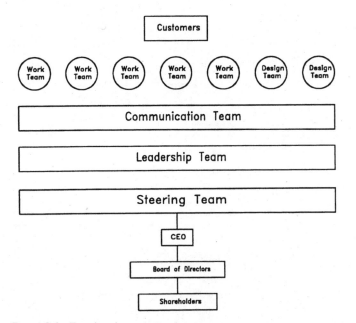

Figure 8.4   Team-based organizational structure

Interestingly, many have discussed the team-based structure using the labels *open networked* organization, *relational* organization, *cluster* organization, *human networking*, etc. In many of these discussions, there seems to be no awareness of the need for the coexistence and the overlapping of the two organizational structures. You see, Fig. 8.4 could be the organizational structure only for a company that had every line and staff function covered by a self-managing work team. This is neither practical nor desirable.

Therefore, what will exist in Genesis Enterprises is both a hierarchical, pyramidal organizational structure, to represent certain organizational relationships, and at the same time, a team-based organizational structure to represent other organizational relationships. It is only by understanding both of these structures and their overlap that an organization can gain a true understanding of the role of individuals and teams in an organization, and thus the magnitude of the shift from individuals to teams for that specific organization at that specific time. Genesis Leaders will rely on individuals to be accountable for certain tasks, and on teams for other tasks. Everyone within a Genesis Enterprise will know which teams are accountable for which tasks, and which individuals are accountable for which tasks.

CAUTION: CREATING TEAMS DOES NOT AUTOMATICALLY ALTER JOB DESCRIPTION OR RESPONSIBILITIES

A Steering Team was created early in October. A Leadership Team and Communication Team in mid-October. By mid-November, three cross-functional work teams were norming to performing and two functional work teams had been chartered. All was fine. By mid-December, the company and the process were approaching chaos. How could this have happened?

Easy. A single person had a misunderstanding of the authority of teams, and in an attempt to move forward, upset many middle managers—who then fought back. Let me be more specific.

Richard Span was a natural leader on the C Track assembly line. He was told in mid-November that he was to be the C Track Assembly Line Team Leader. Bob Hendry from data processing was to be the Team Liaison. Richard is an excellent communicator, well respected in the shop and a good thinker with an action orientation. Richard believed in the team concept and, in fact, had read a few empowerment books. Bob was very quiet, very intelligent, new to the company, and uncertain of the team process. The C Track Assembly Line Team charter was weak. The charter didn't define the level of the team, the constraints, or the time involvement expectations of the Team Members. The Leadership Team had addressed all these issues for the initial cross-functional work teams, but for some reason didn't think functional work teams needed this guidance as "everyone knows what we want to achieve." Well, Richard and his team got it on. In the first three weeks, they

1. Changed the layout in two subassembly areas without interaction with Industrial Engineering, which is responsible for the layout.

2. Purchased two new fans, and mounted them over the line to improve air circulation. The fans were bought directly, without the support of purchasing, and the fans were connected without input from maintenance. Purchasing and maintenance are responsible for these functions.

3. Changed from a size-eight screw to a size-nine screw for motor mounting, without approval from Engineering, which controls product design and documentation.

4. Changed the inspection process on subassemblies without approval from the people responsible in Quality.

Well, guess what? Industrial Engineering, Purchasing, Maintenance, Engineering, and Quality all went bananas. What's going on here? Who's in charge? If the teams can do anything they want, then what is *my* job? Etc., etc. World War III.

What went wrong? Well, for starters, a weak charter, then a weak team liaison, then an overanxious team leader, and finally no outside facilitator to run interference. In short, a mess. How was it fixed? A strong charter was written, the team leader and team liaison were provided with support from an outside facilitator, and an apology was issued to Industrial Engineering, Purchasing, Maintenance, Engineering, and Quality.

How did it work out? Richard did fine, as did the team, Industrial Engineering, Purchasing, Engineering, and Quality. The Maintenance guy never agreed to this team stuff, and as this book goes to press is still a question mark. Bob Hendry, the data-processing guy, left the company, and was replaced by Sue Carnevale from Quality as Team Liaison. Sue is doing well and has helped the team to stay focused.

Was all this a major mistake? Yes. Did it hurt the company? No. Was it good for the company? Yes. They learned from this mistake and to this date have not again approved a weak charter or allowed a team to automatically alter the responsibilities of others just because the team exists.

8.3   Avoiding Team Failures

As stated in the introduction to Part 3, many organizations are not being successful with teams. Since we have worked to make teams successful in many organizations, and truly understand how hard it is to shift an organization from individuals to teams, it's a no-brainer that organizations that adopt a cavalier attitude to creating teams will fail. The creation of successful teams is very complex. Just as it would be a mistake for you to do surgery without an experienced surgeon, so it's a mistake for you to pursue teams without an experienced team expert. Thus, the following list of team-based mistakes will be helpful in allowing you to understand the challenge of making teams successful, but it isn't possible to create a comprehensive list. In fact your organization, your people, and your teams will think of new and unique ways for teams to fail, and it is only by seeing things through the eyes of an experienced team-based facilitator that you can avoid team failure. Nevertheless, the following list of the 10 most dangerous team-based mistakes should be studied closely, as one key to an organization achieving team-based success is to avoid team-based failure!

1. *The team-based process is not customized.* Although this book advocates a specific process to become a Genesis Enterprise, the simple truth is that the process explained herein has never been followed. The process presented herein is an excellent baseline, but you see, each organization has a unique culture, a unique history, a unique group of leaders, managers, and people, and a unique team-based background that must be taken into consideration when designing and refining a specific organization's team-based process.

   Rarely will we find an organization that is beginning the team-based process. For better or worse, the process has been evolving for years. This evolution may have involved Employee Involvement, Participative Management, Quality Circles, Job Enrichment, Organizational Development, etc. It is critical that this past be understood and considered when implementing the team-based process in the pursuit of becoming a Genesis Enterprise. This past may result in a change in the Model of Success terminology and/or format. It may result in the combining of the Steering Team and the Leadership Team. It may result in knowledge of how the Communication Team evolves. It may mandate the adoption of existing teams or the prioritization of early teams, and on and on. It is critical for an organization to customize its team-based process while maintaining the essence of the process to create the required shift from individuals to teams.

2. *The Steering Team is not actively steering.* The Steering Team must actively and visibly demonstrate a focus on an alignment with the Model of Success. It must actively, visibly, and consistently exhibit a support of the Leadership Team, and clearly communicate to the entire organization that the team-based process is not a fad or "another program." The Steering Team must be cautious to avoid the sickness as well as the symptoms of the leadership disease "attention span deficit disorder." Because of past bouts with this disease, an organization requires an ongoing assurance that the organization will become team-based and that there is no turning back.

A test of a Steering Team occurs when a member of the Steering Team changes. When a key person or even *the* key person leaves an organization, the Steering Team should stay the course and demonstrate its commitment not only to the Genesis Enterprise pursuit but also to bringing the new key person up to speed on how the organization functions.

THE ROCKET SHIP IS LEAVING THE LAUNCH PAD

The President of the over 500-person company knew he had to place a stake in the ground. His company had pursued many fads and had done the hat, lapel pin, banner, etc. thing. He needed to let the entire organization know that this was different, that this was not a program but how the company was going to function. He called a meeting for the last five minutes of first shift and the first five minutes of the second shift. This type of meeting was unprecedented. In fact, there was no place to hold such a large meeting. The President set up a microphone on the shipping dock, and all the people stood outside in the truck wells. (Fortunately, it was a nice day.) The President introduced the entire company to the Model of Success, the team-based process, the membership of the Steering Team, and the Leadership Team, then made this statement:

> We have done many programs here. I want you to know that this is different. This is not a program, but the beginning of the process that will define how we do business forever. Folks, we will become a Genesis Enterprise and, here today, we are making a first step. A new beginning. The rocket ship is leaving the launch pad and there is no turning back. This is how we will run our business. This is how we will all be successful. I appreciate and expect your active involvement, and look forward to working with you as we begin anew. Thank you.

The impact was amazing. The results six months later were even more amazing. The rocket ship truly *did* leave the launch pad, and not only was there no *turning* back, there wasn't even any *looking* back.

---

3. *Middle management/supervisors roles are not changed.*   Middle managers and supervisors are threatened by teams. Middle managers and supervisors feel that teams will undercut their authority, power, and control. The self-esteem of the middle manager and supervisor is tied to their jobs as it used to be. They believe they have earned their positions, and now they are losing these positions. Their career path seems broken.

When looked at from these perspectives, it isn't hard to understand why middle managers and supervisors are against teams. At the same time, middle managers and supervisors have had a lousy job, and their satisfaction is among the lowest in industry. Middle managers and supervisors typically have all the responsibility for performance, but little authority to achieve performance. It is time we all realized that, in general, the middle manager/supervisor job is broken. When asked to describe their job, middle managers and supervisors use words like *firefighter, policeman, power broker, paper pusher, stock chaser, baby-sitter, disciplinarian, problem fixer,* and *priority settler.* When asked which of these roles they enjoy, the majority of all middle managers and supervisors say "None of the above."

This is a major problem, because the people who fill these positions are "promoted" because of good performance and tremendous potential. So what we do is take our best workers and promote them into a job that is broken. How intelligent is that? In fact, one of the important results of becoming a team-based organization is the recapture of all the talent that is today wasted on middle-management and supervisory positions. In a Genesis Enterprise, there will be fewer middle managers and no supervisors. This doesn't mean people will be fired. To the contrary, these people are some of the best in our companies, and they will be moved into much more satisfying, relevant, value-added work where their talents may be more fully utilized. Some of these people will fulfill the role of coordinator, where a coordinator will support the team process. Instead of the words like *firefighter, power broker,* etc., used to describe the old middle manager/supervisor role, the new coordinator job will be described as *coach, planner, trainer, motivator, people developer,* and *sounding board.* These coordinators will really feel good about themselves and their contributions, and they will never want to go back to their old positions.

The challenge, however, is to make the middle manager/supervisor-to-coordinator transformation in sync with the evolution of the teams. Depending upon the team and the middle manager/supervisor, this synchronous transformation may be easy or difficult. For example, if a middle manager/supervisor has evolved with a Natural Group and has a positive relationship with that group, a clear understanding of the required role transformation, it is possible he or she could still retain the role as middle manager/supervisor, be a Suggestion Team member and an Improvement Team member, then become a coordinator and work as a member of a Semi-Autonomous Team and ultimately a Self-Managing Team. The middle manager/supervisor would transition with the team and become the coordinator while serving as a member of the team. The team would define the roles, and the transformation would be straightforward.

To the contrary, there will be some traditional groups where the middle manager/supervisor is not able to transition to a Natural Group. Here, when the Suggestion Team is formed, the middle manager/supervisor should not serve on the team, as this would prevent the team from evolving. The Team Liaison and Team Leader should work with the middle manager/supervisor to help them evolve their interaction with the team. As the team transitions to an Improvement Team, the team will need to work through the Team Liaison and Team Leader to transition the middle manager/supervisor's role. Depending upon the team and the middle manager/supervisor, this may involve the middle manager/supervisor joining the team, or may not. Each circumstance needs to be assessed and synchronized by the Leadership Team, with the inputs of the Team Liaisons and Team Leaders.

Eventually, the transformations all will be complete, and all Self-Managed Teams will have coordinators. Managing this team and role transformation is the responsibility of the Leadership Team. This responsibility requires that at every point in time each middle manager/supervisor/coordinator and each corresponding team must have a clear definition and understanding of roles. Roles that need to be assigned include the following:

a. *Scheduling*—work prioritization, assignments, and reporting
b. *Quality*—addressing quality problems, coordinating quality improvements, and reporting
c. *Administration*—attendance, overtime, vacation, work schedules, and payroll reporting
d. *Human relations*—performance reviews, hiring, and training
e. *Maintenance*—housekeeping, maintenance problem solving, and coordination
f. *Safety*—addressing safety problems, coordinating safety improvements, and reporting
g. *Materials*—coordination with purchasing, receiving, warehousing, and material handling

4. *Team charters are not effective.* An ineffective Team Charter is a charter that does not focus or motivate a team. The following are some reasons for ineffective charters:

a. The Team Charter is not tied to the Model of Success. Team Members don't see how fulfilling the charter will help the company.
b. The Team Charter is not understood by the team. The Team Members simply don't know what the charter says.
c. The Team Charter is so broad that it doesn't provide any focus to the team deliberations. The charter can be interpreted many different ways, so there is a lack of team direction.

     d. The Team Charter Evidences of Success aren't measurable, understood, or relevant. Evidences of Success in the Team Charter don't relate to the Evidences of Success in the Model of Success.

     e. The Team Charter has not clarified the role of the team. Is the team a Design Team or a Work Team? Is the team a Suggestion Team, an Improvement Team, a Semi-Autonomous Team, or a Self-Managing Team?

     f. The Team Charter does not identify a topic for team deliberations, but rather an attempt is made to use a team to rubber-stamp a solution already identified by leadership. The team will see through this charter, and will be unwilling to be used in this manner.

5. *Teams are improperly staffed.* A key to the success of a team is the staffing of the team with the correct people. Useful guidelines to consider when staffing a team include the following:

     a. People should not be placed on teams as a reward or a favor. Teams should not be staffed with people because of their loyalty to company leadership.

     b. People should be placed on a team only when they have personal knowledge about the topic the team is pursuing. Team Members should have a stake in the outputs of the team.

     c. People should not (in fact, cannot) be forced to be a part of a team. If a person doesn't want to be on a team after the team orientation, he or she should be allowed, without negative repercussions, to not serve on the team.

     d. People with diverse perspectives, talents, age, and personalities should be placed on a team. It is the diversity of Team Members that results in the synergistic evolution of the team.

6. *Team Leader and/or Team Liaison isn't doing his/her job.* Team recommendations should be handled in a timely fashion and, for the most part, should be accepted. Team Leaders and Team Liaisons should support a team to help them get results. Not getting these results will result in

     a. A loss of team energy and enthusiasm

     b. A sense of helplessness

     c. A lack of direction

     d. A loss of focus to discussions

     e. Ineffective meetings

     f. Cynicism and mistrust

     g. The failure of the team

7. *Teams are not allowed to work.* The three things that will prevent a team from being successful are

    a. Members of early teams are subjected to peer pressure, and the Leadership Team doesn't properly handle this pressure.

    b. Teams are prevented from obtaining the information they need to address their tasks.

    c. Adequate time is not allocated for Team Members to participate in the teams.

8. *The Leadership Team isn't working.* The Leadership Team doesn't provide for the proper management of the team evolution (Suggestion Team, Improvement Team, Semi-Autonomous Team, and Self-Managing Team) or development (Forming, Storming, Norming, Performing, and Maturation). Or, to the contrary, the Leadership Team attempts to micro-manage the teams and doesn't allow the teams to evolve. The micro-management challenge for the Leadership Team typically is a result of the Leadership Team and/or the Steering Team lacking patience. Although the whole purpose of the team-based process is to create peak-to-peak performance, care must be exhibited early in the process not to place too much early emphasis on results at the expense of the evolution of the team. The teams will be expecting the leadership to take charge and "make something happen." The Leadership Team must sit tight and allow the cultural transformation and team evolution to take its natural course.

PATIENCE IS A VIRTUE: BUT IT ISN'T EASY

The Leadership Team charters a team with a focus on company cost reduction. The first thing the team tackles: the paper towels in the bathrooms. After four weeks of team meetings, a recommendation comes forth to replace the paper towels with cloth towels. No investment required, and an annual savings projected at almost $150. That's correct, not $150,000 but $150. The Leadership Team went bananas, they went nuts. Finally, cooler heads prevailed and they decided to replace the paper towels and to just be patient.

The second project the team tackled: the cups used for coffee in the company. After six weeks of deliberations (think eight people, one hour a week, for six weeks), the recommendation was to stay with the present cups.

The Leadership Team wanted to fire someone, anyone. They were crazy with anger. The outside facilitator kept them under control and they decided to do nothing and to be patient. The third project had to do with tool life, and it saved the company about $55,000/year. The fourth project involved the reduction of set-up time in the press department. Annual savings? Around $490,000.

The moral of the story? You sometimes have to live through the paper towels and the coffee cups before a team believes in itself. Patience, patience, patience!

---

9. *The Communication Team isn't working.*   As explained in Sec. 6.2.3, it is the responsibility of the Communication Team to ensure that everyone in the organization has a clear understanding of the Model of Success, the status of teams, and the organizational status. When the Communication Team doesn't work, it means that people within the organization are lost, uninformed, or both. This is totally unacceptable, and will result in Team Members not being able to contribute effectively at their team meetings. This will result in ineffective team meetings, which will then result in an ineffective team-based process. The Communication Team *must* be effective, and thus must apply several of their available tools to ensure organizational awareness and understanding.

10. *The legal aspects of teams are poorly handled.*   Appendix D contains a description of the legal aspects of teams. Although this continues to be an evolving issue, the bottom line is that teams should not be used as a mechanism to deal with "grievances, labor, disputes, wages, rates of pay, hours of employment, or conditions of work." As long as teams are restricted from these topics, there shouldn't be any difficulties in either a union or a nonunion shop with proceeding with teams. Nevertheless, Appendix D should be read, and any current legal aspects of teams reviewed, so as not to undermine the effectiveness of teams.

8.4   Achieving Team-Based Success

Most of this book up to this point has been focused on achieving team-based success. Part 1 set the stage, Part 2 defined the role of leadership, and this Part 3 has presented the fundamentals of teams (Chap. 6) and empowerment (Chap. 7). In this chapter, I have explained how to have successful team meetings, how to organize for success, and how not to fail. Thus, the methodology for achieving team-based success has been presented. What remains to be done here is to define the steps to be followed to shift an organization from individuals to teams. These steps are presented in Table 8.1.

Table 8.1   The Steps to Shift an Organization from Individuals to Teams

Step	Who	What
1.	Steering Team	Genesis Enterprise orientation
2.	Steering Team	Define Model of Success
3.	Steering Team	Charter Leadership Team
4.	Steering Team	Refine Model of Success
5.	Leadership Team	Genesis Enterprise orientation
6.	Leadership Team	Charter Communication Team
7.	Leadership Team	Define priorities for Cross-functional Work Teams
8.	Leadership Team	Charter Cross-functional Work Teams
9.	Cross-functional Work Teams	Genesis Enterprise orientation
10.	Cross-functional Work Teams	Pursue charter
11.	Communication Team	Genesis Enterprise orientation
12.	Communication Team	Pursue charter
13.	Steering Team	Support Leadership Team and overall process
14.	Leadership Team	Liaise, support, and evolve teams
15.	Leadership Team	Charter new teams
16.	New teams	Genesis Enterprise orientation
17.	New teams	Pursue charter
18.	All	Go to step 12

Steps 1, 5, 9, 11, and 16, as shown in Table 8.1, all have the same Genesis Enterprise orientation. This orientation is a review of the first eight chapters of this book. In addition to these orientations, if there is a union in the organization it would be a good idea to conduct exactly this same orientation for the local union leadership, between Steps 5 and 6. Steps 1, 2, 3, and 4, in Table 8.1, are preparation steps for the Steering Team, as are Steps 5, 6, 7, and 8 for the Leadership Team. Typically, the first work teams created should be Cross-functional Work Teams (Steps 8, 9, and 10), as Cross-functional Work Teams allow for the greatest exposure and cultural transformation. Once these early Cross-functional Work Teams have moved into a norming phase, then new teams should be created (Steps 15, 16, and 17). This then begins the continuous process of Steps 12-13-14-15-16-17-back-to-12, and so forth. This process will never end, but will cycle through the creation and completion of Cross-functional Work Teams and Design Teams and the creation and evolution of Self-Managing Functional Work Teams. This will lead an organization to peak-to-peak performance and will be the ongoing process of the Genesis Enterprise.

Step 14, in Table 8.1, involves the Leadership Team, through the Team Liaison, supporting the team development through the phases of Forming, Storming, Norming, Performing, and Maturation. Appendix C presents three tools that can be used to assess team progress. The results from these team assessment tools can be used by the Team Leaders and Team Liaisons to help teams to develop and to identify and to take the appropriate action when a team reaches Maturation.

8.5 Becoming a Learning Organization

We all have heard about the solution for the 1990s, the Learning Organization. In fact, I even danced around this topic in the introduction to this chapter, as I attacked the training-based approach to implementing the team-based process and the formal-educational mental model of learning. But what *is* a learning organization? In the popular book by Peter Senge, *The Fifth Discipline: The Art and Practice of the Learning Organization,* he tells us the answer, but then he gets wrapped up in an intellectually stimulating treatise on learning and never gets back to the process of creating a learning organization. Let me delay for a moment in telling you what Senge says, and instead see if I can get you to think this through with me.

First, can organizations learn? Well, what does it mean to learn; what is learning? According to the dictionary, learning is "the acquiring of knowledge or skill." D. H. Kim adds insight to this definition by pointing out that knowledge is "knowing why," which implies the ability to understand concepts, and that skill is "knowing how," which implies the physical ability to produce. For example, a carpenter who is good at woodworking (skill) but lacks any conceptual understanding of how to build a table (knowledge) hasn't really learned to be a carpenter.

Or, to the contrary, a carpenter who has the conceptual knowledge to design tables, but not the skills to *produce* the tables, hasn't really learned how to be a carpenter. It is from this perspective that D. A. Kolb defines learning as "the process whereby knowledge is created through the transformation of experience." Kim defines learning as "increasing one's capacity to take effective action."

Now, in answer to our first question, "Can organizations learn?" the answer is no, not really. Only individuals can learn. Which leads us to our second question: "If only individuals can learn, not organizations, what is 'organizational learning'?" The scholars have had no shortage of thoughts on this one. Garvin has compiled the following definitions from over 10 years of discussions:

- "Organizational learning means the process of improving actions through better knowledge and understanding."

- "An entity learns if, through its processing of information, the range of its potential behaviors is changed."

- "Organizations are seen as learning by encoding inferences from history into routines that guide behavior."

- "Organizational learning is a process of detecting and correcting error."

- "Organizational learning occurs through shared insights, knowledge, and mental models."

The dilemma, then, is how can there be organizational learning, if only individuals can learn. Argyris and Schon pose this issue as follows:

> There is something paradoxical here. Organizations are not merely collections of individuals, yet there are no organizations without such collections. Similarly, organizational learning is not merely individual learning, yet organizations learn only through the experience and action of individuals. What, then, are we to make of organizational learning? What is an organization, that it may learn?

This leads to the third and the target question: "What is the definition of a learning organization?" Garvin's answer to this question is

> A learning organization is an organization skilled at creating, acquiring, and transferring knowledge, and modifying its behavior to reflect new knowledge and insights.

Wick's answer to this question is

> A learning organization is an organization that continually improves by rapidly creating and refining the capabilities needed for future success.

Senge's answer to this question is

> A learning organization is an organization where people continually expand their capacities to create the results they truly desire, where new and expansive patterns of thinking are nurtured, where collective aspiration is set free, and where people are continually learning how to learn together.

Then, to be certain the meaning is clear, Senge really tells us what we need to know:

> Team learning is vital because teams, not individuals, are the fundamental learning unit in modern organizations. This is where "the rubber meets the road"; unless teams can learn, the organization cannot learn.

Thus, a learning organization is a team-based organization in which teams are pursuing peak-to-peak performance. Amazing as it may seem, when one does a thorough review of the five "component technologies" of the Senge learning organization (Systems Thinking, Personnel Mastery, Mental Models, Building Shared Vision, and Team Learning), what is understood is that this book presents a process that fully defines how to do these five things. Similarly, if one does a thorough review of Garvin's five building blocks (Systematic Problem Solving, Experimentation,

Learning From Past Experience, Learning From Others, and Transferring Knowledge), once again we see that this book defines how to do these five things. So in a way this book is the "How-to" guide to becoming a learning organization. In fact, given a robust definition of a learning organization, a Genesis Enterprise *is* a Learning Organization.

At the same time, caution must be exhibited, as there are holes in the learning organization literature that have resulted from the lack of actually pursuing a Genesis Enterprise. For example, although Senge understands the issue of alignment (see Sec. 3.4), he does not understand empowerment. He states:

> Alignment is the necessary condition before empowering the individual will empower the whole team. Empowering the individual when there is a relatively low level of alignment worsens the chaos and makes managing the team even more difficult.

We know that alignment is the necessary condition before empowering a team, but that a team will never be empowered if first the individuals are empowered. Similarly, although Kim defines learning as "increasing one's capacity to take effective action," he also says

> All organizations learn; whether they consciously choose to or not, it is a fundamental requirement for their sustained existence. Some firms deliberately advance organizational learning, developing capabilities that are consistent with their objectives; others make no focused effort, and therefore acquire habits that are counterproductive. Nevertheless, all organizations learn.

This is not true. All organizations are not increasing their capacity to take effective action, any more than all organizations are improving teamwork or performance by creating teams. To create a shift from individuals to teams, to become a team-based organization, to become a Learning Organization, to become a Genesis Enterprise is not something that will just happen. To the contrary, if leadership does not properly carry out a methodical process, these things will *not* happen.

AT CITICORP, LEARNING AND INNOVATION GO HAND-IN-HAND

Citicorp has long been thought of as a bank of innovation. The Citicorp record on certificates of deposit, automated teller machines, bank credit cards, foreign banking, electronic funds transfer, and on and on, is one of aggressive pioneering. The stimulation for this innovation was an emphasis on learning. Among the stories told about Citicorp:

- Leadership authorizes many experiments. Almost any good idea is supported.

- Leadership believes "Having a lot of activity going on and learning from it" is the best way to improve the bank.

- Bright, nonconventional nonbankers are brought in, and encouraged to experiment. When they succeed, they are promoted; when they fail, they are assigned to a routine job for a while, allowed to recover and recharge, and then assigned to another experiment.

- Mistakes are viewed as opportunities for learning.

Is it any wonder that Citicorp continues to learn and, therefore, be successful?

A benefit to thinking about a Genesis Enterprise as a Learning Organization is the pondering of the following learning issues, which need to be fully embraced by the Genesis Enterprise:

1. In the introduction to this chapter, the concept of Just-In-Time learning and the philosophy of learning Uncover-Discover-Recover was presented. It is this philosophy of learning that explains the criticality of organizational alignment with the Model of Success. It is only when an organization uncovers the gap between the present organizational position and the Vision that the organization has a true understanding of why the organization must become a Genesis Enterprise.

2. A Genesis Leader will be intimately involved with learning. In Chap. 2, I said that "the first task of a Genesis Leader is to shape the organization's culture." A key element of a peak-to-peak performance culture is learning, so obviously the Genesis Leader must shape the organization's culture to encourage learning. In Sec. 4.3.2, the importance of the Genesis Leader personally learning was stressed, and then throughout Chaps. 6, 7, and 8, the role of the Genesis Leader in providing the leadership to the learning process of the team-based process is explained. It is clear that the Genesis Leader is a leader who has a total awareness of learning.

3. There is an old saying that "Success breeds success." This is a nice saying, but unfortunately it isn't true. More often than not, success breeds complacency which eventually breeds failure. In fact, it is more true to say that *failure* breeds success. If that seems funny to you, consider that

   - Babe Ruth not only had 714 career home runs, he also had 1330 career strike outs.
   - R.H. Macy failed in retailing seven times before he became a success with his store in New York.
   - Pete Rose holds the record not only for the most hits in baseball, 4192, but also the most outs, 9518.

Abe Lincoln, Thomas Edison, and on and on, all had many more failures than successes. But we call them all successful. The point, however, is not to try to fail but rather not to be afraid of failing and, if you do fail, to learn from it. In fact, in a Genesis Enterprise, where risk-taking is encouraged, a failure is seen as a learning opportunity. When no one is failing, when no one is making mistakes, there is no risk-taking, no growth, and no learning. In a Genesis Enterprise there will be lots of failures, lots of mistakes, lots of learning, and yes, lots of success.

4. Directly related to the saying "Failure breeds success" is the topic of active learning. Active learning says that the best way to learn is by doing, by being involved, by participating. Allow me to adopt an old Chinese proverb by thinking from a team perspective: "We hear and we forget; we see and we remember; we do and we understand." As I said in Sec. 4.1.5 ("Go, Go, Go"), the more you try, the more you learn.

5. Genesis Enterprises certainly learn by making mistakes and by being involved, but they also can learn by observing and understanding the experiences of others. By watching others' successes and failures and adapting what was learned to one's own situation, there is an opportunity to learn. This may be done by visiting plants, reading trade publications, attending industry meetings, conferences, and seminars, retaining consultants, and participating in benchmarking studies. The experts in this type of learning have been the Japanese. Prior to each trip, they receive training on "How to look, How to listen, and How to ask." During each trip large amounts of information, audiotapes, videotapes, and pictures are taken, and after each trip detailed debriefing and trip reports are prepared. We never want to miss an opportunity to learn, and if we are aware of what is happening around us, we certainly can learn from the success and failure of others.

6. An important type of learning that is very difficult for some to accept is *unlearning*. Unlearning is the process of discarding old knowledge and skills and adopting new knowledge and skills. A term that has become popular as a result of the excellent video *The Business of Paradigms* by Joel Barker is *paradigm*. A paradigm is a model, a framework, a way of thinking, or a scheme for understanding reality. Unlearning is a process that may be likened to a *paradigm shift*, the throwing off of an old way of thinking and adopting a new. I believe many misunderstand the process of paradigm shifting and unlearning, in that people think only about the acceptance of new ways of thinking and forget the equally important aspect of leaving behind old ways of thinking. Certainly, Genesis Leaders will fully understand *all* aspects of unlearning and paradigm shifting.

7. A distinguishing characteristic between a Genesis Leader and a Traditional Manager will be the outlook on learning. A Genesis Leader will

seek out every opportunity to learn, whereas a Traditional Manager will wait to be taught. The Genesis Leader understands that learning is a part of every day, whereas the Traditional Manager believes that learning occurs only in a classroom. The Genesis Leader believes that he/she is personally accountable for his/her own learning, whereas the Traditional Manager doesn't really think about accountability for learning but certainly doesn't think it is his/her job. The Genesis Leader sees each day as a part of his/her lifelong learning process, whereas the Traditional Manager sees his/her learning as largely being complete. The Genesis Leader is concerned with his/her entire organization's learning, as he/she believes that learning is required for continued business success, whereas the Traditional Manager is not concerned with organizational learning and doesn't see any linkage between business success and learning. In fact, a good measure of a Genesis Leader may be obtained by simply asking the person about learning within his/her organization. Within minutes, you will know if you are speaking to a Genesis Leader or a Traditional Manager.

MOTOROLA: THE LEARNING ORGANIZATION

Motorola spent the 1980s focusing on quality, and as a result of their six sigma defect-reduction program and excellent basic and statistical process control training, won the Malcolm Baldrige National Quality Award and, even more importantly, the finest reputation for quality in Corporate America. But the leaders have understood that as the competition catches up, quality will have gone from a goal to a strategic advantage to a given. Motorola believes that the next set of weapons to win the competitive war will be responsiveness, adaptability, and creativity, and to arm with these weapons, what will be required is a focus on teams and lifelong learning. The goal is a work force that is disciplined yet free-thinking, with a depth of understanding and an independent-mindedness.

Two keys to Motorola's focus on learning are how they link learning to business strategies, and what they call "embedded learning." This ensures that Motorola people aren't just learning for the sake of learning, but that learning is done so as to achieve peak-to-peak performance. The learning being tied to business strategies results in the uncovering the need for knowledge, and the learning resulting from the embedded learning process of both team-based learning and apprenticeship learning results in the Discovery and Recovery phases of the education process. It is clear that Motorola is a learning organization and, in fact, probably *the* prototypical Genesis Enterprise.

8.6 Conclusion

Genesis Enterprises will shift from "I" to "we," from individuals to teams. There are two approaches to pursuing this shift: the process-based approach and the training-based approach. The training-based approach is wrong, will not work, and cannot be made to work. It is based upon an obsolete definition of organizational learning. What is needed to create the shift from individual to team is real organizational learning through a process of team-based peak-to-peak performance. This chapter has focused on the "how-to" of making this happen by

1. Having successful team meetings

2. Creating an understanding of how the traditional, hierarchical organizational structure and the team-based organizational structure must work in harmony

3. Avoiding team failures by avoiding team-based mistakes

4. Following a methodical individual-to-team shift process

5. Becoming a learning organization in which it is understood that a learning organization is a team-based organization where teams are pursuing peak-to-peak performance

References

Argyris, C. and D. Schon, *Organizational Learning: A Theory of Action Perspective*, Addison-Wesley, Reading, MA, 1978.

Belasco, J. A. and R. C. Stayer. *Flight of the Buffalo*, Warner Books, New York, 1993.

Belbin, R. M., *Management Teams*, Butterworth-Heinemann, Oxford, England, 1981.

Bennett, J. K. and M. J. O'Brien, "The Building Blocks of the Learning Organization," *Training*, June 1994.

Bennis, W. and B. Nanus. *Leaders: The Strategies for Taking Charge*, Harper and Row Publishers, New York, 1985.

Galagan, P. A., "How to Get Your TQM Training on Track," *Nations Business*, October 1992.

Garvin, D. A., "Building a Learning Organization," *Harvard Business Review*, July–August 1993.

Gerber, B., "From Manager into Coach," *Training*, February 1992.

Holpp, L., "5 Ways to Sink Self-Managed Teams," *Training*, September 1993.

Katzenbach, J. R. and D. K. Smith, *The Wisdom of Teams*, Harvard Business School Press, Boston, MA, 1993.

Kelly, K., "Motorola: Training for the Millennium," *Business Week*, March 28, 1994.

Kim, D. H., "The Link Between Individual and Organizational Learning," *Sloan Management Review,* Fall 1993.

Kolb, D. A., *Experimental Learning: Experience as the Source of Learning and Development,* Prentice-Hall, New York, 1984.

Kouzes, J. M. and B. Z. Posner, *The Leadership Challenge: How to Get Extraordinary Things Done in Organizations,* Jossey-Bass Publishers, San Francisco, 1991.

Neusch, D. R. and A. F. Sienbenaler, *The High Performance Enterprise,* Oliver Wight Publications, Essex Junction, VT, 1994.

Popoff, F., "The Seven Deadly Sins of Process Improvement," *Chief Executive,* June 1994.

Sayles, L. R., *The Working Leader, The Triumph of High Performance Over Conventional Management Principles,* The Free Press, New York, 1993.

Schaffer, R. H. and H. A. Thomson, "Successful Change Programs Begin with Results," *Harvard Business Review,* January–February 1992.

Senge, P. M., *The Fifth Discipline: The Art and Practice of the Learning Organization,* Doubleday Currency, New York, 1990.

Tapscott, D. and A. Caston, *Paradigm Shift: The New Promise of Information Technology,* McGraw-Hill, New York, 1993.

Tompkins, J. A., "Team-Based Continuous Improvement: How to Make the Pace of Change Work for You and Your Company—Part 3," *Material Handling Engineering,* March 1993.

———, "Team-Based Continuous Improvement: How to Make the Pace of Change Work for You and Your Company—Part 4," *Material Handling Engineering,* April 1993.

Van Aker, E. M. and D. S. Sink, "Addressing Problems and Implementation Issues," 1992 International Industrial Engineering Conference Proceedings, Institute of Industrial Engineers, Norcross, GA, 1992.

Wick, C. W. and L. S. Leon, *The Learning Edge: How Smart Managers and Smart Companies Stay Ahead,* McGraw-Hill, New York, 1993.

There Is More to Partnerships Than Working Together

We have a lot of work to do. To become a Genesis Enterprise, we must be able to make the shift from the traditional supplier/customer relationship to Genesis Partnerships. The four phases that we must traverse are the following:

1. Customer-driven organizations

2. Invincible customer service

3. Cooperative relationship

4. Genesis partnership

The analogy that is used to describe these four phases relates to a couple:

1. Dating

2. Going steady

3. Being engaged

4. Getting married

Unfortunately, many organizations today have a desire to get married, but don't even understand the basics of dating. It's perfectly clear that any marriages that occur under such circumstances are sure to be headed for divorce or annulment. Part 4 will show you how to pursue relationships in a logical, mindful manner, so as to bring about only positive, mutually rewarding marriages.

Chapter 9 begins by setting the record straight on customer service and customer satisfaction. It then goes on to explain how to become a customer-driven organization, and then how to provide invincible customer service. It is invincible customer service that will serve as a foundation upon which to pursue Genesis Partnerships. Chapters 10 and 11 both attack the rhetoric of partnership and explain the process of evolving Genesis Partnerships. A Genesis Partnership is defined as *a long-term relationship based upon trust and a mutual desire to work together for the benefit of the other partner and the partnership.* The evolution of a Genesis Partnership occurs by applying the Part 3 team-based process of creating peak-to-peak performance to the integrated, linked, boundaryless, seamless relationship between two partners. Just as Part 3 provided unique and in-depth understanding of how to really make teams work for your organization, Part 4 provides a unique and in-depth understanding of how to expand the team-based approach outside of your organization to form Genesis Partnerships.

9

Understanding Customer Service

I have been overwhelmed by the seminars, books, articles, videotapes, audiotapes, software packages, and newsletters that have been crossing my desk on the topic of customer service. From one perspective this is good news, as it appears that we are beginning to understand that the whole reason to be in business is to service the customer. It's really quite simple: If you don't have satisfied customers, you won't be in business over the long term. From another perspective, however, this is bad news, because virtually all of the customer service materials available today are basic sales tips that have more to do with business etiquette than satisfying customers. For example, consider the following personal attributes that often are presented as keys to achieving customer satisfaction:

1. *Smiling.* A secret to customer service is smiling. If you smile a lot, even when on the telephone, the customer will feel good about doing business with your company.

2. *Liking yourself.* If you like yourself, the customer will like you, and be more inclined to do business with your company. You are a special person, so be happy with who you are.

3. *Dressing well.* You are how you look. You gain confidence by looking your best. If you dress correctly and are confident, customers will be more likely to do business with your company.

4. *Listening.* Listen to your customers, and especially to their complaints. Complaints are good for the company, as they let you know where you can improve.

5. *Empathizing.* Always put yourself in the customers' shoes. When you take their perspective, customers will be less dissatisfied when they have complaints.

6. *Listening to complaints.*   The beginning of a satisfied customer is a complaint that has been attentively listened to. By listening and empathizing, we turn complaints into opportunities for customer service.

7. *Empowering.*   Give customer service people the authority to handle all customer complaints. It is through empowerment that customer service gains its ability to respond.

8. *Not overpromising.*   Be sure not to promise more than you can deliver. It is always best to under-promise and over-deliver.

9. *Speaking well.*   Customer satisfaction will result from how loudly you speak, how fast you speak, how clearly you speak, and how you use the right words and phrases for customer satisfaction.

10. *Having a positive attitude.*   When you have a positive attitude, so will your customers. This will result in happy customers, which will make *you* happy.

11. Etc.

One recent piece that came across my desk described a good server of customers as

1. *An acrobat,* with the ability to balance customer wants and company needs.

2. *A mind-reader,* reading between the lines of what a customer says, so that you know just how to respond.

3. *A juggler,* keeping the conflicting facts and reality all in the air at once.

4. *A lion tamer,* knowing how not to put your head in the lion's mouth with the wrong words or tone of voice.

5. *A ringmaster,* keeping the customer's anger in one ring, your own anger in another, and the actual problem in a third.

6. *A magician,* making everyone happy as you deal with a huge variety of customers—and problems—simultaneously.

What are we doing here? Have we decided that, independent of the quality of the product we produce, or independent of the selling price of the product, or independent of the quality of the value-added support we provide, the key is to smile, like ourselves, look good, listen well, empathize, solve complaints, empower people, under-promise, speak clearly, and have a positive attitude, and customer satisfaction will follow? Baloney! Have we decided that all we need to do is practice our circus acts and the audience will clap? Come on! This is all *fluff*! This *fluff* is not bad and, in fact, we should probably do some of these things (I'm not against smiling, for example), but the problem lies in the myth that this *fluff* has something to do with customer service. It is in fact a focusing on this *fluff* rather than a true emphasis on customer service that has resulted in our current very sorry state of customer service satisfaction.

Well, what do you think? Is customer service a priority? How is your customer satisfaction? Do you want my stories, or will your own suffice? Let me see, in the last week

- A rental truck wasn't available, even though I had reservations to help my daughter move.
- A motel reservation was lost, so I paid $149 a night to sleep on a pull-down bed.
- I was given airplane food that the flight attendant told me she wouldn't eat either.
- A bank teller was on the telephone, ordering concert tickets, while happily ignoring the line of customers.
- Mail order arrived with the wrong color shirt.
- I got home with my fast food and was one sandwich short.
- A rude check-out person told me, in a monotone voice and no eye contact, "Have a nice day."

Where does it stop? Some people say we are moving to a service economy; to me it seems more like a nonservice economy. Customer service isn't a smile. Customer service isn't a department. Customer service is a way of doing business, and it is a prerequisite to beginning to think about creating peak-to-peak performance.

9.1 Defining Customer Service

Perhaps the core of the challenge concerning customer service is the definition of customer service. Customer service may be defined as *everything done to enhance customer satisfaction*. But a problem can arise with this definition, due to a misunderstanding of the definition of *customer satisfaction*. The reason for this is that the meaning of *customer service satisfaction* changes as the customer's expectations grow. New customers for a product have low expectations, and therfore to them, customer satisfaction has to do with the fundamental aspects of the product. These Level I customers define satisfaction in terms of product features and cost.

As customers' experiences grow, so too do their expectations. As they enter Level II, they begin to take features and cost for granted, and turn their attention to quality. This is a real challenge, as the elements defined as *quality* by different customers will be different.

In the David Garvin book, *Managing Quality: The Strategic and Competitive Edge,* the elements of quality are identified as given in Table 9.1 As customers' experiences continue to grow (Level III), they expect features, cost, *and* quality, and they turn their attention for satisfaction to other value-added support such as special handling, special delivery, extra services, training, etc. So what we need to understand is that customer satisfaction depends upon the level of the customer experience. Therefore customer service is not something you can define for the marketplace, but something that each customer will define for you.

Table 9.1   Elements of Quality

Element	Definition	Automobile Illustration
Performance	The operating characteristics of the product	Acceleration
Secondary features	Characteristics that supplement the product's basic features	Air conditioning
Reliability	The anticipated failure rate of the product	Length of time to failure of the starter
Conformance	The lack of defects in the product when delivered	Fitting of trunk, hood, and doors
Durability	The useful life of the product	Number of years before car deteriorates to the point where it should no longer be repaired
Serviceability	The ability to obtain satisfactory repair	Availability of engine parts, and ease of installation
Aesthetics	The customer's feeling about appearance of the product	How the customer views styling
Perceived quality	The customer's overall feeling about the product	Subjective judgment of the customer as to which is the best automobile

A formula for customer satisfaction is

$$\text{Customer satisfaction} = \text{Perception of customer service received} - \text{Expectation of customer service}$$

To illustrate the use of this formula, consider a situation in which a company produces an excellent product, at a competitive cost, with high quality but little extra value added. Let's say the perception of the customer service received was 100 points. Then, for a Level I customer whose expectation of customer service was only 40, their customer satisfaction is very high, at a 60 (100 − 40 = 60). However, the Level II Customer, who expected an excellent product, competitive cost, and high quality, had an expectation of customer service of 90, so their customer satisfaction is low, at only 10 (100 − 90 = 10). Still worse, a Level III customer, who expected an excellent product, competitive cost, high quality, and considerable value-added support, had an expectation of customer service of 110, so their customer satisfaction is −10 (100 − 110 = −10). To put it another way, his/her customer *dis*satisfaction is at 10.

This illustrates the customer service inflation that many have experienced. The comment often heard today is, "I'm delivering better customer service now than at any time in the history of our company, but the level of customer satisfaction is at an all-time low." This is because the customer is more demanding than he/she has ever been before. Guess what? The customer will be more demanding still in the future.

SCANDINAVIAN AIRLINE SYSTEM: CUSTOMER SERVICE BASED ON THE CUSTOMER'S PERCEPTIONS

When Jan Carlzon took over Scandinavian Airline System (SAS), the company had an $8 million loss on top of a $20 million loss the year before. The next year, SAS made $72 million, and it has continued to be successful ever since. What was the key?

According to Carlzon, the key was and continues to be customer service. Rather than continuing a trend of having customer service be defined by marketing, Carlzon delegated customer service to the frontline SAS employees, the people who have direct contact with the customers. Carlzon explains: "Last year, each of our 10 million customers came in contact with approximately five SAS employees, and this contact lasted an average of 15 seconds each time. Thus, SAS is created in the minds of our customers 50 million times a year, 15 seconds at a time. These 50 million 'moments of truth' are the moments that ultimately determine whether SAS will succeed or fail as a company. They are the moments when we must prove to our customers that SAS is their best alternative."

It is the customer's perception of these moments of truth that will result in the customer service perception of SAS. It is not that SAS defines customer service. The customer, and the basis for the customer's perception of customer service, is not a corporate slogan, program, or outreach, but rather those 50 million "moments of truth." SAS has great customer service because it truly understands that it is the customer who defines customer service.

Table 9.2 Growing Customer Satisfaction

Customer level	Perception of customer service received	Expectation of customer service	Customer satisfaction	Description of customer satisfaction
I	0	40	(40)	Lost
I	20	40	(20)	Dissatisfied
I	60	40	20	Satisfied
I	80	40	40	Appreciative
I	100	40	60	Delighted
I	120	40	80	Invincible
II	50	90	(40)	Lost
II	70	90	(20)	Dissatisfied
II	110	90	20	Satisfied
II	130	90	40	Appreciative
II	150	90	60	Delighted
II	170	90	80	Invincible
III	100	140	(40)	Lost
III	120	140	(20)	Dissatisfied
III	160	140	20	Satisfied
III	180	140	40	Appreciative
III	200	140	60	Delighted
III	220	140	80	Invincible

Another way to view the formula for customer satisfaction is to grow the customer expectation for service, but grow the customer's perception of customer service at even a faster rate. Table 9.2 illustrates this scenario. As may be seen for a Level I Customer, a Perception of Customer Service Received of 100 results in a Delighted Customer. For the same Perception of Customer Service Received of 100 for a Level III Customer, we have a lost customer. At the same time, growing the Perception of Customer Service Received for any level of customer allows for the progression from Lost Customer–Dissastified Customer–Satisfied Customer–Appreciative Customer–Delighted Customer–Invincible Customer Service.

9.2   Laying a Customer Service Foundation

The foundation for customer service must be laid by leadership. Leadership must adopt a customer service culture and define the organization's Model of Success and motivation, which includes the customer point of view. Leadership must be certain that everyone in the organization knows the answers to the following three key questions:

1. Who is the customer?

2. What does the customer want?

3. How do we increase customer satisfaction?

In many companies, there is disagreement over who the customer is. If you're a brewery who sells through a distributor organization, who is your customer: the distributor, the retailer, or the person who drinks the beer? If you're a pharmaceutical firm that sells controlled drugs, who is your customer: the wholesaler, the doctor, the pharmacist, or the person in need of your product? If you produce baby food, who is your customer: the wholesaler, the retailer, the mother, the father, or the baby? In each of these situations, the answer is "all of the above." All of the options presented are customers, and they are the ones who define customer service.

At the same time, the question "Who is the customer?" is answered by many as "the king" or "the boss." The attitude here is that "the customer is always right." This "customer-driven" attitude is dangerous. Your customer *is not* always right, is not the king, and *certainly* is not the boss. There have been many "customer-driven" organizations that believed the customer was always right, and those organizations went bankrupt through pleasing their customers. A better way to think about the customer is that the customer is your mother, or the memory of your mother. With this attitude, service is put forth not from a platform of weakness or submissiveness, but from a platform of honor, respect, and love. Despite the fact that your mother wasn't always right, you were always interested in her best interest because without your mother (the customer), you wouldn't exist.

The second question, "What does the customer want?" can be answered in several ways. First, as was stated in the introduction to this chapter, the customer does not want *fluff*. Second, as defined in Sec. 9.1, the customer wants more features, lower prices, higher quality, and more value-added support. Third, and most accurately, the answer to this question should be "Don't ask me, ask the customer." In fact, it is only once we have really understood that it is the customer who answers the question, "What does the customer want?" that we can tackle the third question, "How do we increase customer satisfaction?"

The three-part answer to the third question is straightforward for an organization in pursuit of becoming a Genesis Enterprise:

1. Leaders define culture, direction, and motivation for increased customer satisfaction.

2. A team-based process of creating peak-to-peak performance is installed.

3. Organizations listen to customers and then, via the team-based process, improve the organization's performance so as to increase customer satisfaction.

The greatest challenge to listening is found in the so-called "iceberg of listening." The iceberg of listening indicates that only 8 percent of all opportunities to improve customer service are known by upper management, 16 percent by middle management, 32 percent by supervisors, 64 percent by your staff, but 100 percent by your customers. To whom are you going to listen?

First and foremost, listen to the customer. Then, respond to and take action based on the customer input, the people closest to the firing line, and the teams involved with the opportunities for improvement. How should you listen to your customers?

The most popular but the least useful method is through their complaints. Complaints tell you about problems that should be addressed and about things causing dissatisfaction, but complaints don't tell you anything about improving customer service. In addition to complaints not being a source of ideas for creating peak-to-peak performance, they represent only a very small percentage of your dissatisfied customers. Most dissatisfied customers will complain to their friends and take their business elsewhere, but rarely will they be so outraged as to go through the process of submitting a complaint.

Customer interviews also tend not to result in an accurate understanding of customer satisfaction. The problem with interviews is that people aren't willing to truly speak their mind or to commit the time to sharing their thoughts, and they desire to avoid controversy.

Therefore the best approach to listening to the customer is through a customer survey. However, the benefit one receives from a customer survey has a lot to do with the design of the survey. The surveys used by many motels and restaurants are excellent examples of ineffective designs. The only people who complete these cards are customers who are either very satisfied or very dissatisfied. These two groups don't represent the majority of customers, and rarely will they provide information relevant to creating peak-to-peak performance. The only real benefit to come from these surveys is in the area of identifying real problems, but that's it.

By contrast, a properly designed survey will provide you with a clear understanding of the customer's satisfaction in all the aspects of your relationship. Here are some key considerations in the design of a customer survey:

1. Keep it simple, straightforward, and short. Your customer's time is valuable. Don't expect him or her to spend a lot of time on the survey.

2. Make most questions multiple-choice. That makes it easier for the customer to complete, and for you to compile and analyze.

3. Always leave some room for open-ended questions. Many great ideas have been obtained from customers.

Appendix E presents the Tompkins Associates, Inc., base customer survey. The customization of this base survey may be used to obtain an excellent understanding of customer satisfaction. There are three approaches to disseminating the customer survey.

The first approach is the easiest, but results in the poorest response rate. This approach is to include the customer survey with the customer order. The second approach is to mail the survey so that it will be received by the customer a few days after the order. This approach will result in an improved response rate, but requires additional coordination. The best approach from both a customer satisfaction and a response-rate perspective is to call the customer a few days after he/she has received the order and to ask him/her:

1. Were there any problems with the order?

2. Who would be the best person to receive the customer survey?

3. Would this person be willing to complete a customer survey?

Then send the survey, and refer to the telephone conversation.

This third approach is recommended, and will result in the best feedback from the customer on their satisfaction. It is based on the feedback from these customer surveys that opportunities should be given to teams, or teams should be created to address these opportunities. The team-based response to these opportunities will lead to the improvement of customer satisfaction.

"MAYBERRY BUYS BIGGEST BANK IN TEXAS"

This was the *Dallas Morning News* headline when NationsBank, then NCNB, announced its acquisition of First Republic of Texas. Since then, the Charlotte, NC–based bank has grown to more than 1900 branch offices in nine states and the District of Columbia, and to assets of $165 billion. The leadership of Chief Executive Hugh McColl has been key to vaulting NationsBank to the number-five position in the nation. In addition to First Republic, the bank has had a string of well-timed strategic acquisitions and investments, such as C&S Sovran, MNC Financial, Chrysler Financial, and Dean Witter. Critical to NationsBank's success has been its devotion to customer service.

At NationsBank, customer service takes the form of Model Banking. Model Banking is shaped around the simple premise that providing superior products and responsive and reliable customer service leads to satisfied customers and profitable relationships. "We must be completely dedicated to understanding and satisfying the needs of our customers," says Ken Lewis, President of NationsBank. "This process has to shape the way we think and do business every day." A few of the initiatives this thinking has led to include:

- A streamlined organization that allows NationsBank associates to immediately do what's best for the customer
- Staffing requirements based on customer arrival times
- Products and services designed with direct input from customers
- A personal computer system designed to assist associates in the identification of customer needs, and the appropriate products and services to meet those needs

These initiatives are important in and of themselves, but their individual importance is overshadowed by the peak-to-peak performance process which they represent. "You can't look at the Model Banking Program as just one program," explains Steve Callaghan, Model Banking Program Executive. "It's really a neverending, continuous process." According to Amy Brinkley, Director of Marketing, iterative improvement is integral to everything NationsBank does. She sees the Model Banking program as a circular process beginning with learning, leading to implementation, and generating results that can be learned from and applied to the next implementation.

Teamwork drives the peak-to-peak performance process at NationsBank. "I can't think of anything we do that doesn't involve cross-functional teams," says Brinkley. "Teamwork is a value in our company. It is definitely part of our structure." One example is the Acquisitions Team. For every NationsBank acquisition, a team of managers navigates the perils of each acquisition, folding the new operation into the overall corporation. Throughout the team-based process, serving the customer remains the focus of the bank. "The General Bank is concentrating on several primary business objectives," explains Brinkley. "One, we want to increase the retention of our current customers. Two, we want to continue to attract new customers from bank and nonbank competition. Three, we want to broaden and deepen all of our customer relationships." Jim Trigg, Change Management Executive, adds, "The first question we ask ourselves is, 'How do we satisfy customers?'"

To answer this question, NationsBank must find out what their customers want. According to Amy Brinkley, direct input from customers through customer surveys plays a big role. In addition, NationsBank concentrates on what Brinkley calls the "behavior of the customer." The bank examines the type and volume of customer transactions. Follow-up research is then done, for customers who remained with the bank as well as those who left. Based on this type of information from its customers, NationsBank develops fairly accurate predictive models, helping the bank choose which products or services to introduce or modify. NationsBank uses this type of database-modeling to tailor products and services to fit specific customer segments. In the Washington, D.C., area, for example, the bank experimented with special video/telephone banking for customers whose hectic lifestyles don't fit bankers' hours. In another area, modeling helps the bank to consider the location and customized services of their automated teller machines (ATMs), such as allowing customers to print out interim bank statements.

Right now, the Model Banking Program only directly involves the NationsBank General Bank area, which operates full-service banking centers, and commercial bank and business offices. The process of creating peak-to-peak performance, however, touches the bank's Institutional Group and Financial Services area as well. In fact, as Brinkley states, Model Banking "has implications for customers no matter where they are." The team-based process represented by the Model Banking Program allows NationsBank to concentrate on the customer and maintain its leadership role in the banking industry.

9.3   Creating Invincible Customer Service

What do customers really buy? Customers of Tompkins Associates, Inc., do not buy consulting services, they buy confidence in the solutions implemented. Customers of IBM do not buy hardware or software, they buy solutions to business problems. A TGIF restaurant does not sell food, they sell a good time, they sell a celebration, they sell an opportunity to unwind. At Rubbermaid, it has been discovered that yes, customers want quality products, low prices, and product innovation. But these are not the things that allow Rubbermaid to provide invincible customer service. According to the Vice President of Management Information Systems and Invincible Customer Service (a real title!), what the retail chains buy from Rubbermaid is quality, prices, innovation, and, most importantly, information about the satisfaction of the ultimate customer, the consumer. It is this information that differentiates Rubbermaid from the competition.

What do your customers really buy? Do all your customers buy the same thing? As a starting point to invincible customer service, understand what your customer buys. Invincible customer service understands that knowledge is service. Information, as in the Rubbermaid case, innovative ideas, suggestions that help a customer to achieve success, business experience, and technical expertise—all these are a part of value-added support that leads to invincible customer service.

Interestingly, customer satisfaction isn't a surrogate for customer retention. While it might seem logical that increased customer satisfaction would result in increased customer retention, it isn't true. Between 65 and 85 percent of customers who change suppliers say they were satisfied or very satisfied with their former supplier. In the automobile industry, although satisfaction scores range from 85 to 95 percent, repurchase rates average only 40 percent. Companies that provide invincible customer service know that customer loyalty today is not tied to customer satisfaction as much as it is to

1. Consistently delivering invincible service

2. Consistently improving the customer service provided

3. The cumulative impact of many, many successful interactions

4. Ease of working together

5. Loyal relationships between people in the organizations

6. No-hassle problem resolution

Customer loyalty will be a frequent topic of discussion among firms that wish to provide invincible customer service.

STATE FARM'S INVINCIBLE LOYALTY-BASED SYSTEM

Consider the following statistics:

- State Farm insures more than 20 percent of the nation's households.
- State Farm has the lowest sales and distribution costs among insurance companies of its type.
- State Farm agents' incomes are generally higher than those of agents working for other insurance companies.
- State Farm has one of the fastest growth rates of any multiple-line insurer.
- State Farm agents remain with the company at a much higher rate than the rest of the industry.
- State Farm agents have 50 percent higher productivity than industry norms.
- State Farm customer loyalty is reflected in the highest customer retention rates in the industry, in excess of 90 percent.

How does State Farm achieve such phenomenal results? They say it all has to do with their Loyalty-Based System. They have actually built a system that grows loyalty! What is this Loyalty-Based System? Here are a few of its elements:

- State Farm agents work from neighborhood offices, which allow them to build long-lasting relationships with their customers and to provide personal service.

- State Farm agents are rooted in the community. They become a part of their customer's family, proudly offering discounts for honor-roll performance and sternly warning young drivers about the responsibilities of driving.

- State Farm pricing policies are a magnet that retains good customers by offering discounts for accident-free customers.

- State Farm agent commissions are designed to encourage long-term relationships. Commission rates are the same for both new and renewal business.

- State Farm provides a full-life-cycle product line, giving the agents an advantage in economically servicing multiple-line customers.

- State Farm agent retention is a result both of a lengthy recruiting and selection process before appointment, and of the fact that State Farm agents are independent contractors who exclusively sell and service State Farm products.

- State Farm business systems measure customer retention and defections, and are distributed throughout the organization.

The result of the invincible Loyalty-Based System at State Farm is invincible customer service. State Farm has built a super business, one in which agents benefit and, most importantly, customers obtain outstanding value.

A sales tool that was used for many years has now become an invincible customer service tool. This tool, customer training, has undergone significant changes as it has progressed from sales tool to invincible customer service tool. The traditional sales-tool training consisted of seminars, books, and videos that focused on how to use a supplier's product, and why the product is the best product to be used. Today, in companies providing invincible customer service, the customer training is focused on helping the customer be successful. In many cases the supplier will not only recommend how to use the product, but also will provide guidelines and suggestions on how to reduce costs, increase safety, improve quality and performance. A much more holistic approach is now taken to customer education, often with the specific product being sold included only as a secondary consideration.

SMITHKLINE BEECHAM OFFERS BOTH INVINCIBLE CUSTOMER SERVICE AND INVINCIBLE NON-CUSTOMER SERVICE

The animal-health division of Smithkline Beecham has run many educational programs over the years, on how to use a specific product to prevent or cure a specific disease. In 1991, several beef-packing plants reported problems with meat quality because some cattle vaccines had been incorrectly administered. John Landon, the Smithkline Beecham marketing manager for the company's cow/calf products, said, "Because we manufactured some of those products, we felt a challenge to train the customer in the proper use of the product so the image of beef wasn't damaged. The producers' livelihood depends on that image, and ultimately ours depends on it too." Therefore Smithkline Beecham developed an education program that not only helped beef producers to administer vaccines, but also included information on the value of good facilities, how to make sure animals don't become bruised, how to process cattle with as little stress on the animal as possible, and other practices for working cattle to produce the best end product.

The education program was offered throughout the United States and was sponsored by 40 states. The education was flexible, in that it consisted of wall charts, video, slide show, brochures, and other written materials. The materials could be used in a self-taught mode, a presentation, or a demonstration in which Smithkline sales representatives delivered the seminar while working with live animals.

Due to the success of the initial education, Smithkline has added a second program for producers who raise calves, and a third that presents the advantages of communication among various groups in the industry. Possibly the only questionable portion of this educational outreach was Smithkline's decision to include not only customers but also producers who don't use Smithkline products. Smithkline Beecham explains this approach as follows: "Rather than selling a product, we're more interested in selling a solution to a problem over the long term. We aren't interested in a one-time sale."

This approach is working, as evidenced by what Mike Smith, director of animal health and education for the Colorado Cattle Feeders Association, says: "Personally, I find that these programs clearly testify to the Smithkline commitment to the beef-cattle industry. It is a bold step to offer this to noncustomers, but I think it sets up a win-win situation for the entire industry."

So, although product features, price, quality, and value-added support are important factors, for today's sophisticated customer they're, for the most part, a given. To move beyond good customer service and achieve invincible customer service, we must focus on

1. Understanding what the customer really buys
2. Providing knowledge to our customers
3. Customer loyalty
4. True customer training

9.4   Conclusion

More often than not, customer service is treated as something done in the customer service department, and has to do with handling complaints well. This is *not* customer service, and in fact is the mindset that has resulted in the poor level of customer satisfaction that exists in many companies today. Customer service is defined as everything done to enhance customer satisfaction, where customer satisfaction is a moving target that is defined as *the gap between the Perception of Customer Service Received and the Expectation of Customer Service.* As customers grow in sophistication, their expectations evolve from product features, price, quality, and value-added support to invincible customer service.

The foundation for customer service is an organization's leadership's commitment to customer service. From this commitment must flow a true understanding of what the customer wants, and then a process of creating peak-to-peak performance focusing on exceeding customer expectations. These expectations should be understood by listening to customers on an ongoing basis via customer surveys. These surveys should be used to provide teams with the opportunities for improvement to be addressed. This will result in good customer service and delighted customers. To go one step further and achieve invincible customer service, the motives of customers must be understood, customers must gain knowledge from their suppliers, customer loyalty must be pursued, and true customer training must be implemented. It is invincible customer service that will serve as a foundation upon which to pursue the Genesis Enterprise.

References

Belasco, J. A. and R. L. Stayer, *Flight of the Buffalo,* Warner Books, New York, 1993.

Davidou, W. H. and B. Uttal. *Total Customer Service,* Harper and Row Publishers, New York, 1989.

Denton, D. K., "Total Customer Satisfaction: The Next Step," *Industrial Management,* November–December 1993.

Kaeter, M., "Customer Training: More Than a Sales Tool," *Training,* March 1994.

Lane, D. A., "Customer Service Is Not a Department," *APICS: The Performance Advantages,* February 1994.

Reichheld, F. F., "Loyalty-Based Management," *Harvard Business Review,* March–April, 1993.

Tompkins, J. A., "Team-Based Continuous Improvement: How to Make the Pace of Change Work for You and Your Company—Part 7," *Material Handling Engineering,* October 1993.

——, Tompkins, J. A., *Winning Manufacturing: The How-to Book of Successful Manufacturing,* IIE, Norcross, GA, 1989.

10

Understanding Partnerships

It has been reported that a major corporation provided the following instructions to its purchasing managers:

1. Offer exaggerated growth projections.
2. Establish very early long-term contract rules, but don't negotiate in detail.
3. Resist all suggestions that some costs are controllable and others are not.
4. Focus all activity on reducing the immediate price dramatically.
5. Destabilize the supplier with repeated meetings and "urgent" demands for information.
6. Set deadlines for suppliers to meet, but increase anxiety by deferring decisions.
7. Tie up the short-term price, but keep nibbling at the eleventh hour.

These seven guidelines were referred to as "The Purchasing Vice," in reference to squeezing their suppliers. Is it surprising that this same company has had a problem with supplier loyalty? Is it surprising that this company has both an internal and an external challenge with trust? At the same time, many companies are leveraging and negotiating their way to success on their suppliers' backs. The whole Just-In-Time thing has often been twisted, and used as a hammer to force suppliers into a "survival of the fittest" contest. Consider the traditional maxims adopted by purchasing:

1. The best way to cut costs is to maximize competition.
2. Suppliers are interchangeable.
3. Multiple sourcing allows us to maximize our supplier leverage.

4. Share only the information required to address the contract on the table, and be sure to hold confidential information on product designs and production schedules.

5. Maintain arm's-length relationships.

6. Pursue short-term contracts, to keep the suppliers on their toes and to maximize your flexibility.

7. Evaluate all contracts on cost, and play suppliers off each other.

Interestingly, many of the above practices have been pursued while pursuing strategic alliances. Is it surprising to you that several studies have reported the failure of strategic alliances? For example, just in the automotive industry, failed alliances include: General Motors and Daewoo Corporation; General Motors and Isuzu Motors; Chrysler and Mitsubishi Motors; Chrysler and Maserati; Fiat and Nissan; and more. It is time for a restart, a shift, a new relationship. There has been some movement here, but it's not clear that organizations have truly understood the magnitude of the challenge. What is needed is partnerships, but as Tom Peters has said, "The fact that the rhetoric of partnership outstrips the reality is really no surprise; not so long ago we didn't even have rhetoric." The shift here, just like the shift from manager to leader and the shift from individual to team, is a fundamental shift that must take place if an organization is to become a Genesis Enterprise. For this shift from customer/supplier to partners to take place, we must begin with a true understanding of the word *trust.*

When most people think of the word *trust,* they contrast it with the word *distrust.* The idea is, you either trust or distrust someone. That's wrong. There are actually three possibilities:

Trust—assured reliance of, or confidence in, character, ability, and truth

Distrust—no trust, no assurance or confidence

Lack of trust—neither trust nor distrust; a void

You can trust or distrust someone only after you have repeatedly tested a relationship. While testing the relationship, you have a lack of trust. After many positive tests, you develop trust; after many failed tests, you develop distrust. Thus we see that trust is evolutionary.

Why is trust so critical to establishing partnerships? Because it is out of trust that relationships grow and prosper. Consider the upward progression shown in Fig. 10.1. It is from trust that comes respect. From this respect comes a willingness to really listen to what others are saying. From this listening grow understanding, concern, participation, and then open communications. It is open communications that lead to positive results,

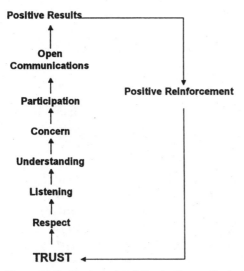

Figure 10.1 Trust as a foundation for the growth of relationships

which acts as a positive reinforcement for even greater trust. Therefore without trust there is no partnership, and no true collective win-win evolution of those mutual objectives, mutual strategy, mutual rewards, and mutual sharing of risk that are required to build partnerships.

Interestingly, trust doesn't occur between companies but among people. Therefore it must be understood that *partnerships* don't occur between companies but among people. Thus partnerships require a fundamental shift in relationships, one that occurs over time as the trust between people evolves.

10.1 Partnership Definition

Just as a relationship between a man and a woman goes through the phases of dating, to going steady, to being engaged, to marriage, so too a partnership relationship evolves (see Table 10.1). The partnership equivalent of dating is the "customer-driven" organization. The shallow *fluff* of customer service—"focus on the customer," "the customer is always right," "the customer comes first," "the customer is king"—was discussed in Chap. 9, and the traditional customer/supplier interactions were defined in the introduction to this chapter. In these traditional relationships, there is little commitment to one another.

A step above dating is going steady. The partnership equivalent of going steady is invincible customer service, and although this is an important step in the beginning of the evolution of a trusting relationship (just like

Table 10.1 Relationship Evolution

Between a man and a woman	Among people within two organizations
Dating	Customer-driven organization
Going steady	Invincible customer service
Being engaged	Cooperative relationship planning for partnership
Marriage	Partnership

going steady), it is only that, a beginning. With invincible customer service the relationship is above the traditional relationship, as there is genuine participation in it, but it is still a long way from being a partnership.

To move beyond this relationship, just like the step up from a couple going steady to being engaged, each of the parties must step up their commitment to one another. The partnership equivalent to being engaged is a cooperative relationship in which significant planning for partnership (marriage) occurs. The ultimate commitment, of course, is the marriage/partnership. Alas, just like happy marriages, partnerships sometimes result in divorce. A key result of being a Genesis Enterprise, as opposed to a traditional organization, is that as long as partnerships are made with other Genesis Enterprises, a divorce will be very rare.

Although it's obvious, many organizations haven't seemed to understand that, just as it takes two to be married, it takes two to create a partnership. Therefore in each relationship we must have a supplier who is ready for partnership, and a customer who is ready for partnership. An important thing to reflect on here is that every organization is the customer to some organizations and the supplier to others. Thus, each organization has some firsthand experience of playing on both sides of many potential partnership relationships. We want to learn about our fitness for partnering by understanding how we partner as a supplier and how we partner as a customer.

Although I generally turn off when people start in on the "Japan is great" stuff, there is certainly no better illustration of partnerships than the partnerships in Japan. In fact, consider the following quote from the Japanese Ministry of International Trade and Industry (MITI):

> Japanese manufacturing industry owes its competitive advantage and strength to its subcontracting structure.

In a study of Japan's competitive advantage, Dyer and Ouchi conclude that

> Evidence from an increasing number of industries and sources suggests that much of Japanese success can be attributed to Japanese-style business partnerships.

In another study by Clark and Fujimoto, on the role of Japanese-style business partnerships during product development, they concluded

> In U.S. companies, the projects in our sample were heavily influenced by the traditional system, in which suppliers produced parts under short-term, arm's-length contracts and had little role in design and engineering. In the Japanese system, in contrast, suppliers are an integral part of the development process: they are involved early, assume significant responsibility, and communicate extensively and directly with product and process engineers.

So, what *is* a Japanese-style business partnership? A Japanese-style business partnership is *an exclusive supplier/customer relationship that focuses on maximizing the efficiency of the entire business system.* The goal of these partnerships is to maximize quality while minimizing the total cost. The partners work to create a "see-through" business system, in which both partners can see costs, problems, and opportunities. Then both partners can work together to create peak-to-peak performance. The Japanese-style business partnerships attempt to capture the synergies that would exist if the two organizations were combined under common ownership. The key characteristics of Japanese-style business partnerships are

1. Long-term relationships

2. Frequent communications

3. Mutual cooperation on creating peak-to-peak performance

4. Willingness to invest in the future of the partnership

5. In-depth and regular sharing of technical and cost information

6. Trust-building practices such as owning stock, transferring employees, and having flexible legal contracts

7. Fewer suppliers handling more work

8. Elimination of waste and true Just-In-Time

So what can we *learn* from these Japanese-style business partnerships, and what should be the characteristics of a Genesis Enterprise Partnership? Genesis Partners believe in

1. Rejecting the notion that business relationships should be based on antagonism, leveraging, hammering, and negotiating.

2. Long-term relationships based on trust and a true understanding of their partner's business.

3. The sharing of information, planning, scheduling, risk, rewards, problems, solutions, and opportunities for creating peak-to-peak performance.

4. Working together toward improved performance on quality, lead times, new product development time, inventories, waste, and costs.

5. Building on each other's strengths, growing their partner's business, and investing in the long-term partnership relationship. (Due to this commitment, Genesis Partners will deal with fewer and fewer suppliers.)

6. The integration of systems and the interdependence of their organizations, while still retaining their individual identities so as to assure innovation and creativity.

7. Frequent communications at all levels of the organization, and frequent, structured interaction on creating peak-to-peak performance. (Partnership proximity is therefore important and will be mutually addressed.)

8. Getting their partners involved early in any new innovations, and working with their partners with the utmost flexibility to ensure the best overall performance of the partnership.

In discussions of Genesis Partnerships, some seem to believe that this partnership holds only when dealing up the supply chain to the level below the ultimate consumer. The belief is that the Genesis Partnership doesn't include the ultimate consumer. To the contrary: Although there will be some differences, there are many examples where a Genesis Partnership is formed directly with the consumer. Coke does this with their Customer Advisory Board, and Apple has their User Groups. The Lotus spreadsheet was developed when an MIT student found he couldn't use existing spreadsheets. Luggage carriers with wheels and handles that fit in airplane compartments were an idea that came from a pilot who just couldn't find any luggage that fit his needs. Mountain bikes were created by Californians who couldn't find bikes designed for their trails and therefore created the first mountain bikes by putting together components to create their own bikes. And on and on.

CAUTION: IT ISN'T CLEAR THAT MOVING FORWARD IS ALWAYS GOOD

Packaged-goods manufacturers have for years wooed consumers through product innovation and advertising. This built brand awareness, and thus pleased retailers by increasing sales. Packaged-good manufacturers treated the retailers as a necessary evil, and often would say with pride, "We don't sell *to* the retailers but *through* the retailers."

Now, however, under the banner of partnerships, the large retail chains are trying to gain a competitive advantage by changing their relationship with manufacturers. The large retailers are demanding lower prices, better service, and customized promotions. The packaged-goods manufacturers are responding, but in order to meet the demands, they are making major cuts in their consumer-related and advertising budgets. The pendulum has shifted to manufacturers thinking, "We don't sell to *consumers* but to *retailers.*" This has cut costs, but at what cost? Many believe the loss of focus on the consumer will squelch innovation and ignore consumer needs. This will lead to all brands becoming equal, a growth in private labels, and further pressure from the retailers for the manufacturers to cut costs.

Is this a partnership? No. Is this good for the packaged-goods manufacturers? No. Is this good for the consumer? No. Is this good for the large retailers? Some say yes, some say no; time will tell. Nevertheless, it's important to realize that what is *called* a partnership *isn't* always a partnership, and that a trend that is said to be "moving forward" isn't always good.

Genesis Partnerships, then, are long-term relationships based upon trust and a mutual desire to work together for the benefit of the other partner and the partnership. Genesis Partnerships play a key role in the evolution of Genesis Enterprises, and should be pursued as soon as an organization is worthy of partnering.

10.2   Creating Genesis Partnerships

The best way to think about the process of creating Genesis Partnerships is to realize that a Genesis Partnership is the successful application of the team-based process between organizations. In fact, the objective of creating Genesis Partnerships is to create the same synergy between organizations as the synergy that resulted from the creation of teams within an organization. Therefore, the process that was followed to shift an organization from individuals to teams may be used as a guide to shift two organizations from supplier/customer to partners. Prerequisites to beginning the process of creating Genesis Partnerships are that the individual organizations have already shifted from management to leadership and from individuals to teams. Once this has occurred, then the organizations must begin the customer/supplier-to-partner transformation by throwing off the traditional customer/supplier win-lose mindset and adopting a win-win mindset.

It is the difficulty in throwing off the win-lose mindset that is at the root of most broken relationships. With the win-lose mindset, each party is afraid that the other will gain an upper hand if they cooperate in good faith. Since they believe in win-lose, it is clear that if the other party wins they must lose. Thus there is no cooperation, as offering this cooperation is seen as being just a step away from losing. Unfortunately, since there is no cooperation, there is no winning and in fact. no partnership.

An evaluation of the payoff matrices given in Table 10.2 provides an interesting insight into the win-lose mindset. In Table 10.2*a*, Party A indicates that from its perspective either both parties cooperating or both parties not cooperating there is no win-lose. So, although both cooperating results in a higher payoff to A (60), than both not cooperating (50), this increase is not nearly as significant as the loss that would be incurred (to 30) if Party A cooperated and Party B did not, win for B and a lose for A. In fact, the only big win (80) is if Party A did not cooperate and Party B did cooperate, a win for A and a lose for B.

The exact opposite is true with Party B, as seen in Table 10.2*b*. It is clear that the win-lose mindset predefines anyone who cooperates as a person asking to lose. To the contrary, Table 10.3 illustrates the payoffs that exist under a win-win mindset. For both Parties A and B, there is a loss involved when the two parties do not act in unison. Interestingly, the loss typically still is perceived as greater if you cooperate and the other party does not, than vice versa. Nevertheless, both parties are better off if you agree not to cooperate together, or much, much better off if you both cooperate. Some might suggest that if you agree not to cooperate, you are in fact cooperating on this. This is true, and such are the positive thoughts to be gained once you adopt a win-win mindset.

The win-win mindset, when fully embraced, results in powerful relationships. A win-win mindset supplier realizes that its opportunity to grow

Table 10.2   Payoff Matrices, Given a Win-Lose Mindset

a. Payoff Matrix for Party A; *b*. Payoff Matrix for Party B

		a. Payoff Matrix for Party A	
		Party B	
		Cooperate	Not cooperate
Party A:	Cooperate	60	30
	Not cooperate	80	50

		b. Payoff Matrix for Party B	
		Party B	
		Cooperate	Not cooperate
Party A:	Cooperate	60	80
	Not cooperate	30	50

Table 10.3   Payoff Matrices, Given a Win-Win Mindset

a. Payoff Matrix for Party A; *b.* Payoff Matrix for Party B

a. Payoff Matrix for Party A

		Party B	
		Cooperate	Not cooperate
Party A:	Cooperate	100	30
	Not cooperate	40	50

b. Payoff Matrix for Party B

		Party B	
		Cooperate	Not cooperate
Party A:	Cooperate	100	40
	Not cooperate	30	50

lies in the growth of its customers. As its customers grow, so do its suppliers. Therefore, in a win-win mindset relationship, the supplier is totally focused on the success of its customers, as it is only by achieving its customer's success that it may succeed. The supplier will do whatever it can to bring about the success of its customers. This is at the core of a Genesis Partnership.

Once your organization has shifted from management to leadership, shifted from individuals to teams, and adopted a win-win mindset, then you are ready to identify potential Genesis Partners. Identification of potential Genesis Partners can be done by the customer looking at their suppliers or by the suppliers looking at their customers. In either case, the identification of potential Genesis Partners should not be based upon the sales volume done in the past or projected for the future. The identification of potential partners should be based upon the opportunity for additional contribution to profit over a five-year planning horizon.

Contribution to profit may be obtained either by increasing revenues or reducing costs. Factors that come into play in a potential partner's ability to contribute to additional profits include the following:

1. Quality of leadership

2. Quality of team-based process

3. Understanding of partnerships

4. Focus on quality

5. Level of innovativeness

6. Understanding of time compression

7. Volume of present and potential business

8. Acceptance of change

9. Stability of personnel

10. Technical competence and creativity

11. Level of information systems

12. Geographical location/responsiveness

13. Honesty, ethics, and trust

14. Organizational consistency

15. Level of distribution expertise

16. Understanding of Just-In-Time

17. Openness of communications

18. A win-win mindset

19. Flexibility

20. Level of desire to create peak-to-peak performance

21. Focus on value

22. Product design skills

23. Profitability

24. Attitude toward growth

25. Clarity and timeliness of decision/investment process

26. Performance track record

27. Willingness to experiment/take risks

28. History of organizational learning

29. Willingness to accept feedback

30. Cultural fit

31. Quality and accuracy of cost information

32. Ability to run/participate in effective outreach

33. Industry reputation

34. Awareness of competition

These factors should be evaluated (a questionnaire that may help with this evaluation is provided in Appendix F) and a preliminary list of potential partners should be generated.

This list of potential partners should be further refined by conducting an on-site visit with the potential partner. This visit should be positioned with the potential partner as a get-together to more fully understand the relationship and to review future opportunities. It should not be positioned as the first step toward partnering. Many visits will result in a decision not to pursue a Genesis Partnership and thus, not labeling the partnership concept will minimize the disruption with those suppliers with whom it is best to retain a traditional relationship. Additionally, announcing up front the potential for the creation of a partnership may very well scare off good potentials, in much the same way as a young man would scare off a young lady if on the first date he began to talk about marriage.

The on-site visit should include a plant tour, some relationship-building, and a lot of discussion of the following types of issues:

1. What are the keys to your success?
2. Why do customers select your product?
3. What changes do you see in your business?
4. What do you see in the future that will change your business?
5. What are you doing now to prepare for the future?
6. What are the greatest opportunities for improvement?
7. What is the one thing that if you could change you would like to change?
8. What can we do to help you?
9. What can we do to make our relationship easier?
10. What can we do together to reduce costs?
11. What are the cost drivers?
12. What can we do together to increase revenues?
13. What can we do together to increase margins?
14. What can we do for each other to increase profits?
15. What can we do for each other to enhance growth?

The results of some of these on-site meetings will be joint projects. The on-site meetings that do not net joint projects should not be forced to a next level of partnership. Allow these relationships to evolve at a pace both parties are comfortable with. The on-site meetings that do result in some joint projects should still be considered as potentials for partnership. Every effort should be made to pursue the joint efforts while demonstrating trust, openness, and a win-win mindset. It is important to realize that much like the forming, storming, norming, performing, and maturation phases of team development presented in Chap. 6, the same evolution of a partnership will take place for many of the same reasons. Many successful meetings, interactions, and projects will need to take place before a relationship can evolve into a Genesis Partnership. Especially early in the process, the focus should be on building trust, clearly communicating, and creating peak-to-peak performance.

As relationships between individuals evolve, so too should the level of interaction between the potential partners. This escalation of trust, openness, and success will naturally lead to the sharing of Models of Success and strategic business plans.

Once a win-win mutual mindset has been adopted by both parties, a Partnership Workshop should be developed. The purpose of this Partnership Workshop is to officially establish a Cooperative Relationship. The Partnership Workshop should be held off-site, and should include leadership from both companies as well as the people most closely involved with the successful joint projects. The agenda for the off-site workshop should include time to share experiences, successes, and failures, to build a relationship, to establish a letter of intent for a cooperative relationship (see Appendix G), and to establish a mutual plan toward partnership. The elements of the Cooperative Relationship Mutual Plan should include the following:

1. Mutual objectives for business levels

2. Mutual objectives for cost reduction

3. Mutual strategies to achieve mutual objectives

4. Mutual agreement on how to share risks and rewards

5. Mutual agreement on a time frame for the evolution of the partnership

6. Mutual agreement on the process of evolving to partnership

7. Mutual agreement on the priorities to be pursued, the teams to address these priorities, and the charters of these teams

8. Mutual agreement on the communications to take place between meetings and the schedule for meetings

9. Mutual agreement on how to share information about the Cooperative Relationship both inside and outside of the company

10. Mutual agreement on confidentiality and restrictions on business relations

The purpose of these mutual understandings is to ensure that there are no surprises and to maintain a comfort level with what is not a natural relationship for many business people. The Cooperative Relationship should then be pursued as the relationship evolves. As this evolution occurs, many of the team-based lessons explained in Part 3 will be applicable. The teams consisting of members from each of the partners will develop their own identities. The identity of suppliers/customers will become blurred, and first individuals, then teams, and finally entire companies will be Genesis Partners. The supplier/customer distinctions will

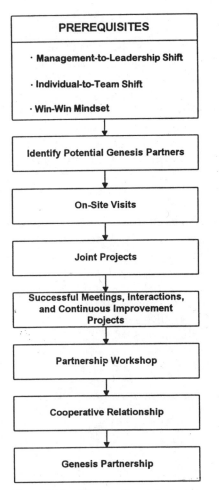

Figure 10.2 Creating a Genesis Partnership

disappear, and the Genesis Partners will act as one to improve, grow, and prosper while still maintaining their own corporate identities.

Figure 10.2 illustrates the process explained in this section. Please keep in mind that it is not the process but the *people* who make this work.

PARTNERSHIPS: WINNING RELATIONSHIPS FOR PENNY PARTS AS WELL AS $300 MILLION FACILITIES

Ford Motor Company was facing the design/construction/commissioning of one of the largest automotive paint-finishing plants in the world. The 730,000-square-foot, 75-car-per-hour, paint-finishing plant was to be attached to the Ford Oakville, Canada, assembly plant. This $300 million facility was to utilize leading-edge, paint-finishing technology, while being completed for 25 to 30 percent less investment than similar operations. In addition, Ford had a tight timeline and a need to significantly improve paint-finishing quality while addressing several difficult environmental challenges. Sound like an impossible task? Well, it was, and if a traditional approach had been adopted, success wouldn't have occurred. Nevertheless, success *was* achieved, and it all had to do with partnerships.

ABB was formed by the merger of the Swedish ASEA and the Swiss company Brown Boveri. ABB, with a market value of $11 billion, is a global electric company whose portfolio of expertise includes power generation, power transmission, power distribution, mass transportation, environmental controls, and industrial process optimization. In the mid-1980s, ABB made a commitment to pursue business with automotive companies in the design, building, and commissioning of automotive paint-finishing facilities. It pursued this commitment by acquiring small companies, recruiting experienced engineers, developing and demonstrating a partnership model, and forming a construction project management partnership with Fluor Daniel. As Ford reviewed its situation, it decided to pursue a partnership with ABB/Fluor Daniel to achieve its objectives. At the core of this partnership was a deferred fixed-price contract that consisted of the following three phases:

Phase One	The design of a process to establish the price and scope of the facility, the definition of a base price of 90 percent of the original ABB bid, and the exact makeup of this price; the agreement that after Phase Two each party had the right to withdraw.
Phase Two	A cooperative engineering effort, whereby a final scope and design was established; the sharing of the savings from the base price; the mutual improvement, innovation, and cost reduction of the facility.
Phase Three	The contracting for a fixed definition and cost project; ABB presenting a bid for 75 percent of the original bid, and Ford accepting this contract.

The results were very, very good. Ford accomplished all of its objectives, and ABB and Fluor Daniel were able to achieve their desired profit while having a significantly lower level of risk. The facility was implemented on time, at budget, and achieved all design objectives. The most interesting part of this effort lies in the Ford/ABB/Fluor Daniel relationships. Consider the following quotes from an article on these relationships:

- "ABB/Fluor Daniel and Ford managed to create a new way to conduct their business that resulted in a genuine win-win outcome."
- "Both the Ford/ABB and the ABB/Fluor Daniel relationships were dependent on trust."
- "Beyond the apparent need for a cooperative relationship, the companies created the necessary trust as a result of the process they employed for working together. They formed a governance structure that brought about repeated encounters; they used the passage of time to their advantage; they created open and simple structures for sharing financial benefits."
- "Only sustained relationships allow time for cross-fertilization, the compression of total project time, and the achievement of exceptionally tight schedules."
- "By establishing a well-defined means for dividing mutual gain, all parties were able to focus their attention on how to create that gain rather than on the distractions of claiming those gains before they were even created."
- "Purchasing focused more on acquiring a system rather than on acquiring component parts; more on minimizing total cost than on minimizing elemental costs; more on capturing process knowledge than on just buying hardware; more on developing meaningful relationships with a few suppliers than on enlarging the supplier base."

The partnership lessons that follow from the win-win-win Ford/ABB/Fluor Daniel relationships and that may be applied to all partnerships include the following:

1. Acknowledge, respect, and utilize mutual strengths.
2. Maintain a broad perspective and a view of the big picture.
3. Use time as an ally. Don't force a contract until all factors have been resolved; mutually minimize risks.
4. Structure the process of interaction around a succession of transactions. This builds trust.
5. Don't negotiate price. This is a win-lose process. Establish a process that allows the development of price in a win-win context.

These lessons are as applicable for partnerships buying penny screws as $300 million facilities. Don't overlook the potential for partnerships in any relationship. Partnerships work for all parties, and are at the core of Genesis Enterprises.

10.3 Conclusion

To date, the rhetoric of partnerships has outstripped the reality. What is required to achieve Genesis Partnerships is a fundamental shift from the traditional supplier/customer relationship to a partnership relationship. A foundation upon which partnerships are built is trust. This trust must evolve as individuals from the partnership companies repeatedly test their relationship and gain confidence in one another. Partnerships evolve by going through the following four phases:

1. Customer-driven organization

2. Invincible customer service

3. Cooperative relationship

4. Genesis Partnership

Genesis Partnerships are the application of the team-based process defined in Part 3 between organizations. Prerequisites for pursuing a Genesis Partnership are

1. A shift from management to leadership

2. A shift from individual to team

3. An acceptance of a win-win mindset

Once these prerequisites are in place, the process of creating a Genesis Partnership involves

1. Identifying potential Genesis Partners

2. On-site visits

3. Joint projects

4. Successful meetings, interactions, and continuous-improvement projects

5. Partnership workshop

6. Cooperative relationship

7. Genesis Partnership

The synergy and benefits that result from Genesis Partnerships are great. A Genesis Enterprise cannot be an island unto itself, and can only be a Genesis Enterprise by partnering with other Genesis Enterprises. Once you are ready to partner, all barriers to partnering should be removed and a clear path toward Genesis Partnership pursued.

References

Belasco, J. A. and R. C. Stayer. *Flight of the Buffalo,* Warner Books, New York, 1993.

Clark K. B. and T. Fujimoto, *Product Development Performance,* Harvard Business School Press, Boston, 1991.

Conway, B., "Partnering for Quality Improvement," *Quality,* April 1994.

Dyer, J. H. and W. G. Ouchi, "Japanese Style Partnerships: Giving Companies a Competitive Edge," *Sloan Management Review,* Fall 1993.

Frey, S. C. and M. M. Schlosser, "ABB and Ford: Creating Value Through Cooperation," *Sloan Management Review,* Fall 1993.

Gulat, R., T. Khanna, and N. Nohria, "Unilateral Commitments and the Importance of Process in Alliances," *Sloan Management Review,* Spring 1994.

Hanan, M., *Growth Partnering: How to Build Your Company's Profits by Building Customer Profits,* Amacom, New York, 1992.

Hillman, G. P., "Partnering in Practice," *ASQC 48th Annual Quality Congress Proceedings,* ASQC, Milwaukee, WI, 1994.

Johnson, H. T., *Relevance Regained: From Top-Down to Bottom-Up Empowerment,* The Free Press, New York, 1992.

Moody, P. E., *Breakthrough Partnering: Creating a Collective Enterprise Advantage,* Oliver Wight Publications, Essex Junction, VT, 1993.

O'Brien, J. M., "Are Consumers Being Jilted?" *Direct,* July 1994.

Peters, T., "The Boundaries of Business Partners—The Rhetoric and Reality," *Harvard Business Review,* October 1991.

Remich, N. C., "Big-Time Partnering," *Appliance Manufacturer,* June 1994.

Stein, M., "The Customer-Driven Organization," *Corporate Meetings and Inventories,* May 1994.

Tapscott, D. and A. Caston, *Paradigm Shift: The New Promise of Information Technology,* McGraw-Hill, New York, 1993.

Tompkins, J. A., *Winning Manufacturing: The How-to Book of Successful Manufacturing,* IIE, Norcross, GA, 1989.

Urban, G. L., "How Partnering with Lead Users Can Impact Product Development," *The Planning Forum Network,* April 1994.

Williams, G. and L. Reid, "Enhancing Customer-Supplier Relationships," *Quality,* April 1994.

11
Shifting from Traditional Customer/Supplier Relationships to Partnerships

The opening sentence of Chap. 6 stated, "Possibly the biggest challenge in creating a successful team-based organization is overcoming all the existing paradigms of teams." In a similar fashion, possibly the largest challenge in creating successful partnerships is overcoming the existing paradigms of partnerships. Much in the same manner that people throw around the words *consortium, acquisition, merger, strategic alliance,* and *joint ventures,* the word *partnership* is used to describe many different relationships. Some of these relationships have merit, and some do not. Some of these relationships work, and some do not. Some of these relationships are pursued with sincerity and openness, and others just use the word *partnership* to gain some competitive advantage. Just as it was stated in Chap. 10 that "Just-In-Time has often been twisted and used as a hammer to force suppliers into a survival-of-the-fittest contest," so too with partnerships. There are many documented cases in which companies have used the partnership rhetoric to gain advantage over a supplier. It is for this reason that, just as with the use of the words *teams* and *empowerment,* care must be used when using the word *partnership.* It is critical not only that you know what you mean by the word, but also that the people to whom you speak have the same understanding of the word. From this perspective, it is important to understand that

1. A relationship between similar companies in the same type of business who ban together to pool their resources to do research, evaluate technology or lobby for a political position is not a partnership. This is a *consortium.*

2. A relationship between two companies in which the companies lose their independence by becoming one corporate entity is not a partnership. This vertical integration is either an *acquisition* or a *merger.*

3. A relationship between two companies in which the companies work together to pursue a specific, single focused business objective is not a partnership. This is a *strategic alliance.*

4. A relationship between two companies in which the companies form a separate entity with joint ownership to pursue a specific business objective is not a partnership. This is a *joint venture.*

5. A true partnership, a Genesis Partnership, is a long-term relationship based upon trust and a mutual desire to work together for the benefit of the other partner and the partnership.

WHEN THE SUM OF EIGHT I's EQUALS ONE WE

In an excellent July–August 1994 *Harvard Business Review* study of relationships, Rosabeth Moss Kanter presented the following eight I's as criteria for achieving true partnerships:

1. *Individual excellence.* A win-win mentality exists between two strong partners who have something of value to contribute and gain from the partnership.

2. *Importance.* The partners believe the relationship is important for their mutual long-term success, and therefore they are each committed to the success of the partnership.

3. *Interdependence.* The partners need each other. Neither can do alone what the two of them can do together.

4. *Investment.* Both partners demonstrate their long-term commitment by devoting significant resources to the partnership.

5. *Information.* Communications are open. Partners share information with full confidence of the protection and security of that which is shared.

6. *Integration.* The partners develop linkages that integrate their businesses and minimize the difficulties with information and materials flowing across boundaries.

7. *Institutionalization.* The relationship is formally recognized and broadly understood. The partnership encompasses all aspects of the partner's business and cannot be ended on a whim.

8. *Integrity.* The partners work like a team, with a focus on the continual escalation of trust. The partners honor both the law and the spirit of the relationship, and practice the golden rule.

11.1 Growing a Partnership

In Chap. 10, the evolution of a partnership was likened to the evolution of a relationship between a couple dating, going steady, being engaged, and getting married. To fully understand the shift from a traditional supplier/customer relationship to a partnership, the evolution of the relationship as organizations go from dating to getting married needs to be fully understood. In addition to the couple analogy demonstrating the evolution of a partnership relationship, it is also relevant in that

1. No two relationships ever evolve in the same manner.

2. The evolution of a relationship is not a cold-blooded business negotiation, but a comfortable personal relationship between individuals.

3. There exists a positive chemistry between the two portions of the relationship.

4. Just as with a romance, the evolution involves the hopes, dreams, and anticipation of what the future may hold.

5. A certain way to kill a relationship (either between organizations or couples) is to get third parties (lawyers, accountants, bankers, mothers-in-law, brothers-in-law, etc.) intimately involved with the evolution of the relationship.

6. A key to a long-term relationship is the basic compatibility of the parties. People or organizations that come from drastically different backgrounds, or have drastically different values or goals will not be able to find the basis for a positive long-term relationship.

7. For a relationship to work, both parties must know themselves and what they are looking for in the relationship.

8. The relationship has at the very foundation the well being of the other party, as well as the relationship between the parties.

9. For a relationship to progress to a successful marriage/partnership, there must be not only an acceptance by the primary parties. Also, the

people around these parties need to accept the evolution of the relationship. With a couple, the people around the relationship may include family and friends. With two organizations, the people around the relationship may include the subordinates, stockholders, government, and other parties.

10. Each party in the evolving relationship must have shared expectations of how and when the relationship shall evolve. There will be no major surprises.

During the dating phase, the relationship between two organizations is very traditional. The *fluff* of customer service, described in Chap. 9, is the foundation of the relationship. A typical commitment between the two organizations at this level of evolution includes

1. A well-defined customer quality standard.

2. Quarterly review meetings between purchasing and customer service.

3. Annual scheduling meetings to negotiate price and understand schedule.

4. Sharing of each organization's Model of Success.

The step above the dating relationship is going steady, and from an organizational relationship perspective, this is equivalent to the invincible customer service relationship defined in Chap. 9. This participative relationship is the beginning of the mutual commitment between the parties in the relationship. A typical commitment between the two organizations at this level of evolution involves

1. The adoption of a win-win mindset.

2. A well-defined, jointly defined quality standard.

3. Monthly review meetings between purchasing and customer service.

4. Semiannual scheduling and price review meetings.

5. Sharing of each organization's Model of Success, strategic business plans, and improvement initiatives.

6. Annual leadership interaction.

7. Annual review of business plans, forecasts, and new-product plans.

8. Sharing of each other's distribution requirements.

9. For organizations where a partnership is viable, the conducting of a Partnership Workshop to further the relationship and to develop a letter of intent for a cooperative relationship and a mutual plan toward partnership.

The step above going steady is being engaged, and from an organizational relationship perspective this is equivalent to the cooperative relationship defined in Chap. 10. This cooperative relationship is a significant step up in the organization's commitment, and like the engagement indicates the intention to be married (partnership) at some future time. This level of commitment is made public and is treated with a much greater level of seriousness, as it indicates a mutual willingness to be married (become partners). It is often at this point in a relationship that difficulties surface. Because there is now an awareness of the intention to be married (become partners), there are many people who step forward to speak against and, yes, even sabotage the relationship. It is important for the principal parties to remain strong to their commitment, while bringing along those people around them who have questions and/or concerns about the relationship. It is during the cooperative relationship phase that the mutual understandings of the partnership, as defined in Chap. 10, are pursued. Typical activities to occur during the cooperative relationship phase include the following:

1. The adoption of a mutual improvement initiative for all existing products

2. A mutual quality improvement process

3. Real-time review meetings between purchasing and customer service

4. Monthly scheduling and price review meetings

5. Monthly cooperative relationship progress assessments and interactions

6. Semiannual leadership visits

7. Semiannual review of business plans, forecasts, and new product plans

8. Joint pursuit of distribution improvements

9. Annual engineering review of product plans and product improvements

10. One-way Electronic Data Interchange (EDI)

The ultimate relationship is the marriage (partnership), in which the parties agree to a long-term, mutually beneficial relationship. This relationship should maintain some mutually agreed-to flexibility but nevertheless should be a binding, lasting relationship that can be ended only by going through a formal divorce (dissolution of the partnership). Parties need to be aware of the fact that, just as in a new marriage, the early days of a new partnership require considerable patience and understanding. As with newlyweds, once the celebration is over, the reality of marriage sets in. As more and more people from the two organizations participate in the partnership, the positive relationship established to date may be challenged because

1. Many people within the organizations have not been involved with the partner, so although some people have developed close ties, others have no ties and therefore question the relationship.

2. Many people aren't comfortable working with people outside of their organization. So, even though they have heard about partnering, they are not personally comfortable with the relationship.

3. Many people will have a full list of internal organizational challenges, and a well-defined internal organization performance criteria that does not involve the partner. So, although they may buy into the concept, they don't have adequate time to be involved with their partners.

4. Some people within the organizations may not support the partnership, and therfore openly resist being forced to participate.

5. The organizations have different cultures which sour the relationship due to differences in decision-making style, timing, documentation, levels of authority, etc.

6. Although leadership has adopted a win-win mindset, there still exist people within the organization who have a win-lose mindset.

7. Although the cooperative relationship letter of intent was ratified, there hasn't been a clear understanding established over money. Leadership understands the need for flexibility depending upon the issue at hand, but others in the organizations don't understand this and confrontations over money take place (kind of like a new marriage).

8. The organizations have different economic analysis and justification criteria, and they both believe their criteria are best. Recommendations get lost in financial white water, and frustration and resignation result.

Leadership must anticipate these challenges and ensure an abundance of open communications to resolve these issues as they arise. After the initial start-up, three or four months during which communications should be very frequent, typical activities that should be put in place to assure the health and evolution of the partnership include

1. The adoption of a mutual peak-to-peak performance effort for all existing and future products

2. A real-time, joint quality improvement process

3. Real-time production requirements via two-way EDI

4. Joint price setting and cost reduction goals, as a result of the ongoing joint peak-to-peak performance process

5. Quarterly leadership site visits to assure partnership success

6. Quarterly review of business plans, forecasts, and new product plans

7. Joint responsibility for distribution

8. Semiannual engineering review of product plans and product improvement

9. Annual partnership strategic retreat

11.2 Efficient Consumer Response: A Partnership Mandate

The grocery industry consists of manufacturers who sell to wholesalers who sell to retailers who sell to consumers. The evolution over the last 20 years of how the manufacturers, wholesalers, and retailers worked to please the customer has resulted in some very poor business practices. At the heart of the problem in the grocery industry are the nonintegrated logistics practices that have evolved. The manufacturers have taken to a neverending promotion of their products. These promotions are done in an attempt to push product during slow seasons. To help justify this practice in their minds, the manufacturers and wholesalers called it *forward-buying, strategic purchasing,* or *promotional selling.*

What happened was the manufacturers would create a super price for quantity purchases a couple of times a year, and the wholesalers would load up. The wholesalers would build or rent facilities to hold all this inventory, and obviously would not buy again until they had unloaded this excess inventory to the retailers and the next deal came along. Interestingly, while waiting for the next deal, many wholesalers would back-order items to the retailer, which would result in the retailer being out of stock. Not surprisingly, the manufacturers found themselves building large inventories, awaiting the announcement of the next deal. All this occurred while encountering a massive buildup in the number of items being offered. So what happened was, the manufacturer had very erratic demand as they pushed inventory onto the wholesalers. This erratic demand resulted in inefficiency and waste in their distribution of an ever-increasing number of products. At the same time, wholesalers came to depend upon the forward-buying for their profit margin, so they too built large warehouses to hold their erratic ebbs and flows of an ever-increasing number of items.

The result of this practice was that the retailers had to pay more for poor service, which resulted in their overcharging and under-servicing their customers. Then, as if this weren't a big enough mess, the manufacturers started to work promotions directly with the consumer to attempt to pull goods from the retailers, who were being supplied from a wholesaler, who was being pushed goods from the manufacturer. The ultimate in stupidity resulted when the manufacturer paid to advertise to consumers who came to stores to buy products that were out of stock, even though the distribution costs from manufacturer and wholesaler were excessively high.

What's wrong with this picture? Well, what we have here is not a lack of synergy, but *anti*-synergy. Think about anti-synergy this way:

- Synergy says that 2 + 2 = 6.
- Lack of synergy says that 2 + 2 = 4.
- Anti-synergy says that 2 + 2 = 0.

The interesting thing is that everyone saw and understood this anti-synergy. But the manufacturer was afraid to change, because if it stopped doing deals and its competition didn't, it would lose business. The wholesaler was afraid to change, because the majority of its profit came from the forward-buying. The retailers didn't really have a choice, and so they lived with the situation and continued to overcharge and under-service the consumer. This is how it was, until. Until the mass merchandise clubs and super-centers changed the game. Until Wal-Mart, K-Mart, and others rang a loud and clear wake-up call.

The grocery industry has banded together to balance the benefits of replenishment and promotion, to eliminate waste in distribution, to increase consumer value, and to work together as partners. The banner under which they are attacking the problems of the last 20 years is Efficient Consumer Response (ECR), with ECR defined as *a grocery-industry strategy in which manufacturers and wholesalers are committed to working together to bring about better value to the grocery consumer.* ECR obtains results by having the customer and supplier jointly focus on the efficiency of the total grocery supply system, rather than the efficiency of individual components. The purpose of ECR is to reduce total system costs while improving the consumer's choice of high-quality, fresh grocery products. The ultimate goal of ECR is a responsive, boundaryless supply chain, in which manufacturers and wholesalers work together as partners to maximize consumer satisfaction at a minimal systems cost. Interestingly, the four core initiatives of ECR are

1. *Continuous replenishment inventory systems.* The capturing of point-of-sale (POS) data and the transmission of this data on a daily basis via electronic data interchange (EDI) to the wholesaler, to bring supply in line with demand.

2. *Flow-through distribution systems.* The increased efficiency of handling products from the manufacturers to the wholesalers and to the retailers. Transportation and warehouse management systems to eliminate waste, and speed the product flow through distribution.

3. *Pipeline logistics organizations.* The creation of more integrated manufacturing organizations, wholesaler organizations, and retailer organizations, and the adoption of a broader total supply chain view.

4. *Pipeline performance measures.* The development of performance measures that focus on costs and service across the supply chain, and the application of management techniques that take into account the total supply chain performance.

Now this is all fine, but is ECR missing something? Here are a few thoughts from around the grocery industry:

- "One stumbling block is that many wholesalers and retailers question the motives of manufacturers in pushing ECR."

- "Mentally, wholesalers and retailers need to come to grips with being partners more than they have historically."

- "We are having a terrible time getting ECR down through the system. Everybody talks fine at industry meetings. But when we get back home and talk to manufacturers' reps, they don't know what we're talking about."

- "The industry has studied the retailer backward and forward on stores and distribution. We hear we are inefficient, but we don't know about the manufacturer's efficiency. This lack of trust on allowances can destroy ECR before it starts. How about a study of the manufacturers?"

- "I read in *The Wall Street Journal* that manufacturers who have moved to continuous replenishment are posting earnings up 15 percent and 20 percent, but then I pick up *Supermarket News* to find that supermarkets are just making ends meet. Something's not right."

- "ECR is about creating a true system of teamwork through alliances among grocery industry trading partners. But who, I wonder, makes the first move? Manufacturers? Retailers? Or wholesalers?"

- "Even if we buy the idea that we are going to create a system of teamwork through alliances among grocery industry trading partners, the question is, do I give up my margin? Do you give up your margin? Or do we both give up some of our margin?"

- "The problem of getting it done is leadership. The technology is easy, the culture is hard. Without leadership, this cannot be done. ECR comes with obstacles and pain."

- "The primary challenge is not big investments in technology, like EDI; rather, it is the human commitment to change business practices."

The challenge in making ECR a reality is the challenge of becoming a Genesis Enterprise. The technology of ECR is fine, but before it can even begin to pay a true dividend, there must be a shift from management to leadership, then a shift from individual to team, then a shift from the traditional supplier/customer (manufacturer/wholesaler/retailer) relationship to a Genesis Partnership. If this is not done, ECR will never be made to work. An organization can't partner until it has become team-based, and an organization can't be team-based until it has become leadership-driven. Manufacturers, wholesalers, and/or retailers cannot make ECR work until they have adopted an *internal* culture of creating peak-to-peak performance, so that they may then adopt an *external* culture of creating peak-to-peak performance. This external culture of creating peak-to-peak performance is the essence of a Genesis Partnership, and it is a prerequisite for success with ECR.

11.3 Integrated, Linked, Boundaryless, and Seamless

Section 11.2 focused on ECR, but it would have been just as easy to talk about Quick Response (QR), Fluid Distribution (FD), Continuous Flow Distribution (CFD), etc. The essence of all of these outreaches is the same: the real-time capture of information on demand, so that supply may be fully responsive to the needs of the marketplace while minimizing the total system costs. All of these have at their core both a technology component and a partnership component. The technology component is well defined, and given the proper expertise it isn't a major problem. The partnership component requires a shift from the traditional supplier/customer relationship to a Genesis Partnership, and it is a major hurdle for most organizations. If organizations are to melt together, have success with ECR, QR, FD, CFD, etc., it is crucial that they truly understand partnerships. All of the talk about "virtual organizations" and "virtual enterprises," which although they really don't exist act as if they do, is absolutely impossible without Genesis Partnerships but straightforward with Genesis Partnerships. If ECR, QR, FD, CFD, and all other virtual enterprise types of solutions are to achieve their potential, the following must occur:

1. All partners must shift from management to leadership.

2. All partners must shift from individuals to teams.

3. All partners must fully embrace and implement the reality of Genesis Partnerships to become

a. *Integrated.*   Where the partners trust, understand, and are compatible with each other, and are mutually working toward the same objectives. Where both partners are focused on the well-being of their partners and the partnership.

b. *Linked.*   Where the partners are both interdependent, but still independent. Interdependent in that the partners need each other, have good relationships, and share a win-win mindset. Independent in that they do their job well, do valuable work, maintain their own identity, and are independently creative and innovative.

c. *Boundaryless.*   The partners have open, frequent communications, totally shared information, and see-through business. The partners see the same costs, problems, and opportunities.

d. *Seamless.*   The partners have mutual participation in creating peak-to-peak performance, and a joint relationship that is based upon synergy. The partnership is flexible, and free from interfering rules or bureaucracy.

11.4   Conclusion

The word *partnership* is often misused. A Genesis Partnership is *a long-term relationship based upon trust and a mutual desire to work together for the benefit of the other partner and the partnership.* The analogy of a couple evolving through dating, going steady, being engaged, and getting married not only demonstrates the evolution of a Genesis Partnership, it also is relevant in that partnerships are personal, emotional, and unique. As relationships between organizations evolve, so should their levels of interaction, participation, and trust. By the time two organizations have become partners, the organizations should have an integrated, linked, boundaryless, and seamless relationship. Many of the outreaches being pursued today between organizations are being pursued without a proper understanding of the foundations upon which partnerships must be built. The steps that must be pursued are first to shift from management to leadership, then to shift from individuals to teams, and then, and *only* then, to evolve a relationship through a mutual, synergistic, peak-to-peak performance process to achieve a Genesis Partnership.

References

Brooker, D., "Faster Food, How Just-In-Time Techniques Can Cut Supermarket Distribution Costs," *Materials Management and Distribution,* May 1993.

Herlitz, A., "Partnering May Not Be All It Seems," *U.S. Distribution Journal,* October 1993.

Kanter, R. M., "Collaborative Advantage: The Art of Alliances," *Harvard Business Review,* July–August 1994.

Lipnack, J. and J. Stamps, "The Best of Both Worlds," *Inc.,* March 1994.

Mathews, R., "ECR Initiatives Threatening Margins Unacceptable to Wholesalers," *Grocery Marketing,* November 1993.

——, "ECR Opens Door to New Era of Supplier/Distribution Interface," *Grocery Marketing,* October 1993.

Messing, A., "What It Takes to Be a Virtual Enterprise," *U.S. Distribution Journal,* October 15, 1993.

Nannery, M., "Forging Relationships: Retailers and Manufacturers Are Allying Themselves in the Pursuit of ECR's Goals," *Supermarket News,* January 17, 1994.

Sansolo, M., "Formula for Success," *Progressive Grocer,* November 1993.

Ticky, N. M., "Revolutionize Your Company," *Fortune,* December 13, 1993.

Tompkins, J. A. and D. Harmelink, *The Distribution Management Handbook,* McGraw-Hill, New York, 1994.

Weinstein, S., "Small Firms Need Help," *Progressive Grocer,* February 1994.

PART 5

Yes, But What's in It for Me?

Why should managers shift to become leaders? Why should individuals shift to become teams? Why should separate organizations shift from their traditional relationship to become partners? All good questions. All answered in Part 5.

It is important for us to begin Part 5 with a recognition that in most organizations today, the compensation system is broken. What is needed is not a refinement of the traditional compensation plans, but a shift to a whole new approach to compensation. Chapter 12 lays the foundation for this shift, by explaining what's wrong with traditional compensation plans and the psychology of rewards and recognition. Chapter 13 then defines Genesis Compensation as consisting of a recognition element and a rewards element. The recognition element consists of a formal individual goal assessment portion and an ongoing informal emotional recognition portion. The rewards element consists of base pay, pay-for-skill, individual bonus, and goal-sharing.

A key with respect to Genesis Compensation is the reality that there will never be two Genesis Compensation Plans that are alike. One size does *not* fit all. Therefore it is critical that organizations understand the process whereby they can design their own unique Genesis Compensation Plan. This is the topic of Chap. 14. It is by following this participative process that great performance will be rewarded, that all employees will believe there is a balance between their contribution and their compensation, and that companies will prosper. Part 5 answers the question, "What's in it for me?" Once managers have shifted to become leaders, individuals to become teams, organizations to become partners, then peak-to-peak performance will result, which when rewarded and recognized by Genesis Compensation will drive even greater performance, which will merit even greater rewards and recognition by Genesis Compensation, which will ...

It's a wonderful story, peak-to-peak performance created by a leadership-driven, team-based process and true partnerships, and driven to even higher peaks by rewards and recognition. Once you have understood Part 5, you will fully understand how to keep the Genesis Enterprise creating peak-to-peak performance.

12

You Get What You Pay For

A Genesis Enterprise has now shifted from management to leadership, from individual to team, and from a traditional supplier/customer relationship to partnership. Is there any doubt that there must now be a shift in compensation? In fact, once the above shifts have begun to take hold, isn't it common sense that without a compensation shift, the impacts of the prior shifts will be dampened? Without a shift in compensation the prior shifts cannot be expected to hold, as individuals will still be driven by the traditional individual compensation system. The confusion will surface with comments such as these:

- "You ask why I'm not working on my team assignment? Well, let me tell you, my raise depends not on our team but on how well I do on the performance appraisal. And secondly, my boss doesn't have a clue what I'm doing on the team. Do teams really matter?"

- "My boss has asked me to devote my energy to a partnership with our supplier on our new product X, but my bonus is still based on the budget conformance of my old department. What am I to do?"

- "They asked me to work on a team, but my efforts on teams aren't even *on* my performance appraisal. Believe me, if they really wanted me to support teams, it would be on my appraisal."

It's clear that the shift, or lack of a shift, in compensation can have a major impact on the reinforcement or negation of the leadership, team, and partnership shifts.

In many organizations, the compensation plan hasn't been significantly changed in the last 20 years. With the exception of the addition of some form of a retirement plan, the rewards, recognition, and performance appraisals are the same today as they have been for years. Often employees don't understand the compensation structure, but are more than glad to be critical of how it functions. Although there have been and continue to be study after study of compensation, little changes, and it is as if no one is willing to change something as fundamental as how people are compensated. So life goes on with a traditional compensation structure that is ineffective but similar to what others are doing. There has been little innovation, and the focus tends to be more on how to refine our methodology of doing the wrong things rather than shifting to do the right things.

Isn't this amazing? A key area in all companies, and what we have settled for and continue to settle for are compensation practices that try to minimize employee dissatisfaction while keeping our costs in line. What is needed is not a new approach to the traditional compensation practices. What is needed is new, innovative approaches to compensation. For the most part, today's compensation practices will not support a Genesis Enterprise. A Genesis Compensation structure is needed to fully shift to becoming a Genesis Enterprise.

For better or worse, the title of this chapter is true. Companies *do* get what they pay for. For example, Sears used to pay their automobile mechanics based upon their volume of repairs. In 1992, the attorneys-general in 41 states alleged that Sears mechanics were repairing things that weren't broken. Sears settled the charges for $15 million and eliminated commissions for mechanics.

The purpose of this chapter is to look back at what we have been paying for. Not only does this chapter define what we have traditionally been doing, it also presents an overview of the conflicting psychological views of compensation.

12.1   Traditional Compensation

Traditional compensation consists of a pay scale and little or no recognition. The pay scale may be based on incentive pay or merit pay. Merit pay may be an hourly rate or a salary, both of which are initially tied to the base pay for a specific job, which is then adjusted in accordance with seniority and/or a performance appraisal. The next three subsections will discuss the applications and challenges of incentive pay, merit pay, and performance appraisals.

12.1.1   Incentive Pay

The ultimate pay-for-performance plan is incentive pay. Incentive pay involves the employee being paid a given piece-rate for each piece he/she produces. The essence of an incentive pay plan has to do with a task being so boring, repetitive, simple, and routine that there is no intrinsic motivation to perform it. Since the task is paced by the employee, the use of an extrinsic motivation of paying a certain amount of money per piece is a way of keeping employee productivity high.

In the 1920s, 1930s, and 1940s, incentive pay was the most common approach for compensation. Since the 1950s, however, fewer and fewer incentive pay plans have existed, and today most have been eliminated. Their demise has to do with the increased talents of workers, the unbearable hassle associated with the plans, and the changing work environment.

Unfortunately, the increased talents of the workers were not used to contribute to the well-being of the company, but rather to outsmart, beat, and cheat the incentive pay system. Everyone associated with incentive plans can tell a large number of stories about the way workers could work together to beat the system. To try and catch the outsmarters, beaters, and cheaters, large staffs were employed to control, monitor, update, fight grievances, and administer the incentive pay plans. Tremendous adversarial relationships developed between workers and management, as the fights over piece rates continued. The incentive rates became limits on productivity, with all workers agreeing to the level at which all would produce so as to protect their jobs and their pay.

Then too, in today's work environment of high quality, mass customization, a highly-skilled work force, and team-based participation, incentive pay really doesn't fit. So although there are still some companies that successfully use incentive pay, this approach won't be found in a Genesis Enterprise.

12.1.2 Merit Pay

In theory, traditional merit pay plans are also pay-for-performance plans. The essence of a merit pay plan lies in a job-based pay table, a performance measurement system, and an increase in pay based on merit. The job-based pay table is a series of pay ranges for different levels of jobs. These pay ranges may be salary ranges or hourly wage ranges. Typically, these job-based pay tables are the result of a job evaluation system that consists of job description, job factors, allocation of points to jobs based on the factors, and job point scores, which are then translated into the pay ranges. The pay received by a person on a job will be within the pay range for the job and will be demonstrated by a combination of past merit, seniority, and recent merit. A person then will be evaluated for his/her recent merit (typically the last year) and an increase in his/her pay will be defined.

There are five intrinsic problems with traditional merit pay that will lead to fewer and fewer firms using this approach:

1. There are fairness, credibility, and accuracy problems with the performance measurement system in use in most companies today, upon which merit increases are based. The reviews that result from the performance measurement system don't accurately assess performance, and thus the basis for merit increases is faulty. (More on this in Sec. 12.1.3.)

2. The performance measurement system is used to evaluate individuals and not teams, but organizations want to encourage teams. Giving merit increases to individuals based upon a review of their individual efforts is counter to the objectives of teams.

3. Due to the first two problems with merit pay, the difference in merit-pay increases from the worst to the best employee are small. It would not be unusual for the best employee to receive a 4 percent pay increase and the worst to receive a 2 percent pay increase. Is this small difference supposed to be a motivation?

4. Since in a merit pay plan the past merit increases become a part of the person's new base pay, this past performance becomes an annuity. This results in a system that is supposed to pay on merit but in which the people who are really performing the best are rarely paid the best. In fact, in most merit pay plans, the top performers rarely receive the top pay.

5. Due to the pay ranges for specific jobs, individuals will reach a point where they will hit the upper limit of pay for that job. When this occurs, there will be no potential for pay increases until the pay ranges have been adjusted. Unfortunately, when an individual hits the upper limit, what often happens is that to give this person further merit increases, the only choice is to promote him/her. Thus, the reason for the promotion is not that the person *should* be promoted, but that this is the only way to increase the person's salary. This is a problem, as often the wrong person is promoted.

Most organizations will relate to and agree with these five problems. It is for this reason that even though traditional merit pay is the most popular approach to compensation today, this approach must be significantly altered if the objectives of the Genesis Enterprise are to be achieved.

A BROKEN PAY PLAN: SAD STORY NUMBER 3268

The ten-year-old California company had grown quickly, and hadn't been consistent with its human resource types of things. There were pay problems. What a person got paid had more to do with when he/she was hired than with what he/she did or how well he/she did it. During its fast growth period, the company had to pay some pretty high wages just to get people in the door. There were no real quantifiable goals or performance criteria. There was a need to implement a new pay plan, and a compensation expert was hired to do this.

Well, after everyone had taken tests, filled out forms, and sat through an interview, the day of the pay raises arrived. Everyone had talked about this for weeks. Everyone had told their spouses about the pay raises, and the whole company was poised for a celebration.

Alas, it wasn't a happy day. Some people got no raise. Some people were told they were making more money than they should be. Some got very small raises, some got good raises, and some got great raises. All the people in the test department came out very well. All the people in assembly got nothing. The average pay in test was higher than the highest pay in assembly! Everyone was told that these were not pay increases, but "adjustments." The pay raises would be done in December, and done based on merit, but these adjustments weren't done on merit, just based upon the pay ranges for the point totals for each job. To get a feel for this situation, look at this snapshot of the company two weeks after the big day:

President:	"We give out over $600,000 in annual pay increases, and I have the most unhappy people in the world."
Human resource manager:	"This has not gone well. I can't believe the compensation expert let me down like this."
Vice president, operations:	"I can't even walk out on the floor or go to the cafeteria without getting beat up over this pay thing."
Assembly person:	"They think I will accept this? I'm looking for another job, and as soon as I find one I'm gone."
Test person:	"It isn't fair that I got such a big raise and many others got nothing. I'm embarrassed to even talk to the people in production. This is not good!"

What went wrong? Consider that

- People were allowed to have expectations of a big pay increase. Although this was never *said*, this is what the people *heard*.
- There was no participation by the employees in the design, refinement, or implementation of the plan.
- The new plan was poorly implemented. There was no phase-in plan.
- People didn't understand what was done, why it was done, or where the plan would go from there.

■ People felt betrayed, manipulated. They were now being rewarded or punished based upon assignments that were made arbitrarily when they were hired.

What happened next? The plan was eliminated, the company ate crow, all pay increases were left in place, all people who did not get a significant pay raise were given one, the Human Resources Manager was fired, and as of today, there is no plan in place to manage compensation. Isn't this sad? I guess what's even worse is that this story is being repeated, repeated, and repeated all around the world. Let's quit playing with this stuff and shift to Genesis Compensation!

12.1.3 Performance Appraisal

A good starting point for a discussion of traditional performance appraisals is for each of us to think back in our career to the performance appraisals we have received. How did you feel about those appraisals? Most of us weren't pleased. At the core of our displeasure was, and is, a problem with the objectives of the performance appraisals. Isn't it obvious that if the objectives of the organization, the appraiser, and the appraisee are different, then the performance appraisal won't be a success? Well, what are the objectives of a performance appraisal? Here are a few:

1. Career guidance and counseling
2. Improving job performance
3. Improving motivation
4. Improving alignment with the company
5. Clarifying present job requirements
6. Improving appraiser and appraisee communications
7. Enhancing skills
8. Defining training needs
9. Defining performance for pay purposes
10. Creating a complete human resources file on the individual

Not included in that list of valid objectives are objectives that may also exist, such as to get even, to show who is in control, to fulfill an order from my boss that I do this, to straighten out a troublemaker, to tell someone in authority how underpaid I am, to try to get some action on a problem that has not been resolved, to speak up for my coworkers, etc. To combat the lack of success of performance appraisals, organizations are continually revising their performance appraisal systems. A normal cycle goes like this:

1. *Year 1.* Begin developing a new performance appraisal system. Revise the old system by adding categories, eliminating, or other cosmetic things.
2. *Year 2.* Implement new system, and debug.
3. *Year 3.* Obtain feedback that the new system has problems and that people are not happy with their performance appraisals.
4. Go back to Year 1, while still using the last system for one more year.

The problem is not with the cosmetics of the performance appraisal system, but at a deeper level. Here are the questions that need to be asked but too often aren't:

1. What are the objectives of the performance appraisal? Do both the appraiser and appraisee share those objectives?
2. What should be the frequency of performance appraisals?
3. Are the people doing the performance appraisal comfortable with their role? Do they support the process?
4. What lasting impacts on communications, relationships, and egos will result from the appraisal?
5. What are the legal implications of performance appraisals?
6. How much time should be allocated to preparing and presenting performance appraisals? Is this time available?
7. What is the role of teams in and on performance appraisals?
8. What should be the level of participation by the appraisee before, during, and after the appraisal?
9. Should appraisers be held to a predefined distribution of appraisal results? How should the "halo effect" be handled?
10. What form should be used? Are the rating factors subjective or objective? Do the appraisers have a choice or input on forms used?

Typically these issues are not addressed well, and hence the problems with traditional performance appraisals. Performance appraisals are a key feedback mechanism of a Genesis Enterprise, but if they are to accomplish the objectives of a true performance appraisal, a significantly different approach must be taken from the approach traditionally used.

WRITE YOUR OWN SIDEBAR

A few days after I finished each chapter, I went back and read the chapter and at that time wrote these little sidebars to illustrate a key point or topic. It's fun doing them.

Well, as I got to this point in this chapter, about 20 sidebars immediately jumped into my mind. So, I needed to make a decision on which one to include. I decided which one to include, and wrote it. It was good. I liked it. However, that night in bed, I decided, "No, I need to do a sidebar on this other experience." This went on and on. I think I could write a book full of nothing but performance appraisal sidebars. As I reflected on this, it occurred to me that you may be in a similar position. So, to resolve my problem, I decided to prepare the following generic performance appraisal sidebar, into which you may insert your own story.

I remember it well. I had been with _____ for about _____ years, when my boss called me in for my annual performance appraisal. Things had been going well. I really didn't see my boss much, as he had always said he would leave me alone as long as I was getting the job done. Boy, was I in for a surprise.

First, when I get there for the review, he's very cold. Then he lays this form on me that I've never seen. He starts off, and to listen to this guy, I was lucky I wasn't being fired. What a jerk! This guy wouldn't know a good operation if he fell on one. Did you see what it says on the form, next to the _____ category? Well, I lost all respect for this guy. Then, he gets around to money, and he says I get a _____ raise. I can't believe I work so hard for these turkeys and then they say _____ about me and give me a _____ raise.

At the end, he asks if I have any questions. Well, I had a bunch, but I wasn't going to talk then. I was so mad, I mght have said something that would cost me. As I sit here now two weeks later, I see everyone else feeling just about like me. On the one hand, I want to do a good job, but to tell you the truth, I'm not sure what my boss wants. On the other hand, I don't want to think about this, 'cause it just gets me mad all over again. Can you _believe_ what it said on my form? Unbelievable!

12.2 Traditional Gainsharing

Traditional gainsharing is a reward system that allows employees to share in a bonus based upon increases in productivity. Gainsharing has existed for over 60 years, and typically has been used in manufacturing organizations. Over the last 10 years, with the shift to teams, many organizations have gotten into gainsharing. Unfortunately, the organizations that have pursued traditional gainsharing plans haven't been successful.

All traditional gainsharing plans require that a historical standard of expected labor be computed. Then, any improvement in labor performance nets a gain, which creates the bonus that is shared. Most gainsharing applications will split the bonus, half to the company and half to everyone involved in increasing the productivity. The three most popular traditional gainsharing plans are the Scanlon plan, the Rucker plan, and Improshare.

The Scanlon plan is based upon an allowable payroll cost as a percent of the value of production (where value of production is sales minus returns, plus increases or decreases in inventory). For example, consider a company that in the last period spent $1.8 million on payroll and has an allowable payroll cost of 20 percent. Given that the value of production last period was $10 million, the allowable payroll cost would be $2 million. Given the labor cost of only $1.8 million, a labor savings of $200,000 existed last period, and a bonus percentage of 11.1 percent ($200,000/$1,800,000) would be available to be split between the company and all eligible employees.

The Rucker plan is similar to the Scanlon plan, but instead of utilizing the value of production, which includes work done by outside organizations, the Rucker plan considers only the value added by the organization itself. So, in the example used for the Scanlon plan, let's say the allowable payroll cost of the value added has historically been 40 percent. Then, given the $10 million in sales and the actual payroll cost of $1.8 million, with a cost of outside purchases of

Materials and supplies	$3.6 million
Other outside purchases	$1.6 million
Total	$5.2 million

the value added would be $4.8 million and the allowable payroll cost would be $1.92 million ($4.8 × .4). Given the labor cost of $1.8 million, a labor savings of $120,000 existed last period, and a bonus percentage of 6.7 percent ($120,000/$1,800,000) would be available to be split between the company and all eligible employees.

Improshare is an improvement on the Scanlon and Rucker plans, as it takes into consideration shifts in product mix. The factors required to calculate the bonus percentage available via Improshare are the base productivity factor, the labor standards for each product, and the performance for the period. As an example, let's assume a base productivity factor of 2.0 (this says that for each hour of direct labor, there is one hour of indirect labor). Then, if the labor standards for Product A were one hour/unit and for Product B were two hours/unit, and 100 of each were made, the hours earned would be

Product A ($100 \times 1 \times 2$)	200 hours
Product B ($100 \times 2 \times 2$)	400 hours

for a total hours earned of 600 hours. Then if the actual hours worked was 550 hours, the 50 hours savings would translate into a 9 percent (50/550) bonus percentage, to be split between the company and all eligible employees.

The difficulties with the productivity-based traditional gainsharing programs are 1) their concentration on labor and 2) their assumption that employees can increase productivity by working harder. In many manufacturing organizations today, direct labor is 10 percent or less of the total cost of manufacturing, so the focus of the gainsharing plan on labor is inappropriate. Then too, contrary to incentive pay, where employees can increase their personal productivity by working harder, it is not clear that this will work for entire organizations. Although traditional gainsharing plans refer to cooperation and involvement, the plans don't include a team-based process to make this or allow it to happen. For these reasons, Genesis Enterprises will not find traditional gainsharing plans useful in defining a Genesis Compensation Structure.

NICE TRY, BUT NO CIGAR

The company is located in New Jersey, and they have just hired a new president. The problems are many, but highest on the list are quality, morale, and market share. The new president spends time talking to the people and concludes that the quality and market share problems are a result of the morale problems, and that, at the heart of the morale problems is a lack of pay increases. With the exception of a few random merit increases and promotions, people have not had an increase in three years. The new president doesn't have the funds for a pay increase, so he turns to a gainsharing plan.

The plan selected is a Rucker plan, and with a lot of fanfare and a big speech by the new president about how gainsharing will allow everyone to gain, the plan is implemented. After several periods of little gainsharing understanding, no process to create the gainsharing gains, and no pay-out from the plan, a single large order is responsible for a small bonus being paid at the end of the fifth period. Employees are not excited with what they call "coffee money," but there is an increase in interest in attending the gainsharing meetings. The new president also has been working on several large projects, which begin to bear fruit. Knowing that the company needs a shot in the arm, he implements a $1.00 per hour pay increase for everyone on the floor who had been with the company for more than six months. The company business level is up. In fact, some overtime is needed.

There still has been no process installed to make gainsharing work, and now with the pay increases and the overtime being worked the

Rucker plan goes negative and stays negative. The employees appreciate the pay increase and are happy about the overtime, but as each weekly gainsharing chart is posted and each four-week period is ended, the employees feel worse and worse about gainsharing. A quote from the president's big gainsharing kickoff speech, in which he said, "As the company grows, you grow, as the company gains productivity and quality, you gain money" echoes through the shop. The employees know the company has grown. They see that the numbers are up almost 30 percent. The employees know productivity is up, they are shipping 20 percent more but have only added about 4 percent new people, and look at the quality charts. Everything is great—but no gainsharing payout. What is the president to do?

He decides, just a little over a year after gainsharing was installed, to eliminate gainsharing. So he holds a plantwide meeting and says that gainsharing was a mistake and the meetings are a waste of time and so "there will be no more gainsharing." To support his position, he asks the Chief Financial Officer to make a presentation as to why gainsharing could not be made to work with today's wages and overtime. The employees don't understand much of what the financial guy said, except that "because the people on the floor were making so much money that there is no way the company could have gains to share."

The employees went bananas. Morale hit an all-time low. This impacted both quality and productivity. More overtime was needed to get out the new work, but with the quality problems, they began to lose orders. Two years after taking the job, the new president was fired. The company profits, level of business, market share, and quality were all lower than when he was hired. Morale was shot, there was no trust. As the new president became the old president, his thoughts were, "I did everything right except for gainsharing, and look where it got me."

Well, what did he expect? If you do everything right except lie to the people about their gainsharing check, do you think everything will be fine? No, I think not. We need to be careful. We need to understand that gainsharing, like everything else, can be done well or can be done poorly. In this case, it was a big-time mistake. Some words of condolence to the now ex-president: "Nice try, but no cigar."

12.3   The Psychology of Rewards and Recognition

Well, what do you feel more like, a rat, a pigeon, a dog, a patient in a psychiatric hospital, a child, or an African tribe? There are psychological studies done based upon experiments with all of these, which supposedly explain how you and I act. The thing I find most funny is when one psychologist, who does all of his experiments with patients in a psychiatric hospital, questions the work of another psychologist because all of her work is based on experiments with rats. Personally, I'm not overly impressed with Pavlov's dog, rats in mazes, or how three-year-old children respond. In fact, my in-depth research has allowed me to have sufficient psychological background to prove just about any position I so desire on the subject of rewards and recognition. Take a position, and there's an experiment somewhere that will back your position. It's not my fault that your position is endorsed only strongly by pigeons who like unsalted peanuts!

I have done my best to dig through the literature on the psychology of rewards and recognition, and there seem to be three basic positions:

BEHAVIORIST
With Burrhus Skinner as the visionary, believes that human behavior can be modified and performance improved by rewarding acceptable behavior. Behaviorists believe in pay for performance and that rewards motivate people. Behaviorism may be summarized by the slogan, "What gets rewarded, gets done."

HUMANIST
With Abraham Maslow as the visionary, believes that what will impact human behavior depends upon the individual's level on a hierarchy of human needs. The five levels of human need are food, shelter, belonging, self-respect, and self-actualization. Humanists believe you must understand each person as an individual, and his or her level of development, before you can determine what will motivate him/her. Humanism may be summarized by the slogan, "It all depends."

ANTI-BEHAVIORIST
With Alfie Kohn as a visionary, believes that rewards *punish* and that behaviorists are wrong. Believes that rewards are given in an effort to control people, and that this is bad. Anti-behaviorists are not really sure *how* people should be paid, but they are sure that what motivates people is not rewards but a feeling of inner satisfaction at having done well. Anti-behaviorism may be summarized by the slogan, "What is rewarding, gets done."

Much of the psychological discussion has to do with extrinsic and intrinsic motivation. Extrinsic motivation relates to being stimulated by external sources, such as recognition and rewards. Intrinsic motivation has to do with being stimulated internally and performing because of the challenge, satisfaction, and enjoyment of making a contribution. Behaviorists believe that extrinsic motivation works, and don't have much to say about intrinsic motivation. (How do you ask a rat if he ran the maze for the treat, or just because he enjoyed running the maze?) Anti-behaviorists believe that extrinsic motivation doesn't work (all rewards are just bribes), and that the utilization of rewards will result, in the long term, in a degradation of performance. Anti-behaviorists believe that work needs to be redesigned to ensure that intrinsic motivation exists. Humanists have a belief in both extrinsic and intrinsic motivation, and feel that which will have the biggest impact depends upon the individual's personal development. So, what we have is the behaviorist and the anti-behaviorist at the two extremes, with the humanist in the middle. To more fully understand the dichotomy between the behaviorist and the anti-behaviorist, it is useful to review the following six reasons why the anti-behaviorist thinks the behaviorist is wrong:

1. *Pay is not a motivator.* Too little pay is a demotivator, but increased pay is not a motivator.

2. *Rewards punish.* Rewards have a punitive effect, because just like punishment, they are manipulative. The reward statement, "Do this and you'll get that" is not really very different from, "Do this, or here's what will happen to you."

3. *Rewards rupture relationships.* Competition for rewards will result in a few winners and many losers.

4. *Rewards ignore reasons.* When managers focus on rewards to get results, they lose sight of the things that need to be done to get the results.

5. *Rewards discourage risk-taking.* So as not to lose a reward, individuals will shy away from taking a risk. They will play it safe and play by the rules, to not lose out on the reward.

6. *Rewards undermine interest.* The more a manager stresses what an employee can earn for good work, the less interested that employee is in the work itself.

It's good I'm not a psychologist. If I were, I would have to take a position, and then try to prove to you that I'm right. It's a shame how adamant the behaviorist and the anti-behaviorist are about their positions. If they really listened to each other, they both could probably learn something. Nevertheless, this all has value, and it is now, upon this psychological backdrop, that I may present what all this means to me. Here is my view of all that is known about the psychology of rewards and recognition:

1. *Pay should be related to performance.* This performance should include all aspects of a person's job as the person works to move an organization toward the organization's Model of Success. Only desirable performance should be rewarded.

2. *Rewards and recognition can be done well or they can be done poorly.* If the person being rewarded feels manipulated, that's bad. If the per-

son being rewarded feels respected, honored, and enthusiastic about
even greater performance, the reward is good.

3. *Rewards and recognition should not be exclusionary.* When one person receives a reward, this shouldn't limit other people from receiving
a reward. As appropriate, teams and whole organizations should
receive rewards, but rewards should be well understood and well
justified.

4. *Individuals and teams should participate in designing rewards and
recognition.* Once the reward program has been designed, performance should be measured and communicated against the program,
but the focus should be on the performance, not on the reward.

5. *Leadership must utilize the team-based process to help organizations
improve the intrinsic motivation of all jobs and all employees.* Rewards
and recognition are just one part of this many-part equation.

6. *Performance feedback must be frequent, and be viewed not as an
opportunity to be critical of anyone but to be critical of unacceptable
performance with the objective of defining solutions that will result in
improved performance and advancement.*

7. *Leadership must encourage and reward risk-taking.* Everyone must
understand that at the heart of a Genesis Enterprise is creating peak-
to-peak performance, and that there will be no rewards for anyone if
all we do is keep doing what we have done. There should be no loss
of rewards for trying something that doesn't work.

8. *Leaders should focus not on rewards and recognition, but on peak-to-
peak performance.*

9. *Motivation of individuals is a delicate topic.* All people are different,
and there is no one approach that will result in all people being motivated. The safest approach is to involve people in the design of their
rewards and environment to ensure their motivation. It is important,
independent of what the rats, dogs, pigeons, and/or psychologists
may say, to understand that one size does not fit all. Many of the traditional approaches to rewards and recognition are flawed, but this
doesn't mean that rewards and recognition are unimportant. At the
same time, it is a mistake to think that the upgrade of rewards and
recognition will solve all problems. A Genesis Enterprise must focus
on the four shifts to leadership, teams, partnership, and now Genesis
Compensation. Any one, two, or three shifts will not work. All four
shifts must take place.

10. *Rewards and recognition are a source of celebration.* It is critical that
these celebrations be positive, reinforcing, and inspiring times for all.

12.4 Conclusion

There is no question that, for the full benefit to be obtained by the shifts to leadership, teams, and partnerships, there must also be a shift to Genesis Compensation. In many organizations, the compensation structure has not been significantly changed in over 20 years. It is therefore not surprising that many people throughout their organizations are unhappy and are calling for change. There is a tremendous need to go beyond the refinement of the present methodology and to shift to a whole new approach to compensation. This chapter has laid the groundwork for this shift.

For the most part, incentive plans are either gone or going. Some form of merit pay is most often used today, but unfortunately these plans also are ineffective. Problems exist both in the approach to merit pay and in the ineffective performance appraisal process that in theory is supposed to drive the increases in pay. There is little positive that can be said about most compensation plans in place today.

Some organizations have attempted to upgrade their compensation plans via gainsharing. There are some innovative approaches to gainsharing that hold promise. These will be described in Chap. 13. Unfortunately, the traditional gainsharing plans (the Scanlon plan, the Rucker plan, and Improshare) don't work. These traditional gainsharing plans have an overemphasis on labor, and most of the time include only the reward for improved performance, not the process whereby the improved performance can be achieved. Therefore, traditional gainsharing programs will not be a part of Genesis Compensation.

The psychology of rewards and recognition provides some very interesting conflicting views. The behaviorist believes "what gets rewarded, gets done," the humanist believes "what gets done depends upon the individual included," and the anti-behaviorist believes "what is rewarding, gets done." Believe it or not, out of these diverse views comes a clear psychology of rewards and recognition. This, along with the problems with traditional compensation and traditional gainsharing, form the basis for Genesis Compensation, which is presented in Chap. 13.

References

Banerjee, N., "Rebounding Earnings Star Old Debate on Productivity's Tie to Profit-Sharing," *The Wall Street Journal*, April 1994.

Fierman, J., "The Perilous New World of Fair Pay," *Fortune*, June 13, 1994.

Keenan, W., Jr., "Breaking with Tradition," *Sales and Marketing Management*, June 1994.

Kohn, A., "Why Incentive Plans Cannot Work," *Harvard Business Review*, September–October 1993.

——, *Punished By Rewards,* Houghton Mifflin Company, New York, 1993.

Kouzes, J. M. and B. Z. Posner, *The Leadership Challenge,* Jossey-Bass Publishers, San Francisco, 1991.

Lawler, E., III, *Strategic Pay: Aligning Organizational Strategies and Pay Systems,* Jossey-Bass Publishers, San Francisco, 1990.

McGrath, T. C., "Tapping The Groove in Human Productivity," *Industrial Engineering,* May 1994.

Moore, B. G. and T. L. Ross, *Gainsharing: Plans for Improving Performance,* The Bureau of National Affairs, Inc., Washington D.C., 1990.

Muller, P., "Employee Monetary Systems: The Past or Future in Employee Motivation," *Industrial Management,* November–December 1993.

Pritchett, P. and R. Pound, *High-Velocity Culture Change,* Pritchett Publishing Company, Dallas, TX, 1993.

Zigon, J., "Making Performance Appraisal Work for Teams," *Training,* June 1994.

13

Recognition and Rewards in the Genesis Enterprise

For 10 days, I lectured 9 hours a day to over 100 manufacturing executives from all over China. I found the executives very hungry students. I adjusted to everyone jumping to their feet when I entered or left the room. I started to get used to the standing ovation at the end of each day, and the simultaneous translation difficulties. But I was not ready for the eleventh and last day of my lecture services in Zheng-Zhou, China. I had planned a two-hour session on manufacturing maintenance, then questions and answers, then a round-robin discussion on computerized applications, then a one-hour close on the future of manufacturing. I was told the TV crews would be there at 4 p.m. and that the TV crews wanted to film the end of my lecture and an awards ceremony.

Well, I did the two-hour session on manufacturing maintenance. The executives liked this material, as they hadn't focused on this topic as a key element of their success. After a short break, I asked for questions. Well, I got questions. In fact, the questions didn't end until after 6 p.m. Each of the 147 executives had several written questions. Unfortunately, all of the questions and all of the follow-up questions were of the same nature.

Every question, and I mean *every* question, stated a set of conditions and then asked me for a solution. Here I had spent 10 days teaching them how to plan their business, design their operations, create peak-to-peak performance, and run efficient and effective manufacturing organizations, and these executives weren't asking how to apply the tools they had learned, but rather for a specific solution to a specific and, I suspect, real problem. My goal was not to give these professionals a fish but to teach them how to fish. Here I was on the eleventh day of the world's greatest fishing school and my students had little interest in fishing, but they sure were hungry for me to give them a fish.

Well, to say the least, I was disappointed. The more and more I tried to draw them into the thought process of addressing their own questions, the more and more I realized I was fighting a losing battle. These executives were managers and not leaders, and they were more interested in eating fish than in learning how to catch fish. What did I do? I served them fish.

I tell you this story, for I have learned that whenever we are faced with a challenge we believe is bigger than we can handle, the tendency is to ask for someone else to grab the pole and catch the fish for us. This chapter may offer such a challenge to you. How to do Genesis Compensation? How to do recognition and rewards? These are huge challenges, and we face an almost unlimited number of paradigms and preconceived notions. This makes me think of the old saying, "Talk about anything you want, except politics and religion." I guess I would want to say, "Change anything you want in an organization, but don't touch a person's compensation."

So, what you would like me to do in this chapter is to tell you the answer to Genesis Compensation. To lay it all out, then all you would need to do is implement. By me giving you this fish, you would be absolved of all responsibility. Well, I have worked and worked and worked, to be able to do this for you. Unfortunately, as was said in Sec. 12.3, "one size does not fit all." There is no one correct answer to Genesis Compensation. The correct answer for you is different from the correct answer for another organization. The correct answer depends upon your organization's past compensation practices, your present approach to compensation, your organization's satisfaction with the present approach, the agreements, contracts or guidelines for compensation, and the objectives to be accomplished through compensation.

It is for this reason that Chap. 12 presented the background and psychological views on recognition and rewards. It is based upon this background that in this chapter the framework, the overall architecture, of Genesis Compensation is presented. This framework does not tell you the answer to Genesis Compensation, but, when combined with the background of Chap. 12 and the implementation tools of Chap. 14, will allow your organization to achieve the correct approach to Genesis Compensation for your organization. Whether or not there will be fish for dinner is up to you. Happy fishing!

13.1 The Framework for Genesis Compensation

Genesis Compensation consists of a recognition element and a rewards element. The recognition element consists of a formal individual goal

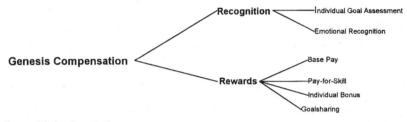

Figure 13.1   Genesis Compensation

assessment portion and an ongoing informal emotional recognition portion. The rewards element consists of the following components:

1. Base Pay

2. Pay-for-Skill

3. Individual Bonus

4. Goalsharing

Figure 13.1 illustrates these components of Genesis Compensation. Although each of these needs to be customized for each organization, the remainder of this chapter presents guidelines for each of these components.

13.2   Genesis Recognition

A key to the success of Genesis Compensation is to realize that there exists an intimate link between recognition and rewards. What works from a recognition point of view depends upon the rewards, and vice versa. Not only does recognition have an impact on rewards, but the rewards also have an impact on recognition.

A key to the success of Genesis Recognition is the proper allocation and understanding of time. Many supervisors, managers, and leaders complain that the whole recognition thing takes too much time. It is true that Genesis Recognition is very time-consuming. It is, however, also true that this time is very, very well spent. Genesis Recognition requires daily involvement from an emotional recognition perspective, and weekly, monthly, or quarterly involvement from an individual goal assessment perspective. It is also important for everyone to understand the role and objectives of the two portions of Genesis Recognition. Without this understanding, the conflict of objectives of performance appraisal described in Sec. 12.1.3 will occur. As a last thought on the big picture of recognition, remember what we learned from the humanist in Sec. 12.3: All individuals are unique. There is no single approach to Genesis Recognition that

will be effective on several different people. Genesis Leaders will understand that a unique, customized approach will be required if they are to
bring out the best in each each person.

13.2.1   Emotional Recognition

In Sec. 4.4, in the basic guidelines for how Genesis Leaders should treat
people, I said, "Say 'thank you': truly appreciate people helping you. A
Genesis Leader will say 'thank you' many, many times every day." The
need for emotional support and emotional recognition is a part of every
person, and requires constant attention. A basketball coach doesn't sit qui-
etly on the sidelines waiting for the game to be over to provide feedback.
He or she is intensely involved in the game, and provides emotional support and emotional recognition on each and every play. So too the Genesis Leader will write notes, verbally recognize in private, verbally recognize in public, and recognize via certificates, plaques, and other tangible
gifts, to demonstrate his or her genuine appreciation for the work done
by individuals and teams.

Shocking as it may seem, however, emotional recognition can be done
incorrectly. You say, how can you recognize someone incorrectly? Well,
consider the following ways:

1. *Lack of genuine appreciation or sincerity.*   A real challenge with emotional recognition evolves from the philosophy, "Catch people doing
   something right and praise them for it," or the poster seen in many
   schools, "Praise every child every day." When recognition lacks spontaneity, a genuine excitement for something done, it will be viewed as
   phony and will undercut the value of all recognition. People will see
   through and resent a strategy of complimenting every person every day.
   When recognition is used as a gimmick, people will view receiving the
   recognition as manipulative and as a demotivator.

2. *Lack of specific recognition.*   We have all met the person who had a
   wonderful spouse, a wonderful family, a wonderful job working for a
   wonderful company, and a wonderful boss. Blah! Phony, phony, phony.
   For recognition to be of value, it has to be specific.

3. *Recognizing the person or team and not the action done by the person
   or team.*   We all have learned, when correcting or disciplining is
   required, that we should do it in private, and that we shouldn't be critical of the person but of the person's actions. Well, guess what? The
   same is true for recognition. Don't say that a person is a good person,
   say that they really do well in planning marketing outreaches.

   Don't take the comment about "in private" to mean that public recognition is bad. To the contrary, public recognition is fine if it is handled

well. What you should understand from this is that you should never recognize something in public that you have not previously recognized in private. Handling recognition in this way will be much more rewarding for the person, as well as reinforcing.

4. *Using Recognition to Establish a Win-Lose Situation.* Recognition should never be done by comparing someone to someone else. Don't recognize anyone by saying, "Here is Sue, my best salesperson." By definition, everyone who hears this comment will then believe he or she is below the best. Therefore, recognition needs to be positive to all by stating, "Here is Sue, the salesperson who last year had a sales volume of over $1,000,000."

5. *Not understanding your motive for recognition.* Who is going to most benefit from the recognition? If the answer is anyone other than the person receiving the recognition, don't give the recognition. The person who must most guard against receiving the benefit of the recognition is the person giving it. For example, the following recognition is better off not said: "I am really excited about Bob's performance, since he has come around to my way of thinking."

6. *Recognizing people for doing their normal routine.* Such recognition is accepted as being condescending. The person receiving the recognition doesn't feel like he/she is being recognized, but rather put down. For example: "I would like to congratulate Bob here, who turned in his expense account on time every month last year." Don't recognize people when doing so will indicate that you have low expectations of the individual's performance.

7. *Recognizing something that has yet to occur.* For example: "Tiffany, I really appreciate the work you're doing on that great new video you're working on." What this recognition has done is place a level of expectation on Tiffany which may be unfair and, in fact, undercut her potential for success.

At the same time, *not* to provide emotional recognition is also a major mistake. Therefore, the Genesis Leader will

1. Continually provide positive reinforcement to recognize peak-to-peak performance

2. Allow his/her spontaneity and genuine excitement for peak-to-peak performance to surface

3. Make a regular habit of saying "Thank you"

4. Provide specific recognition in a real-time mode

5. Recognize both individuals and teams for great performance

6. Be aware of and sensitive to the feelings of both the person or team being recognized and the feelings of others

7. Always recognize first in private and then in public

8. Encourage others to recognize peak-to-peak performance

9. Be consistent and genuine in recognizing peak-to-peak performance

10. Be natural, be his or her self, and have fun while providing recognition

---

MARY KAY ENTHUSIASM: THE POWER OF RECOGNITION

In 1963, Mary Kay sold $198,000 in cosmetics. By 1993 the sales were over $600 million, and the Mary Kay sales force was over 300,000. Even more impressive, over 6000 beauty consultants are now driving complimentary pink Cadillacs and other cars worth over $90 million, and each summer over 30,000 Mary Kay beauty consultants travel to Dallas, Texas, and pay to attend "seminar."

What is "seminar"? Three days of nonstop recognition. There are minks, diamonds, color-coded suits, sashes, badges, crowns, emblems, flowers, jewelry, kisses, hugs, holding hands, tears, and stories of amazing success. The emotional compensation is the secret of seminar success and the success of Mary Kay. Beauty consultants can immediately see by inspecting one another what they have accomplished. Nothing is subtle or hidden here. Salespeople come to seminar for recognition, and it is recognition they get. Between annual seminars, Mary Kay recognizes top performers with five-star vacations. Often Mary Kay Ash herself attends, to get to know her "daughters" better and to develop lifelong relationships.

Some may think this works for Mary Kay housewives but has little to do with the world of business. Well, think again. Two-thirds of these beauty consultants have full-time jobs in addition to selling Mary Kay. Several beauty consultants are lawyers. There are pediatricians, and even a Harvard MBA. When considering the issue of when the Mary Kay reward-by-recognition practice will become mainstream, John Kotter, the Konosoke Matsushita Professor of Leadership at Harvard Business School, says, "The genius of great leaders is that they understand money is only one of the things that make people light up." Applause, prizes, and peer recognition are very, very powerful. Possibly, Mary Kay and Mary Kay Ash are way ahead of the rest of us. Cash is a secondary benefit; *recognition* is the emotional compensation that brings the enthusiasm that creates success.

13.2.2 Individual Goal Assessment

W. Edwards Deming declared war on performance appraisals. He felt appraisals were the number-one problem in American management. Dr. Deming felt that performance appraisals should be eliminated, as they are destructive and actually result in a decline in performance. He felt that the average employee takes six months to get back on track after a performance appraisal.

I believe Dr. Deming was partially correct. I believe poorly designed performance appraisals should be eliminated. I believe any performance appraisal that deflates the person being appraised should be eliminated. However, I also believe that if the objectives of the performance appraisal are clear, if the goals upon which it is based are clear, and the outcome expected to flow from it is predictable and understood by both the appraiser and the appraisee, then performance appraisals are powerful tools for peak-to-peak performance and, in fact, at the very foundation of peak-to-peak performance.

I can understand why Dr. Deming felt as he did. Let's face it, in Japan they don't have annual appraisals but daily feedback, and things work well. In America, the performance appraisals are done poorly. As I said in Sec. 12.1.3., most of us aren't happy with the performance appraisals we have received. But let's not throw out the baby with the bath water! Just because most companies do a lousy job of performance appraisals, that doesn't mean we shouldn't have performance appraisals. What we need to do is to take a different approach to performance appraisals.

As a starting point, I believe we need to eliminate the very words *performance appraisal,* as they have a negative connotation to us all. Instead, what we need is to divide "performance appraisals" into the two separate elements that people think of when they think of performance appraisals and treat the two separate elements *as* two separate elements. Those two elements are *individual goal assessment* and *career guidance.* These should be undertaken at different times, in different ways, by different people, and kept separate. They are two different things, and shouldn't be tied together. In fact, I don't believe career guidance is even a portion of compensation or recognition. I view career guidance as being a benefit, or a training, or development issue. At the same time, career guidance is often thought to be a portion of performance appraisals, so it makes sense that we should at least touch on the subject here.

Careers in business today are not necessarily linear, logical progressions from engineer to project engineer to senior engineer to engineering manager to vice president of engineering. With today's flatter organizations, an upwardly mobile career is unlikely. More often than not, one's career will take a zigzag route. With creating peak-to-peak performance as a motivator, career paths will appear disjointed, but this diversity of backgrounds is what results in perpetual growth for both the individuals and the organization. For this to occur, the following career guidance principles should be understood and practiced:

1. *Career guidance is the responsibility not of the organization but the individual.* Nevertheless, with the individual taking the lead, the Genesis Enterprise will actively support the career guidance of the individual.

2. *Career guidance support will only rarely be done by a person's supervisor.* In today's rapidly changing environment, it wouldn't be surprising if an individual had five supervisors over a five-year period. It's impractical to think about an individual receiving career guidance from five different people over a five-year period. Career guidance support may come from a mentor, a senior person within the organization, a senior person outside the organization, or from human resources.

3. *Career guidance has no impact on rewards.* Career guidance is separate, and should be handled separately from individual goal assessment.

4. *The timing of career guidance will vary tremendously, depending upon the individual whose career is being guided.* Although the Genesis Enterprise should encourage people to think about their careers and should offer them the opportunity to learn about career planning, the timing for career guidance should be left in the hands of the individual. For young employees, a career guidance session might be warranted every six months, whereas a 50-year-old executive might handle his or her own career guidance. Genesis Enterprises should make it clear whom one may turn to for career guidance.

The success of individual goal assessment is based upon people knowing what is expected—feedback about performance against expectation, and financial rewards based upon meeting or exceeding expectations. The following guidelines should be considered when you are ensuring that your people know what is expected of them, and providing feedback about performance against expectation. (Section 13.3.3 describes the individual bonus rewards that should follow from the individual goal assessments.)

1. *Each person's individual goals and individual goal assessment is a highly personalized thing.* Bureaucracy should be minimized, and no attempt should be made to force the individual goals or the assessment of these goals into a rigid format.

2. *Individual goals, and the assessment of these individual goals, should be done to ensure alignment with the organization's Model of Success and the Evidence of Success for all teams in which the individual is a member.* Individual goals should be consistent, and supportive of the organization's and team's path forward. A portion of an individual's

goals should be based upon how well the individual contributes to the organization and team's success, and the overall success of the organization and these teams.

3. *Establishing individual goals, and assessing performance against these goals, should be highly participative.* The assessor and the assessee should interact frequently, during both the establishing and the assessing of individual goals. A format that works is as follows:
   a. Supervisor defines categories and performance criteria for which goals will be established.
   b. Supervisor and employee discuss categories and performance criteria and reach mutual understanding.
   c. Employee sets goals for agreed-to performance criteria and submits these to supervisor.
   d. Supervisor and employee discuss goals and reach mutual agreement on goals and review schedule.
   e. In accordance with review schedule, employee performs a self-assessment and submits to supervisor.
   f. Supervisor and employee discuss self-assessment and reach mutual agreement on goal assessment.
   g. Steps e and f are repeated, until it is time to return to a.

4. *Individual goals should always be objective, observable, and verifiable.* These goals can be either numerical or descriptive. With numerical goals, the issue of objective, observable, and verifiable is straightforward. For example, a goal for an author of three articles that are published this year can clearly be measured objectively, be clearly observed, and verified. With descriptive goals to enssure objective, observable, and verifiable assessment, three factors must be defined:
   a. Who is to make the assessment
   b. The factors to be assessed
   c. Description of what constitutes "meeting expectation"

   For example, a goal of being actively involved with company publications may be objective, observable, and verifiable given the following:
   a. *Who to make assessment:* Rhonda Jones
   b. *Factors to be assessed:* Responsiveness on editing, meeting of deadlines, good thought-provoking titles, unique, provocative materials
   c. *Description of what constitutes "meeting expectation":* Good communications, no surprises, on time, editors who like material, and success in getting published

   Goals which should be avoided are those that are subjective or have to do with traits such as attitude, reliability, friendliness, etc. These traits typically result in problems with communications. For example, the term *reliability* is vague and emotionally difficult. No one wants to be thought of as unreliable. Traits should be translated into behaviors; for "reliable," that would mean "meets deadlines," or "good attendance," etc.

5. The result of an appraisal for each factor must be a rating. These ratings should fall into four to six categories. For example, at Tompkins Associates, Inc., we have Exceptional, Commendable, Satisfactory, Needs Improvement, and Unsatisfactory. Expectation levels should be mutually agreed-upon for each of these ratings at the outset. This is easiest with numerical goals; for example, with the previously given illustration of articles being published, the following scale may be used:

Exceptional: Five articles published in a year

Commendable: Four articles published in a year

Satisfactory: Three articles published a year

Needs Improvement: Five articles submitted for publication, but less than three published

Unsatisfactory: Less than five articles submitted, or less than two published

6. Although an annual overall goal assessment cycle is typical, the review schedule depends upon the individual being assessed. New employees are reviewed much more frequently than established employees. Lower-level employees are reviewed much more frequently than higher-level employees. For example, a review schedule that may be used is

	Duration of employment		
	6 months or less	6 to 18 months	18 months or longer
Hourly	Weekly	Weekly	Monthly
Supervision	Weekly	Monthly	Monthly
Middle management	Monthly	Monthly	Quarterly
Upper management	Monthly	Quarterly	Annually

7. It is important to maintain flexibility with individual goals when circumstances change. For example, if a person were to sell 20,000 books and direct mail was to be one of the avenues for selling the books, and the direct mail budget was cut by 50 percent, it would be fair to change the goal of 20,000. To the contrary, if the direct mail was done and response rates were low, the goal of 20,000 books should not be changed. Although it's important to be flexible, it's also important not to change goals just because things aren't working out.

8. Although it should be obvious, mutual agreement on individual goals should be reached prior to the beginning of the period covered by the goals. Basic as it may seem, I have seen goals that weren't established until after the assessment period was over, or nearly over. This is unacceptable. It isn't difficult to predict who will win a football game when the score is 42 to 0 with only 30 seconds remaining. Without prior agreement to individual goals, there will always be difficulties.

13.3 Genesis Rewards

Just as it is critical for a Genesis Enterprise to upgrade its approach to recognition, it is also critical for it to upgrade its rewards. A Genesis Enterprise must have both Genesis Recognition and Genesis Rewards. Genesis Rewards require innovative approaches to the following four reward components:

1. Base pay

2. Pay-for-skill

3. Individual bonus

4. Goalsharing

The following four subsections present an approach to each of these components.

13.3.1 Base Pay

Base pay in a Genesis Enterprise will be very straightforward. There is just one question to be answered: Should base pay be the same for everyone doing a job, should it have three to five steps based upon seniority, or should some hybrid of these two exist? These base-pay rates should be published and there should be no secrets about base pay. When base pay is not disclosed, speculation runs rampant. If the disclosure of base pay would be an embarrassment, then whatever is the cause of the embarrassment should be rectified and the base pay disclosed. Table 13.1 illustrates a base-pay table for a manufacturing organization.

Base pay should be reviewed annually, and adjusted in accordance with the market.

13.3.2 Pay-for-Skill

Pay-for-skill, also know as *skill-based pay* or *pay-for-knowledge,* is a reward and development program to increase a nonmanager's base pay based

Table 13.1 Base Pay, Hourly and Annually

Position	Fixed	Less than 1-year tenure	1–5 years tenure	6–10 years tenure	11–20 years tenure	Over 20 years tenure
President*	$250,000					
Executive vice president*	$175,000					
Vice president*	$150,000					
Director*	$125,000					
General manager*	$100,000					
Manager*		$60,000	$65,000	$70,000	$75,000	$80,000
Supervisor*		$30,000	$34,000	$38,000	$42,000	$46,000
Level III†		$15.00	$16.00	$17.00	$18.00	$19.00
Level II†		$11.00	$12.00	$13.00	$14.00	$15.00
Level I†		$7.00	$8.00	$9.00	$10.00	$11.00

*Measured by annual pay.
†Measured by hourly pay.

upon the individual's demonstrated capability to perform a variety of skills. Pay-for-skill programs utilize a series of base-pay increases based upon increases in skill proficiency. The method for increasing and documenting skill proficiency is called *competency-based development* or *skill-based training*. Competency-based development is based on the principle of demonstrated capability. An individual either has or does not have the skills required to perform a given task. By giving an individual a test, we may determine if the individual has the required skills or if further training or on-the-job experience is needed. If further training or experience is needed, the results of the test will target the specific needs so as to increase the individual's competency. Thus, with competency-based development, development is based on the level of demonstrated competency.

Figure 13.2 depicts the process of competency-based development. The first activity, *job analysis*, identifies the required tasks that must be successfully performed in a given job. The second activity requires that the skills required for each task be identified. These skills are then used to develop the *competency evaluation criteria*. The evaluation criteria describe what would be measured, or how an individual should perform to demonstrate competency. Often, these evaluation criteria will be categorized by the level of competency demonstrated; i.e., neophyte, operator, expert.

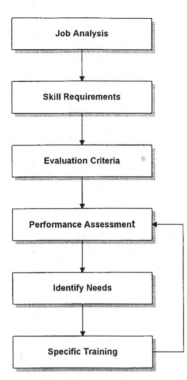

Figure 13.2 The pursuit of competency-based development

Using these evaluation criteria, a test can be developed to check the competency levels of an individual and the quality of the development. Based on this test, individual weaknesses can be identified. Specific training or experience can then be delivered to address these weaknesses. Individuals can be retested and trained, retested and trained, etc. until the individual can be certified as competent and eligible for the pay-for-skill increase consistent with the level of competency demonstrated. For example, building upon the base-pay rates given in Table 13.1, Table 13.2 illustrates how pay-for-skill would increase base pay given different levels of competency.

The most significant benefit to result from pay-for-skill are the increased skill levels of the work force. Additional benefits include the following:

1. Increased work-force flexibility.

2. Increased work-force competency.

3. Increased productivity.

4. Improved customer service.

Table 13.2 Increase in Base Hourly Pay for Demonstrated Competency

Position	Operator in one area	Expert in one area	Expert in one area— operator in one area	Expert in two areas	Expert in two areas— operator in one area	Expert in three areas
Level III			$.25	$.50	$.75	$1.00
Level II		$.25	$.50	$.75	$1.00	$1.25
Level I	$.25	$.50	$.75	$1.00	$1.25	$1.50

5. Increased organizational commitment.

6. Decision making can be pushed to the lowest appropriate level.

7. Reduced turnover and absenteeism.

8. Increased work-force participation.

9. Increased work-force self-esteem.

10. Increased work-force motivation.

13.3.3 Individual Bonus

At the same time that individual goals are established for a person, the bonus-for-performance schedule or formula should also be established. The individual bonus should be based upon the performance against the individual goals. It is the combination of the individual goals and the individual bonus plan that should be mutually agreed upon, prior to the start of the performance period, then signed by the supervisor and the employee to form the "contract" for the performance period. The bonus-for-performance may be as simple as the bonus will be:

■ $10,000 for an overall Exceptional assessment

■ $6000 for an overall Commendable assessment

■ $3000 for an overall Satisfactory assessment

■ $0 for an overall Needs Improvement assessment

■ $0 for an overall Unsatisfactory assessment

Or the bonus-for-performance may be a variable percentage of one's salary or profits. For instance,

■ 20 percent of annual salary for an overall Exceptional assessment

■ 10 percent of annual salary for an overall Commendable assessment

■ 5 percent of annual salary for an overall Satisfactory assessment

- 0 percent of annual salary for an overall Needs Improvement assessment
- 0 percent of annual salary for an overall Unsatisfactory assessment

Or the bonus-for-performance may be some formula based upon the assessment, overall company profitability, base salary, etc. Often the best bonus-for-performance is a hybrid of a couple of different approaches. Prior to the creation of the individual bonus plan, an organization must establish guidelines on the range of funds available for bonus and the pay-out method for bonuses. It would not be unusual for there to be a couple of ranges of bonus, depending upon one's level in the organization. For example, a range of 0 to 40 percent for upper management, 0 to 30 percent for middle management, and for all others 0 to 20 percent of base pay.

The method of bonus payment typically is not just one lump sum. Some organizations are paying 40 percent of the bonus at the end of the performance period, then 20 percent at the end of the first, second, and third quarters. Others are paying 12 percent of the bonus at the end of the performance period, then 8 percent at the end of the next 11 months. A rule in place in many organizations is that there must be one year of employment prior to participating in individual bonuses. Another condition almost always in place is that the person still must be employed. An individual's bonus payout ends at the same time as their base pay.

The individual bonus eliminates the problem of the built-in annuity of the traditional merit pay plans. This results in a fairer overall compensation plan, as individuals are paid based upon their current performance. This allows new employees who are performing at a high level to receive a high bonus, and requires all employees to continue to perform at a high level if they are to continue to receive a high bonus.

13.3.4 Goalsharing

Goalsharing is a type of gainsharing, but it is so different from traditional gainsharing that care must be demonstrated, when discussing it, that negative *gain*sharing feelings do not affect people's understanding of *goal*sharing. The basic concept of goalsharing is the same as the basic concept of individual goals and individual bonuses. The only difference is that goalsharing is based upon the total organization's performance and individuals' rewards; not on their individual performance but on the total organization's performance. Goalsharing is a rewards program that rewards team performance, and accordingly it has at its foundation the organization's Model of Success.

For example, consider an organization whose Model of Success indicates a need to increase productivity, reduce scrap, and improve customer service. For a particular time frame, the following goals and rewards might be established:

Goal #1: Productivity

   Level 1   If increase of productivity of 0 to 5%, a 1% bonus

   Level 2   If increase of productivity of 5.1 to 10%, a 2% bonus

   Level 3   If increase of productivity of 10.1 to 15%, a 3% bonus

   Level 4   If increase of productivity of greater than 15.1%, a 4% bonus

Goal #2: Scrap

   Level 1   If scrap is between 1.5 and 1%, a 1% bonus

   Level 2   If scrap is between .99 and .5%, a 2% bonus

   Level 3   If scrap is between .49 and 0%, a 3% bonus

Goal #3: Customer Service

   Level 1   If a customer service rating of 95 to 96%, a 0.5% bonus

   Level 2   If a customer service rating of 96.1 to 97%, a 1% bonus

   Level 3   If a customer service rating of 97.1 to 98%, a 1.5% bonus

   Level 4   If a customer service rating of 98.1 to 99%, a 2% bonus

   Level 5   If a customer service rating of 99.1 to 100%, a 3% bonus

Then, at the end of each period, the performance would be assessed and a bonus paid accordingly. For the example above, a period of the following would result in an overall bonus of 6 percent of base pay to all employees:

Goal #1: Productivity up 9% results in	2% bonus
Goal #2: Scrap at .76% results in	2% bonus
Goal #3: Customer service at 98.3% results in	<u>2% bonus</u>
Total:	6% bonus

In this manner, teams and teamwork are the basis of an ongoing organizationwide reward for performance enhancement, in the direction of the organization's Model of Success.

VOLVO KALMAR PLANT ANSWERS THE QUESTION: "WHAT'S IN IT FOR ME?"

In the late 1970s, the Volvo assembly plant in Kalmar, Sweden, was brought on-line with a team-based approach linked with Automated Guided Vehicles (AGVs). Participative management and a team-based culture were the drivers of this successful forerunner of the Genesis Enterprise. The 1800 employees were divided into 125 work teams, which had responsibilities to lay out the work area, make work assignments, and design jobs. Communications were open and, on the whole, results were good. However, by the mid-1980s the motivation for peak-to-peak performance was low, and employees didn't see the benefits of improving.

In 1987, a goalsharing program was installed that answered the question being asked by many people at Kalmar: "What's in it for me?" The goalsharing plan was based upon the following six factors:

1. Quality

2. Spoilage and Adjustments

3. Consumption of Materials and Supplier

4. Consumption of Added Materials

5. Man-Hours Per Car

6. Capital Costs for Total Inventories and Other Costs

At the same time that the goalsharing plan was installed, all employees in the shop were given the same hourly wage. Performance against the goals was calculated and communicated every 14 days.

An in-depth series of surveys and studies of Kalmar has revealed the following:

1. The tremendous success of the goalsharing plan as a tool to improve key performance indicators.

2. Positive motivation, through rewarding the teams for their performance.

3. A problem for some in the leveling of all wages. This leveling would have been satisfactory, if an individual bonus plan had been a portion of the total compensation.

4. A need to reward people who increase their ability to contribute. This would have been totally resolved at Volvo had they implemented a pay-for-skill portion to the compensation plan.

The Volvo Kalmar facility has pioneered many innovative concepts, and continues to do so. In this case, they have done well in realizing the need to shift compensation so as to ensure the continuous pursuit of peak-to-peak performances. We have learned and continue to learn from this illustration. However, let's learn not only from what they *have* done, but also from what they have *yet to do*. In this way, your Genesis Enterprise will be able to *move well beyond* Volvo!

13.4   Conclusion

Recognition and rewards, when combined, define compensation. Compensation is a difficult, emotional topic, and therefore any change in recognition or rewards is a difficult one to make. There is no one correct answer. Depending upon the past approaches to compensation and the objectives of the organization, there can be a lot of variability as to what constitutes Genesis Compensation. Certainly, no single compensation plan fits all. Nevertheless, the overall architecture of Genesis Compensation will always consist of

1. Recognition
    a. Individual Goal Assessment
    b. Emotional Recognition
2. Rewards
    a. Base Pay
    b. Pay-for-Skill
    c. Individual Bonus
    d. Goalsharing

Genesis Leadership must allocate a significant amount of resources to achieving Genesis Compensation. This allocation of time, however, is some of the best-invested time of the Genesis Leader, as the investment will return him/her better motivated, focused, aligned, and skilled employees to accomplish the tasks at hand. It is of the utmost importance, in the pursuit of the Genesis Enterprise, that your organization shift from being a traditional compensation organization to one that practices Genesis Compensation.

References

Caggiano, C., "What Workers Want," *Inc.*, November 1992.

Ehrenfeld, T., "The Productivity-Boosting Gainsharing Report," *Inc.*, August 1993.

Farnham, A., "Mary Kay's Lessons in Leadership," *Fortune*, September 20, 1993.

Fenn, D., "Skill-Based Pay Takes Off," *CFO*, January 1993.

Fierman, J., "The Perilous New World of Fair Pay," *Fortune*, June 13, 1994.

Hauch, W. and T. L. Ross, "Expanded Teamwork at Volvo Through Performance Gainsharing," *Industrial Management*, July–August 1988.

Jackson, W. M., "Gainsharing for High Productivity," *Profit*, January–February 1994.

Kohn, A., *Punished by Rewards*, Houghton Mifflin Company, New York, 1993.

Kouzes, J. M. and B. Z. Posner, *The Leadership Challenge: How to Get Extraordinary Things Done in Organizations,* Jossey-Bass Publishers, San Francisco, 1991.

Lawler, E. E. III, *Strategic Pay: Aligning Organizational Strategies and Pay Systems,* Jossey-Bass Publishers, San Francisco, 1990.

McGrath, T. C., "Gainsharing: Tapping the Groove in Human Productivity," *Industrial Engineering,* May 1994.

Peters, T., *Liberation Management,* Alfred A. Knopf, New York, 1992.

——, *Thriving on Chaos: A Handbook for a Management Resolution,* Alfred A. Knopf, New York, 1987.

Rountree, D and J. Yorkutat, "Reward-Results Linkages," *1994 Industrial Engineering Conference Proceedings, Institute of Industrial Engineers,* Norcross, GA, 1994.

Tompkins, J. A., "Gainsharing 1-6," *Industrial Product Bulletin,* September, October, November, and December 1993; January and February 1994.

——, "Team-Based Continuous Improvement: How to Make the Pace of Change Work for You and Your Company," *Material Handling Engineering,* August 1993.

Tully, S., "Your Paycheck Gets Exciting," *Fortune,* November 1, 1993.

Zigon, J., "Making Performance Appraisal Work for Teams," *Training,* June 1994.

14

Shifting from Traditional Compensation to Genesis Compensation

A key objective of Genesis Compensation is to balance each person's contribution with his/her compensation. If this balance doesn't exist, there will be unhappy people who won't make their maximum contribution to the overall performance of the organization. The balance that must be pursued, however, is not an organization balance, but rather an individual balance. Each individual must feel that his/her own compensation is balanced with his/her own contribution.

At the same time, leaders must understand that if they design the compensation plan, they will be held accountable for the compensation plan. Obviously the compensation plan is a highly emotional and important issue which, if designed by leadership, will result in leadership being judged on the fairness of the compensation plan. It is my belief that leadership will *never* be viewed as fair, for each person has his/her own definition of what would be fair compensation. Thus, what is needed to shift from traditional compensation to Genesis Compensation is a highly participative design process. Participation in the design process will

1. Significantly contribute to effective implementation

2. Build understanding of the whole compensation topic

3. Result in a higher-quality compensation plan

It is based upon these thoughts that many compensation experts recommend putting together a "diagonal slice" group, team, or task force to design the compensation plan. Herein lies a major problem with the use of teams and the National Labor Relations Board (NLRB—see Appendix D). Although many compensation experts recommend and utilize a cross-functional, salary, and hourly compensation design team to develop an organization's compensation plan, this may result in a major NLRB problem. The two-part test used by NLRB to determine if management exerts an unlawful domination of a labor organization goes like this:

1. Is the entity a labor organization?
   a. Do employees participate?
   b. Does the team have authority to make decisions without management influence?
   c. Does the team deal with wages and bonus plan?
   d. Do team members represent others, or just themselves?

2. Is the entity unlawfully dominated by management?
   a. Does the entity obtain financial support?
   b. Are members paid for meetings?
   c. Are supplies and meeting places provided?
   d. Does management select members and control voting procedures?
   e. Does management set agendas, lead meetings, or participate?
   f. Did management conceive of the idea for the entity?

Interestingly, the "diagonal slice" compensation design team, as recommended by many compensation experts, would result in a "yes" to all of these questions and, therefore, according to the NLRB, be unlawful. Obviously, this path must not be pursued. Rather, to obtain very beneficial participation in the compensation design, an approach other than a team-based one must be pursued. In union organizations, the desired approach is to work with the union on the design of the compensation plan. If the union refuses to enter into such a design effort, an agreement should be reached on the process to be pursued and the role the union would like to play in the design process. If either the union does not want to be involved or if there is no union, the design of the compensation plan should be done by the organization's leadership, while obtaining significant input and participation from everyone in the company via meetings and surveys in which each individual addresses only his/her specific view and does not in any way represent or speak for others. This chapter presents the process that might be adapted to either a union or a nonunion environment, to allow an organization to shift from traditional compensation to Genesis Compensation.

14.1 The Process of Shifting
from Traditional to Genesis
Compensation

The process of shifting from traditional compensation to Genesis Compensation is defined by the following 10 steps.

1. Lay a foundation for shifting from traditional compensation to Genesis Compensation. The person on the Steering Team most familiar with your company's present compensation plan should accept the role of point person for laying the foundation for the compensation shift. This point person should organize a half-day education session for the Steering Team and the Leadership Team that covers the present compensation plan, the information presented in Chaps. 12, 13, and 14 of this book, and an open discussion of opportunities for improvement. The organization's Model of Success should be used as a focal point during these discussions in aligning the organization and the organization's compensation plan.

   After the education session, the Leadership Team should charter a strategy team of salary personnel to design the Genesis Compensation Plan. If a union exists, the charter for this design team should reflect the role, participation, and interface that should exist between the Design Team and the union. If a union doesn't exist, the requirements of the NLRB should be included in the charter. As a portion of the kickoff of the Genesis Compensation Plan Strategy Design Team, this team should be given the same education session as the Steering Team and Leadership Team received.

2. Define the overall Genesis Compensation plan structure. The Genesis Compensation Plan Strategy Design Team should define the overall structure of the Genesis Compensation Plan. This structure should include factors such as the following.
   a. Base pay will be the same for all people doing the same job, except for a seniority graduation.
   b. A pay-for-skill system will be put in place, based upon competency-based development.
   c. An individual bonus will be put in place, based upon individual goal assessment.
   d. A goalshare plan will be put in place, based upon overall organization performance.

   The structure should *not* include:
   a. Specific base-pay rates
   b. Specific pay-for-skill compensation levels, or any methodology for competency-based development

   c. Specific bonus levels, or procedures for individual goal-setting or assessing

   d. Specific bonus numbers or criteria to be included

At this point in the development of a Genesis Compensation Plan, what is needed is the overall structure of the plan and not the details. Determining factors in designing this structure include the following.

- Problems with the present compensation plan
- Assuring fairness and balance between contribution and compensation
- Providing proper motivation
- Providing for alignment with the organization's Model of Success
- Assuming simplicity of understanding, while still providing responsiveness to market conditions

3. *Obtain an assessment of the present compensation plan, input on the structure of the Genesis Compensation Plan, and feelings on compensation ranges for the Genesis Compensation Plan.* A one- to two-hour session should be held, either with the union and then all employees or with all employees. The background on the present compensation plan should be presented, as well as the structure of the Genesis Compensation Plan. The utmost care must be demonstrated at this point to be certain that false expectations about pay increases are not generated. The last portion of the session should be the completion of a compensation survey. This survey should include an assessment of the present compensation plan and of the Genesis Compensation Plan structure, and a series of questions documenting feelings on specific base rates, compensation levels, bonus levels, or bonus numbers. There should be an opportunity for people to provide comments on the survey, as well as to ask questions at the session. It is very important, at this point of the Genesis Compensation Plan design, that all inputs be solicited.

4. *Refine structure and establish next level of detail.* Based upon the inputs received from the survey, the Genesis Compensation Plan Strategy Design Team should refine the Genesis Compensation Plan structure. The other survey inputs on base rates, compensation levels, bonus levels, and bonus numbers should also be summarized. The Strategy Design Team should then charter a series of teams to develop the Genesis Compensation Plan at the next level of detail. These teams should all be salary employees, and may include:

   a. Individual Goal Setting and Assessing Design Team

   b. Emotional Recognition Design Team

   c. Base-Pay and Pay-for-Skill Rate Design Team

   d. Competency-Based Development Design Team

    e. Individual Bonus Design Team

    f. Goalshare Design Team

The tasks before each of these design teams, with the exception of the Competency-Based Development Design Team and the Goalshare Design Team, are explained in Chap. 13. The path forward for the Competency-Based Development and the Goalshare Design Teams are presented in Secs. 14.2 and 14.3, respectively.

5. *Develop an implementation plan and a communication plan.* As the detail level of the Genesis Compensation Plan is being developed, the Genesis Compensation Plan Strategy Design Team should be developing an implementation plan and a communication plan. The implementation plan is typically quite easy to develop. It consists of the timing for

    a. System refinement

    b. System communication

    c. System start-up

    d. System debug

    e. System improvement

By contrast, the communication plan is anything but easy. At the heart of the challenge with the communication plan is the issue of compensation secrecy. Probably more than any one other single topic, the control over compensation information reflects the traditional power of the authoritarian organization. In some organizations, people can be fired for disclosing their compensation. Unfortunately, this secrecy does much more harm than good. The fact of the matter is that when compensation information is kept a secret, rarely is it *truly* a secret. When the secrecy *is* maintained, rumors and gossip are pervasive.

Although there may be some merit in not disclosing individual compensation information, what is the problem with defining the compensation information for the categories of jobs? Some organizations answer this question by saying that the secrecy is needed because the compensation plan has many inconsistencies. Well, why not clear up the inconsistencies? In fact, a good reason to end compensation secrecy is to eliminate the inconsistencies. Other reasons to maintain compensation secrecy are based on deception, lack of openness, politics, and maintaining paradigms.

In short, there are no good reasons to maintain secrecy, and from the motivation, honesty, openness, and feedback perspectives, there are many good reasons to make compensation by category public information. This having been said, it is interesting to note that most organizations today still do have compensation secrecy, and therefore we all must be patient while this practice is updated. Once the secrecy issue has been resolved, the communication plan should be developed to define specifically in what time frames specific information is to be shared. It is from the combination of the implementation plan and the communication plan that the following types of information should be presented:

a. When are individual goals to be established, and for what time period?

b. When will the new base-pay rates be announced? When will they become effective? When will they be adjusted again? What about future adjustments?

c. When will the individual goal assessments be done, and when will the individual bonuses begin?

d. When will the competency-based development effort begin, and how about pay-for-skill? What is the timing for competency certification, and does this have an expiration date?

e. When will goalshare begin? What is the base goalshare period? When will the employees be eligible for goalshare bonuses? How and when will employees learn about goalshare performance?

f. What is the method of appealing an individual goal assessment?

g. How do I gain more understanding about the compensation system?

6. *Conduct information exchange meetings and refine Genesis Compensation Plan.* Given all the detailed information that results from the teams established in Step 4 and the Implementation Plan and the Communication Plan from Step 5, a series of information exchange meetings should take place in which all employees have the opportunity to understand and provide feedback on the draft of the Genesis Compensation Plan. An open-ended survey should be completed by all employees attending the meetings. The results of the survey should be used to refine both the compensation system and its presentation. A final Genesis Compensation Plan manual and presentation should be created.

7. *Communicate Genesis Compensation Plan to each employee.* A training program should be developed to teach coordinators how to present the Genesis Compensation Plan. This program should include a detailed review of the Genesis Compensation Plan manual and presentation, as well as an in-depth understanding of the plan. Once trained, the coordinators should conduct a series of one-on-one meetings with employees, to ensure their understanding of the system. All questions and concerns about the system should be captured, and feedback given to the Strategy Design Team.

8. *Initiate the Genesis Compensation Plan.* Although relatively minor, further refinements may be made at this point based upon the feed-

back obtained in the Step 7 survey and feedback. Then, in accordance with the Implementation Plan and the Communication Plan, the Genesis Compensation Plan should be implemented. This will involve team and individual meetings. The individual meetings between coordinators and employees are very important to ensuring understanding, awareness, and acceptance of the Genesis Compensation Plan. The importance of these sessions must be stressed to the coordinators, to differentiate the Genesis Compensation Plan from the traditional compensation plan.

Often at this point there will be adjustments in compensation to bring people in line with base-pay guidelines, but the individual bonus, pay-for-skill, and goalsharing portions of the Genesis Compensation Plan won't result in increased compensation but just in the initiation of the individual goal, competency-based development, and goalsharing processes. The team meeting will involve the opportunities available to all to pursue competency-based development, and the encouragement of teams to establish specific plans to use continuous improvement to achieve the goalsharing goals.

9. *Debug the Genesis Compensation Plan.* Even though the design of the system has been very participatory, there will be problems with the implementation of the system. There will be mistakes and disagreements on things as straightforward as seniority. Built into the Genesis Compensation Plan should be an appeal process through which any individual at any time can, without negative repercussions, appeal any part of his/her personal compensation. Early in the implementation this appeal process will be tested, and the test must be handled efficiently and effectively. In fact, employees should be encouraged to probe and question, so as to maximize understanding and minimize uncertainty.

10. *Improve the Genesis Compensation Plan.* The Genesis Compensation Plan Strategy Design Team, and the design teams reporting to this strategy team, should be terminated. The design is now complete. However, the Genesis Compensation Plan is not in its final form. In fact, the Genesis Compensation Plan will *never* be in its final form. As the organization and individuals evolve, so too must the Genesis Compensation Plan.

For this reason, a Genesis Compensation Plan Improvement Team must be established. In a union environment, this improvement team should consist of salaried people and union people. Unfortunately, in a nonunion environment, involving hourly people may create NLRB problems, and so the team must consist only of salaried people. The Leadership Team should charter the Genesis Compensation Plan Improvement Team, and this team should proceed just like all other teams. Often it is this team that will handle appeals. Certainly, this team will be involved with working with the Communication Team in reporting results, making suggestions to the Leadership Team, altering the Genesis Compensation Plan, making policy interpretations, ensuring that all portions of the organization are properly and in a timely manner following the system, and educating new employees as to the functioning of the system.

It is by following these steps that an organization may shift from traditional compensation to Genesis Compensation. Although these steps will be the same for all organizations, and for some organizations even the components of Genesis Compensation will be the same, the Genesis Compensation Plan that flows from this process will be unique for each organization.

EXPECTATIONS CAN UNDERMINE RESULTS

When my second daughter was in high school, we had a problem. She was a quiet, sweet, and active young lady who enjoyed life, but who mentally built unreasonable expectations. It didn't matter if it was a school dance, a date, a vacation, a church outing, or just a meal at a nice restaurant. This young lady would anticipate and mentally rehearse the upcoming event to such an extent that when the event took place, it never quite lived up to expectations. The bad news is that this made many really super events a disappointment. The good news is that she grew out of this phase, and we no longer have to brace ourselves for the backlash after an event.

What does this have to do with Genesis Compensation? A lot. No matter how clearly and how often you explain to people Genesis Compensation, there are those who build up expectations about increases in compensation. This often results in these individuals going shopping for a new car, new living room furniture, a new dress, and so on. Then, when Genesis Compensation is implemented, and either there is no pot of gold or the pot is smaller than expected, there is a lot of disappointment, maybe even hostility and a feeling of having been cheated. It is for this reason that the design of each company's Genesis Compensation Plan must be done in a very participative environment and with clear and open communications. Leadership must not allow elevated expectations, and every effort must be made to underestimate and under-promise the results of Genesis Compensation, so that when the Genesis Compensation Plan is implemented, there is no disappointment or letdown.

14.2 Implementing
Competency-Based Development

The process that should be followed to implement competency-based development as a part of the shift to Genesis Compensation is as follows.

1. *Lay a foundation for implementing competency-based development.* The person on the Genesis Compensation Plan Strategy Design Team most familiar with employee training should develop a presentation that describes all task-specific training that has been done by the organization. This presentation should be made to the Genesis Compensation Plan Strategy Design Team, who should then charter the Competency-Based Development Design Team. The charter for the Competency-Based Development Design Team should require this design team to work closely with the Genesis Compensation Plan Strategy Design Team, as it develops the specific application of competency-based development.

2. *Enhance awareness and understanding of competency-based development.* The same presentation that was provided to the Genesis Compensation Plan Strategy Design Team, or the task-specific training done by the organization, should be given to the Competency-Based Development Design Team. In addition, the following topics should be presented by the Genesis Compensation Plan Strategy Design Team to the Competency-Based Development Design Team:
   a. Relationship of competency-based development to pay-for-skill (see Sec. 13.3.2).
   b. Integration of competency-based development implementation to the implementation of the overall Genesis Compensation Plan (see Sec. 14.1).
   c. The competency-based development design process defined herein.

3. *Establish a Competency Level Skill Requirements Matrix.* The three-step process to define the Competency Level Skill Requirement Matrix is as follows:
   a. Define all job classifications.
   b. Define the functional tasks required by all of the job classifications.
   c. Define the skill level of each functional task for each job, and record these skill levels in a Competency Level Skill Requirements Matrix.

   For example, the job classifications that exist in a warehouse are
   a. Lift truck driver
   b. Lead operator
   c. Supervisor

d. Traffic manager
e. Customer service representative
f. Scheduling
g. Clerical
h. Rework
i. Quality assurance

The functional tasks in this warehouse are

a. Receiving
b. Putaway
c. Picking
d. Shipping
e. Inventory management
f. Rewarehousing
g. Traffic
h. Order administration
i. System administration

The skill levels are as follows:

a. Level I is beginner.
b. Level II is user.
c. Level III is expert.

Then the Compentency Level Skill Requirements Matrix can be designed as given in Table 14.1.

4. *Develop Competency-Based Development functional tests for each skill level for each functional task.* The person on the Competency-Based Development Design Team most familiar with each functional task area should take responsibility for the development questions for each skill level found for the functional tasks in the Competency Level Skill Requirements Matrix. These questions should be multiple choice–type questions. They should be reviewed by the team for their clarity, relevance, and proper definition by skill level. A functional test for each job classification may then be developed by combining the questions at the appropriate skill level for each of the functional tasks.

   For example, for the job classification "Lift truck driver" in Table 14.1, the competency-based test would consist of expert knowledge (Level III) of receiving, putaway, picking, shipping, and rewarehousing; user knowledge (Level II) for inventory management; and beginner knowledge (Level I) for traffic, order administration, and system administration.

5. *Refine functional tests.* A standard test review questionnaire should be developed to collect information from qualified employees in each job classification. This questionnaire, along with the test for each job classification, should be given to two to four people who are recog-

Table 14.1 An Example of a Competency Level Skill Requirements Matrix for a Warehouse*

Job classifications	Functional tasks								
	Receiving	Putaway	Picking	Shipping	Inventory mgmt.	Rewarehousing	Traffic	Order admin.	System admin.
Lift truck driver	III	III	III	III	II	III	I	I	I
Lead operator	III	III	III	III	III	III	II	III	II
Supervisor	III	III	III	III	III	III	III	III	III
Traffic manager	N/A	N/A	N/A	I	N/A	N/A	III	III	I
Customer service	I	N/A	N/A	I	II	N/A	I	III	I
Scheduling	I	N/A	N/A	N/A	III	N/A	N/A	III	I
Clerical	II	I	I	II	III	N/A	II	III	III
Rework	N/A	III	III	N/A	III	III	N/A	N/A	I
Quality assurance	I	N/A	N/A	N/A	II	N/A	N/A	N/A	I

*(I = Beginner, II = User, III = Expert, NA = Not Applicable)

nized as being fully qualified for the job. The purpose of these trial tests and the questionnaire is to identify poorly worded questions and questions for which there might be more than one correct answer. The people who take the trial test should be encouraged to provide feedback on all questions and to suggest additional questions as appropriate. The questions with problems should be refined, new questions added, and, if necessary, additional trial tests performed. This should be continued until valid and encompassing tests have been developed for all job classifications.

6. *Develop Competency-Based Development Scenario Tests for each job classification.*   A scenario test is a 10- to 20-minute test that requires the employee to act out or simulate an answer. Two or three scenarios should be developed for each job classification. For example, looking at the lift truck driver classification scenario, tests may include the following:

   a. You are traveling down an aisle and a pallet is out in the aisle. What do you do?
   b. You are instructed to pick a product from a given location. The location contains another product. What do you do?
   c. You are doing a cycle count and you discover damaged product. What do you do?

   These scenarios, and the answers to them, should be reviewed by the Competency-Based Development Design Team for their clarity, relevance, and proper definition by skill level. A scenario test for each job classification might then be developed by using any combination of the developed scenarios.

7. *Refine scenario tests.*   This step is the same as Step 5, except that here the *scenarios* are refined rather than the questions.

8. *Train people to train people to be competent in each job classification.* Develop training materials for each skill level for each functional task. Combine these training materials to obtain a training manual for each job classification. The Competency-Based Training Design Team should use these materials to train the trainers. The trainers should then be administered both the functional test and the scenario test for the job classifications they are to train. Any questions missed should result in either a change in the test or a change in the training materials.

9. *Train a test group.*   Each trainer should train a small test group of employees. This is important not only to test the materials but also to test the effectiveness of the trainer. Both the functional test and the scenario test should be given to the employees who were trained by the trainers. Any problems identified with the trainers should be addressed.

10. *Develop competency-based development policies on using competency-based development skills, retraining, and retesting.* A difficulty that occurs in some organizations is that people are trained and tested and certified for certain job classifications, receive the appropriate pay-for-skill pay rate, but then never utilize the increased skills they have obtained. The Competency-Based Development Design Team should develop policies on the utilization of job classification skills and the retesting of employees to both update employees and to ensure the paying for skills that still exist. A policy for retraining employees who are no longer competent should also be developed by the Competency-Based Development Design Team.

11. *Implement Competency-Based Development.* Integrate competency-based development with the Pay-for-Skill Rate Design Team results, and implement along with the other elements of the Genesis Compensation Plan. Follow the process as presented in Step 8 of the overall implementation of Genesis Compensation (Section 14.1). Individuals should be encouraged to pursue competency in different job classifications, to broaden their expertise and ability to support the increased performance of the organization.

12. *Debug and participate in the Genesis Compensation Improvement Team.* As people receive training and take the competency-based development tests, the Competency-Based Development Design Team should review results and provide whatever additional support is needed to ensure the success of competency-based development and pay-for-skill. As the start-up difficulties of competency-based development are resolved, the Competency-Based Development Design Team should be terminated. At least one member from this design team, however, should be placed on the Genesis Compensation Plan Improvement Team to help this improvement team

   a. Update and/or upgrade competency-based development tests and training materials as appropriate
   b. Create new competency-based development tests and training materials as appropriate
   c. Encourage people to enhance their value to the organization and their pay rate by pursuing competency-based development.
   d. Oversee the competency-based development policies for the utilization, retest, and recertification of skills

14.3 Implementing Goalsharing

The process that should be followed to implement goalsharing as part of the shift to Genesis Compensation is as follows.

1. *Lay a foundation for implementing goalsharing.* As a portion of the overall shift from traditional compensation to Genesis Compensation, the Steering Team, the Leadership Team, and the Genesis Compensation Plan Strategy Design Team have all participated in an education session that included an overview of goalsharing. Based upon this framework, the Genesis Compensation Plan Strategy Design Team should charter a Goalshare Design Team with the task of designing the specific application of goalsharing. This Goalshare Design Team should report to the Genesis Compensation Plan Strategy Design Team, but will also directly communicate with the Steering Team and the Leadership Team and shall obtain approval of the recommended goalshare plan from the Steering Team.

2. *Enhance awareness and understanding of goalsharing.* Either the Genesis Compensation Plan Strategy Design Team or a consultant should be given the task of developing and presenting a three- to four-hour discussion on goalsharing. Topics to be included should be
   a. Relationship of goalsharing to traditional gainsharing (see Sec. 12.2)
   b. Integration of goalsharing implementation to the implementation of the overall Genesis Compensation Plan (see Sec. 14.1)
   c. The five goalsharing questions presented in Appendix H that will result in the design of a goalshare program

3. *Goalshare Design Team designs Goalshare Plan structure.* The Goalshare Design Team should answer the five questions presented in Appendix H. They should collect history on the goal factors, and do a historical simulation of the bonuses that would be paid if various goals had been in place.

4. *Goalshare Design Team gets input on Goalshare structure.* The Goalshare Design Team should present the goalshare structure and historical simulation to the Steering Team, the Leadership Team, and the Genesis Compensation Plan Strategy Design Team. The people on these teams should provide input via comment and survey. These inputs should be used to refine the goalshare structure and to refine the presentation of the goalshare plan.

5. *Goalshare Design Team defines specific goals and bonuses.* The result of Step 4 will be a refined goalshare structure, and feedback on the historical simulations. Based on this input, the Goalshare Design Team should establish the specifics of the goals and bonuses for the first year of the goalshare plan. These specific goals and bonuses should be presented to the Steering Team, along with a simulation of the range of potential results for the Steering Team's feedback, refinement, and approval.

6. *Goalshare Design Team defines Goalshare Implementation Plan.* In concert with the Genesis Compensation Implementation Plan, the timing for the implementation of the Goalshare Plan should be established. This Implementation Plan should include the date for the Goalshare Plan initiation, the payout periods, and the dates for bonus distribution.

7. *Develop a Goalshare policy document.* This four- to six-page document should explain the why, what, how, and when of goalsharing for the company. This document will be integrated with the materials from other teams to form the basis for the information exchange meetings presented in Step 6, in Sec. 14.1. The survey information on goalsharing obtained at these exchange meetings should be passed to the Goalshare Design Team to further refine the goalshare plan. These refinements should be made to the goalshare policy document and the goalshare presentation package.

8. *Support the communication of the Genesis Compensation Plan to each employee.* Step 7 of the implementation plan for Genesis Compensation (Sec. 14.1) involves the training of coordinators and a series of one-on-one meetings with employees. The Goalshare Design Team should be an active participant in developing goalshare training materials, and in helping coordinators and employees understand the mechanics, procedures, and benefits of the goalsharing plan. The Goalshare Design Team should be a strong advocate in the Genesis Compensation transformation for the organization's team-based process. The Goalshare Design Team should be a loud voice in support of using the team-based process to achieve the goals and obtain the bonuses available from goalsharing. Minor refinement of the goalsharing plan might be made at this point, based upon feedback received from the communication of the plan to all employees.

9. *Implement goalsharing.* As a portion of Step 8 in the implementation of Genesis Compensation (Sec. 14.1), goalsharing will be implemented. At the outset, team meetings should be held with each team to emphasize the goalsharing plan and the opportunity for teams to create peak-to-peak performance to work toward goal achievement. Teams should be encouraged to define their role in achieving the goalsharing goals and to set their own team goals in concert with the goalsharing goals. It is critical to realize that with the individual attention people will be getting with the implementation of Genesis Compensation, goalsharing must be proactively used to continue to focus people's attention on the team-based process.

10. *Debug and participate in the Genesis Compensation Improvement Team.* As the first goalsharing reports and the first goalshare checks

are issued, there will be many questions and concerns. The Gainsharing Design Team should provide whatever support is necessary at this time to ensure understanding of the goalshare plan. When the initial implementation concerns are past, the Goalsharing Design Team should be terminated. But like the overall design of Genesis Compensation, the job is never done. At least one member from the Goalsharing Design Team should be placed on the Genesis Compensation Plan Improvement Team. It is this team that will

a. Report to the Communication Team on the performance of goalsharing
b. Oversee the proper interpretation and application of the goalshare plan
c. Define new factors, and interface with the Steering Team to set goals and bonuses for the next year
d. Continue to stress to all teams the impact of their team efforts on the goalsharing goals, and encourage team goal-setting and achievement in concert with the goalsharing goals

14.4 Genesis Compensation Success Factors

The 10 most important factors that support the success of Genesis Compensation are

1. *Leadership commitment.* The shift from traditional compensation to Genesis Compensation only works after there has been a shift from management to leadership, from individual to team, and from the traditional supplier/customer relationship to partnership. Leadership must drive the organization to become a team-based organization focused on creating peak-to-peak performance, and then must be dedicated to the philosophy of paying-for-performance, paying-for-skill performance, paying-for-skill, and rewarding team initiative of achieving goals. This dedication must be a long-term commitment and not a passing fancy. All employees must understand and observe this leadership dedication. Leadership must be enthusiastic and consistent in its support of the team-based process, partnerships, and Genesis Compensation.

2. *Model of Success.* Everyone in the organization must understand that the Model of Success is the navigation system for the company's evolution. Genesis Compensation must support and reinforce the commitment to the Model of Success.

3. *Quality communications.* The Genesis Compensation Plan Strategy Design Team, the Genesis Compensation Plan Improvement Team, and the Communication Team must be persistent and consistent in presenting the Genesis Compensation message. Communication requirements are ongoing. Each week, there will be new questions and new thoughts that must be addressed. All employees need to be kept up-to-date on the continuous evolution of Genesis Compensation. Quality communications demand calculation accuracy, responsiveness to problems, and clarity of all Genesis Compensation communications.

4. *Trust.* Without trust, there cannot be a successful buy-in to Genesis Compensation. Attempting to use Genesis Compensation to overcome cultural problems, lack of leadership, nonfunctioning teams, or any other problem will not work. Genesis Compensation must not be viewed as a bribe to overcome problems, but rather as a reward to celebrate peak-to-peak performance.

5. *Peak-to-peak performance.* As has been said several times, Genesis Compensation is the rewards portion of peak-to-peak performance. Without peak-to-peak performance in leadership, teams, and partnerships, there are no rewards for Genesis Compensation to distribute. Without peak-to-peak performance, there is no emotional recognition, no pay-for-skill, no individual bonus, and no goalsharing bonus. Peak-to-peak performance is the driver behind Genesis Compensation.

6. *Equitability and Understandability.* The success of Genesis Compensation depends upon everyone understanding Genesis Compensation, and there existing in everyone's mind a balance between contribution and compensation. Genesis Compensation must be fair not only to all employees but also to the organization, and be sufficiently flexible so that as conditions change, so too does Genesis Compensation to maintain equitability.

7. *Employee participation.* Genesis Compensation must be respectful of NLRB requirements, but also must allow significant employee involvement so that all employees own, accept, and are enthusiastic about Genesis Compensation. There should be no barriers to employees providing feedback, having information, or participating in the design and continuous improvement of Genesis Compensation.

8. *Employees must connect peak-to-peak performance with increased compensation.* Employees must understand that when they as individuals perform well, both individually and as a part of a team, this is the basis of Genesis Compensation and increased compensation. At the same time, and just as clear but sometimes not as well accepted, when as individuals or as teams the organization does not perform well, Genesis Compensation will not result in increased compensation.

9. *Flexibility.* All successful Genesis Compensation Plans are custom-designed for the organization. Genesis Compensation must be consistent with and reinforcing of the organization's Model of Success and the team-based process. It is important that the entire organization understand that Genesis Compensation must be fluid, and that it will continuously improve and evolve just as the organization will. It is the responsibility of the Genesis Compensation Plan Improvement Team to be certain that Genesis Compensation is up-to-date and properly reflects the priorities of the organization.

10. *Genesis Compensation success.* At the end of the day, the true measure of Genesis Compensation success is the answer to the question, "Is the organization better off, and are the employees better off?" If for whatever reason the company is *not* more profitable and the employees *worse* compensated, then Genesis Compensation has not been a success. Therefore we must shift from manager to leader, from individuals to teams, from the traditional supplier/customer relationship to partnerships. This will bring the peak-to-peak performance that will result in the success of Genesis Compensation, which in turn will lead to more peak-to-peak performance, and on and on and on, continuously getting better and better.

14.5 Conclusion

A key objective of Genesis Compensation is the balance of contribution and compensation. For this to occur, all employees must understand and to the greatest extent possible participate in the design and evolution of Genesis Compensation. This chapter has presented the following 10-step process for shifting from traditional compensation to Genesis Compensation:

1. Lay a foundation for shifting from traditional compensation to Genesis Compensation.

2. Define the overall Genesis Compensation Plan.

3. Obtain an assessment of the present compensation plan, input, or the structure of the Genesis Compensation Plan, and feelings on compensation ranges for the Genesis Compensation Plan.

4. Refine structure, and establish next level of detail.

5. Develop an implementation plan and a communication plan.

6. Conduct information exchange meetings and refine the Genesis Compensation Plan.

7. Communicate the Genesis Compensation Plan to each employee.

8. Initiate the Genesis Compensation Plan.

9. Debug the Genesis Compensation Plan.

10. Improve the Genesis Compensation Plan.

This chapter has also presented further guidance on the design of the two elements of Genesis Compensation that are totally different from what most organizations have in place today: competency-based development, and goalsharing. The chapter has closed with a compilation of the factors for Genesis Compensation success. It is by adhering to these factors that the last shift of the Genesis Enterprise, the shift from traditional compensation to Genesis Compensation, can be made a reality.

References

Belasco, J. A. and R. C. Stayer, *Flight of the Buffalo: Soaring to Excellence, Learning to Let Employees Lead,* Warner Books, New York, 1993.

Day, M., "Employee Involvement and Gainsharing in the Retailing Industry," *International Industrial Engineering Conference Proceedings,* Institute of Industrial Engineers, Norcross, GA, 1990.

Fierman, J., "The Perilous New World of Fair Pay," *Fortune,* June 13, 1994.

Graham-Moore, B. and T. L. Ross, *Gainsharing: Plans for Improving Performance,* The Bureau of National Affairs, Washington, D.C., 1990.

Hart, J. G., "Gainsharing: The Double-Barreled Solution to Low Morale," *Business Leader,* March 1994.

Lawler, E. E. III, *Strategic Pay: Aligning Organizational Strategies and Pay Systems,* Jossey-Bass Publishers, San Francisco, 1990.

Neusch, D. R. and A. F. Siebenaler, *The High Performance Enterprise,* Oliver Wight Publications, Essex Junction, VT, 1993.

Peters, E., "A New Approach to Systems Training," *Automatic ID News,* July 1994.

Schmid, R. O. "Structuring Gainsharing for Success," *Industrial Engineering,* July 1994.

PART 6

Making It Happen

Part 6 consists of one short chapter that says one simple thing: For your organization to become a Genesis Enterprise, you must begin where you are, and do something. The difference between people who read this book for enjoyment and those who read it for results will lie in the actions they do or do not take when they finish the book. If you want results, if you want to become a Genesis Enterprise, then you must take responsibility for Making It Happen.

15
Becoming a Genesis Enterprise

How do you like a movie to end? Some movies end with the good guy triumphing over Evil, and everybody living happily ever after. Other movies don't really end, but just kind of stop. For days on end my wife and I ask, "Who really did it? What would happen next? Did the couple get back together or not? What did she mean when she said, 'I am really anxious to see you.'?" The movie didn't *end*, it just *stopped*.

How about the books you've read? How do you like them to end? Some nonfiction books end with the *plan*: the seven steps you should follow to do whatever it was the book promised you could do. Other books, like those movies, don't end but just kind of stop.

Now, I know you want your 7-step plan. Unfortunately, this book isn't really a 7-step plan type of book, because what you need to do next depends upon where you *begin*. Two stories come to mind.

The first is from *Alice in Wonderland*. Alice, when lost in the woods and faced with a fork in the road, asks the cat which way to go. The cat says the path selection depends upon where Alice wants to go. Alice doesn't know where she wants to go, so the cat replies, "Then it matters not which path you take."

The other story is credited to Yogi Berra. When asked what to do when facing a decision like Alice's, Yogi is reported to have said, "When you come to a fork in the road, take it."

You see, what you should do next depends upon where you are, and the status of your organization. I think we should learn from Alice and find our path forward by trying to understand both where we are now and where we are trying to go. I think we should learn from Yogi, and realize that it isn't as important for us to decide which path to take as it is for us to take *action*. Make something happen! Move in some direction! Act!

Nevertheless, I know you still want your 7-step plan, so this one's for you:

Step 1	Share this book with others.
Step 2	Determine your organization's present status, with regard to the shift from management to leadership. Find a path forward. Take it.
Step 3	Determine your organization's present status, with regard to the shift from individuals to teams. Find a path forward. Take it.
Step 4	Determine your organization's present status, with regard to the shift from traditional customer/supplier relationships to partnerships. Find a path forward. Take it.
Step 5	Determine your organization's present status, with regard to the shift from traditional compensation to Genesis Compensation. Find a path forward. Take it.
Step 6	Determine your organization's present status, with regard to becoming a Genesis Enterprise. Find a path forward. Take it.
Step 7	Return to Step 2, with enthusiasm!

A COMPANY BECOMES A GENESIS ENTERPRISE: TWICE

The pursuit of becoming a Genesis Enterprise began in 1990. By early 1991, management had become leadership, the organization was team-based, and compensation had been upgraded. Things were good. Sales were up, profits were up, salaries were up, and quality was up. All was great. By early 1992, growth forced the company to pursue an Organizational Design Team and to restructure responsibilities. Growth continued, profits continued to grow, things were good.

When the firm reached twice the size it had been two years earlier, it began to lose control. Because of the level of business, leadership shifted to management and the team process fell into disrepair. Many new people were hired, and the culture became one of static consistency. Innovation and improvements ceased, and most people focused simply on getting through. By 1994, the company was no longer a Genesis Enterprise.

The process was reinstalled in the summer of 1994. Leadership went back to being leaders. Individuals went back to working as teams, and the team-based compensation plan began paying bonuses again. The second go at becoming a Genesis Enterprise was harder, for many had watched the company succeed and then fail. But the second go at becoming a Genesis Enterprise was also easier, for many knew that it worked, liked the process of renewal, and understood where they had gone wrong. The reinstallation of the process took place over a three-month period, and today the organization is once again a Genesis

Enterprise. Guess what? Sales are way up, profits are way up, quality is way up, salaries are way up. In this case, it was proven not only that the Genesis Enterprise works, but that it can be made to work *twice* in the same organization.

15.1 Understanding Boomerangs

I am not sure if the expression "What goes around, comes around" was developed while thinking about boomerangs. I also am not sure if the moral of the Old Testament story about Jacob, "You sow what you reap," was developed from a boomerang perspective. It is, however, by my combined thinking about boomerangs, "what goes around comes around," and sowing and reaping that I want to help you in your pursuit of becoming a Genesis Enterprise. I call these thoughts the Four Genesis Boomerang Principles.

Boomerang Principle I: *What Comes Back Is Exactly What You Put Forth.* When you throw a boomerang, what comes back is not another boomerang but the boomerang you threw. When you plant corn, you get corn. When you plant peas, you get peas. You will never plant peas and get corn. What you harvest is exactly what you plant. What goes around, comes around. As you pursue becoming a Genesis Enterprise, the reactions, responses, and commitment received will exactly mirror the feelings, thoughts, and commitment you put forth. There are no shortcuts. You first must be aligned, and then others will follow. You first must embrace the creation of peak-to-peak performance, and then others will follow. In both words and actions, your dedication to creating peak-to-peak performance will be exactly mirrored in the words and actions of others.

Boomerang Principle II: *What Comes Back Is Always More Than You Put Forth.* A boomerang gains momentum, and returns to the thrower traveling at a speed faster than when it left. When you plant one seed of corn, you can get back many ears of corn. When you plant one pea seed, you can get back many pea pods. As you strive to become a Genesis Enterprise, the synergy that evolves can act as a great multiplier for the evolution of renewal, progress, improvement, growth, and success. A key to the success of a Genesis Enterprise is the synergistic multiplier of creating peak-to-peak performance.

Boomerang Principle III: *You Always Obtain Results* After *You Make the Investment.* There is a timing thing here that is natural, but some people have difficulties understanding it. A boomerang never comes back until after it is thrown. How long it takes to come back depends upon many complex factors, and is very difficult to predict. Most of us just throw the boomerang, watch its flight, and catch it when it returns.

Similarly, you can't harvest corn before it is planted or the day it is planted or the week it is planted or even in the month it is planted. Growing corn takes time. How long it takes to grow depends upon many complex factors and is difficult to predict. Most of us just plant the corn, watch it grow, and harvest it when it is ready.

The same is true with the process of becoming a Genesis Enterprise. You don't read this book and automatically your organization gets better. You don't kick off a cultural transformation, a team, a partnership, etc. and expect to benefit that day or the next day. Growing a Genesis Enterprise takes time. How long it takes to become a Genesis Enterprise depends upon many complex factors and is very difficult to predict. Therefore, what should be done is to start the process, to do something, and then to watch the evolution. The benefits will come. Just like watching the corn grow, it takes patience to watch a Genesis Enterprise grow. And just like the farmer, it is your job to have patience and confidence. The corn will grow and the benefits will come.

Boomerang Principle IV: *The Benefits You Receive Will Be Positive Only If You Know What You Are Doing.* Sometimes you throw the boomerang and it comes back. Sometimes you throw it and it *doesn't* come back. It takes practice to know how to throw a boomerang, and outside help often is useful.

The same with corn. Just planting good seeds and being patient won't result in ears of corn. The farmer needs to be sure the seeds are properly watered and fertilized. The farmer needs to know how to grow corn, and must know when to get outside help.

The same is true of a Genesis Enterprise. There will be mistakes. There will be difficulties. The Genesis Leader needs to know how to nurture the process, how to grow the process, and when faced with difficulties, know when and how to get outside help. Just as it takes a skilled boomerang thrower and a knowledgeable farmer to be successful, so to become a Genesis Enterprise an organization must have a skillful and knowledgeable Genesis Leader.

When you pursue the process of becoming a Genesis Enterprise, it is very important that you think about the boomerang. Genesis Leaders understand that

1. What comes back is exactly what you put forth.

2. What comes back is always more than you put forth.

3. You always obtain results *after* you make the investment.

4. The benefit you receive will work only if you know what you are doing.

MOTOROLA: PUTTING THE BOOMERANG PRINCIPLES TO WORK

Consider the following Motorola accolades:

- "Superbly managed"
- "The company that almost everyone loves to love"
- "Icon of innovation"
- "A worldwide leader"
- "A big company that sizzles"
- "This company is just on a tremendous roll. They're very, very good at everything they do."
- "Motorola is the best-managed company in the world. Nobody else is even close."

What a great success story! Sales jumped up to 27.5 percent in 1993, to a record $17 billion, with 56 percent of those sales coming from overseas. Earnings surged 127 percent, to $1 billion.

But guess what? Leadership isn't sitting back basking in their great success. No, leadership understands the success/fail cycle and so it's saying:

"Fame is a fleeting thing. When the alarm clock rings tomorrow morning, you'd better get up and understand that your customers expect more from you than they did the day before. You'd better find a way to be better."

"Since our inception, Motorola has been managing on the concept of renewal, a willingness to renew our technologies, and to renew the process by which we run the institution."

"We've met the challenge of the Japanese—our quality is high; demand for our product is strong. Our technical people are bordering on being cocky. That keeps me awake at night. I've got to figure out how to keep these people unhappy."

Continuous renewal—being on top but thinking like an underdog, focused on doing a little more and being a little better. Realizing that what comes back is not what they put in two years ago, but what they put in tomorrow. Understanding that they must leverage their expertise, work the global market, and invest in the future. It is clear that Motorola will continue to reap, and reap, and reap. Motorola understands the Boomerang Principles.

15.2 Yes, But ...

Many have read this book, many have heard me explain the Genesis Enterprise, and many have pursued the process. The process works, and it is fundamental to the success of organizations. Nevertheless, skepticism exists and needs to be addressed. I don't view skepticism as negative, but rather as a desire to more fully understand how the process of becoming a Genesis Enterprise really works. This is great. Allow me now to respond to the five questions/concerns most often asked.

> **Question 1.** *I am not in a position in my organization where I can make the decision to become a Genesis Enterprise. What should I do?* This is a good question, as the pursuit of becoming a Genesis Enterprise is a leadership-driven pursuit. The question indicates an awareness of the role of leadership. At the same time, it is important to understand the level of leadership that is required. For example, a plant manager who has 300 people under his/her leadership may not be able to make the shift in compensation, but would certainly be positioned to begin the process of becoming a Genesis Enterprise. Similarly, a distribution center manager who has 40 people under his/her leadership may not be able to make the shift to partnerships or in compensation, but would certainly be positioned to begin the process of becoming a Genesis Enterprise.
>
> By contrast, a branch manager of a bank having 12 employees, or a department manager in a hospital having 80 employees, wouldn't be properly positioned to pursue the organization becoming a Genesis Enterprise. The issue has less to do with size of staff and more to do with the ability of the leader to define a Model of Success, to transform culture, and to pursue a team-based environment. If a leader is positioned to define a Model of Success for his/her operation, to transform his/her culture, and to pursue a team-based environment, then this is the level of leadership needed to begin the pursuit of becoming a Genesis Enterprise. If this level of leadership is not on-board, the next step is to *get* that level on-board. Give that level a copy of this book, and help it to understand how and why the organization should pursue becoming a Genesis Enterprise.
>
> **Question 2.** *I am the right level in the organization, and we wish to become a Genesis Enterprise. What should I do?* There are two different ways to answer this question correctly. The first way is to begin by involving people. Give them a copy of this book. Hold a meeting. Host a presentation on the process of becoming a Genesis Enterprise. Begin by involving people, and have the people define the path forward. Perhaps even follow the 7-step plan.

The second way to answer the question not only is a good answer, but it also helps to explain why the first answer works. The second answer is that it doesn't matter what you do first, as long as you are willing to learn from whatever you do decide to do. If you do something that moves the organization closer to becoming a Genesis Enterprise, great. Do it some more. If you do something that doesn't move the organization closer to becoming a Genesis Enterprise, that too is okay. Learn from the mistake, don't do it again, but try something else. You see, it doesn't matter if you do something good or bad, what matters is that you are doing *something* and that you are learning from your actions. This is the true pursuit of a Genesis Enterprise and no matter what it is that was done, it will allow you to learn and thus be on the path to becoming a Genesis Enterprise.

Question 3. *What are the costs of becoming a Genesis Enterprise?* Once again, there are two correct answers to this question. The first answer may be viewed as being somewhat sarcastic, because it answers a question with a question, but it isn't meant to be. The first answer is, "What is the cost of *not* becoming a Genesis Enterprise?" In a *Fortune* article entitled "Burned-Out Bosses," it is said that "Work no longer energizes; it drains." As companies have downsized and reengineered, a result has been overworked and undermotivated workers who are trying not to improve but rather just to hang on. This doesn't result in improved performance and thus profits are unsatisfactory, which leads to more layoffs, more overworked staff, less performance, less profits, more layoffs, etc. Without the transformation to becoming a Genesis Enterprise, there is no evolution of success and thus, the cost of not pursuing the process of a Genesis Enterprise is huge—such as, the net worth or net value of the organization! Without the movement to becoming a Genesis Enterprise, all is lost, the company will be history.

On the other hand, the more direct answer to the question of what it will cost to be a Genesis Enterprise is that it will cost somewhere between a few days' to a few weeks' payroll for the people contained within the organization being transformed into a Genesis Enterprise. For an advanced organization having in place a leadership-driven, team-based process, the cost will be a few days of payroll. For a traditional organization having a dinosaur culture and no team-based process, the investment could be as much as four weeks of payroll of the people impacted.

At the same time, the bottom-line benefits of becoming a Genesis Enterprise are very large. For an advanced organization, the payback of becoming a Genesis Enterprise will take somewhere between four and eight weeks. For a traditional organization the payback could be much longer, but in no case ever more than six months. Yes, there is seed money that is required to jump-start the process of becoming a Genesis Enterprise, but this seed money will be returned many, many times by the benefits that will result from being a Genesis Enterprise.

Question 4. *How long does it take to become a Genesis Enterprise?* Please excuse what appears to be a flip answer here, but the truth is that it takes about 10 percent longer than leadership estimates to become a Genesis Enterprise. If leadership estimates it will take 10 weeks, it will probably take 11 weeks, if 10 months, it will probably take 11 months, and if 10 years, it will probably take 11 years. The reality is the time leadership projects more often than not will become a self-fulfilling prophecy. The rate at which an organization is transformed is dependent upon how much time an organization believes it *has* to be transformed. An organization that is in financial trouble and on the verge of going out of business, will be transformed in a few weeks if the organization can be transformed. An organization which believes that all is well and, there is no urgency to be transformed can easily take years to become a Genesis Enterprise.

One thing is clear: It's easier to do it quickly. Good advice is to start quickly and then keep accelerating. Becoming a Genesis Enterprise quickly creates a sense of urgency, excitement, energy, and confidence. I can think of no reason not to start quickly and then keep accelerating. Once you have become a Genesis Enterprise, you will look back and observe that it would have been easier and very beneficial to do it more quickly.

Question 5. *What are the risks of trying to become a Genesis Enterprise and failing?* The only way to fail at becoming a Genesis Enterprise is to quit. Sure, there will be disappointments, setbacks, and problems while becoming a Genesis Enterprise, but these difficulties are not failures, they are opportunities to grow, learn, progress, and improve. Therefore, the only risk of trying to become a Genesis Enterprise is the risk associated with the level of commitment by leadership. If leadership is not committed for the long term, there is a significant risk, in that once the organizational transformation begins it is very difficult to reverse. Once leaders begin to lead, and once the transformation from individuals to teams begins, the organization will be very unhappy and uncomfortable with any attempt to return it to its original status. Oliver Wendell Holmes said this best when he said, "Man's mind, stretched to a new idea, never goes back to its original dimensions." So the only risk leadership is exposed to in the pursuit of becoming a Genesis Enterprise is the risk of not maintaining its commitment to and enthusiasm for becoming a Genesis Enterprise. If leadership is uncomfortable with this risk, then it shouldn't pursue becoming a Genesis Enterprise. Otherwise, let's begin, let's do something.

15.3   A Call to Action

In Chap. 1, I suggested an alternative title for this book: "How Are You Gonna Get to Where You Gotta Go?" I guess I would now ask, if you're *not* going to shift from management to leadership, from individuals to teams, from traditional customer/supplier relationships to partnerships, and from traditional compensation to Genesis Compensation, "How are you gonna get to where you gotta go?" You see, I believe you have no choice. I know the process presented in this book works. I know the process is appropriate both for where your organization is today and where it will be in five years. This process is not static but it too, within your organization, will evolve, grow, and improve. For your organization to achieve its potential, you must become a Genesis Enterprise. The next step is yours. You need to do something. You need to start quickly and then keep accelerating. The sense of momentum that will occur from your quick start will pull people into the process. This involvement, while following the process and learning as you go, will result in the synergy needed to create peak-to-peak performance, which will encourage others to be involved. You must take responsibility for making something happen, for doing something now. My recommendation: Go, Go, Go!

References

Belasco, J. A. and R. C. Stayer, *Flight of the Buffalo: Soaring to Excellence, Learning to Let Employees Lead,* Warner Books, New York, 1993.

Neusch, D. R. and A. F. Siebenaler, *The High Performance Enterprise,* Oliver Wight Publications, Essex Junction, VT, 1993.

Henkoff, R., "Keeping Motorola on a Roll," *Fortune,* April 18, 1994.

Pritchett, P., *Firing Up Commitment During Organizational Change,* Pritchett and Associates, Dallas, TX, 1994.

Pritchett, P. and R. Pound, *High-Velocity Culture Change,* Pritchett and Associates, Dallas, TX, 1993.

Riley, P., *The Winner Within: A Life Plan for Team Players,* G.P. Putnam's Sons, New York, 1993.

Smith, L., "Burned-Out Bosses," *Fortune,* July 25, 1994.

Tompkins, J. A., *Winning Manufacturing: How-to Book of Successful Manufacturing,* Institute of Industrial Engineers, Norcross, GA, 1989.

Appendix A

Developing a Model of Success

A.1 Model of Success Development Questionnaire

Agree or Disagree with the Following Statements	True	False
1. A Vision is a description of where we are headed.		
2. An organization's leadership should define the Vision.		
3. A Mission defines how to accomplish the Vision.		
4. An organization's leadership should define the Mission.		
5. A foundation of the success of our organization is the development, commitment, and buy-in of the correct Vision and Mission statements.		
6. A key to successful Vision and Mission statements is that they are simple, straightforward, and easily understood.		
7. Requirements of Success are the science of a business, and define the rules of operating a company.		
8. Guiding Principles are values a company should practice in pursuit of its Vision.		
9. Guiding Principles present a set of standards about how people should be treated.		
10. Evidences of Success are measurable results that will demonstrate when an organization is moving toward its vision.		

11. What changes in our business do you anticipate in the next five years?

12. What changes outside of our business will impact our business in the next five years?

13. What are the most important things to include in our Vision?

14. What are the most important things to include in our Mission?

15. Which of the following Requirements of Success apply to our business?

List here the Requirements of Success for a similar business.	Yes	No

16. Think about a time when you were proud of our company. What values did our company demonstrate?

17. Think about a time when you were disappointed in our company. What values did we fail to demonstrate?

18. Do you feel comfortable with the material presented at the orientation meeting? (If no, please explain).

19. Were you surprised by anything at the orientation meeting? (If yes, please explain).

20. What obstacles do you see in the Steering Team developing a Model of Success?

A.2 Facilitating a Model of Success Development Retreat

The worst way to define the elements of the Model of Success is by asking the Steering Team to define the elements. For example, if you ask the Steering Team, "What is the Vision of this company?" the members will become tongue-tied and apprehensive. An indirect approach will net better results.

After a brief review of the elements of the Model of Success, the outside facilitator should ask the Steering Team members to write on a piece of paper the answer to the question, "What are your aspirations for the company?" After about five minutes, the outside facilitator should go around the room asking each person for one aspiration from their list. These aspirations should be recorded on a flipchart. This should continue until all Steering Team members' lists have been exhausted. This process should be repeated with the question, "How will the company be different in 10 years?" From these two sets of flipchart pages, and the answer provided in the Model of Success Development Questionnaire, the Steering Team and the outside facilitator should define the Vision of the company. If the wordsmithing becomes awkward, the outside facilitator should break the Steering Team into two or three groups and ask each group to craft a Vision.

These two or three Visions should then be combined to define the Vision of the company. In a similar manner, then ask the question, "What must be done to make your 10-year difference come to life?" The answers to this question, along with the leftover answers to the first two questions, should be used to craft a Mission.

Next, the outside facilitator should pass out a draft of the Requirements of Success as defined by the Steering Team in the Model of Success Development Questionnaire (Question 15). The team should review and revise these Requirements of Success so as to establish a viable, applicable set of Requirements of Success.

Lastly, the Steering Team should be asked to record on a piece of paper their answers to the following question: "What do you want the employees to say about your company?" Once the answers to this question have been recorded on a flipchart, the outside facilitator should share with the group the responses to the Model of Success Development Questionnaire "proud" (Question 16) and "disappointed" (Question 17) questions. The flipchart answers to the "employees to say" question and the "proud" and "disappointed" responses should be wordsmithed by the Steering Team so as to define the first draft of the Guiding Principles. It is with the first drafts of the Vision, Mission, Requirements of Success, and Guiding Principles that the Model of Success Development Retreat should be concluded.

A.3   Model of Success
Refinement Questionnaire

	Yes	No
1. Does the Vision statement describe where our organization is headed? (If no, please explain.)	____	____
2. Is the Vision statement inspirational? (If no, please explain.)	____	____

	Yes	No
3. If our organization achieves the Vision statement, will it be successful? (If no, please explain.)	___	___
4. Will our people understand the Vision statement? (If no, please explain.)	___	___
5. Is the Vision statement believable to our people? (If no, please explain.)	___	___
6. Is the Vision statement believable to the outside world? (If no, please explain.)	___	___
7. Can the punctuation or wording be improved on the Vision statement? (If yes, please explain.)	___	___
8. Are there any words that have a double meaning, which could result in misunderstanding of the Vision statement? (If yes, please explain.)	___	___
9. Are there any fad words where meaning may change in the Vision statement? (If yes, please explain.)	___	___
10. Are you comfortable with the Vision statement? (If no, please explain.)	___	___
11. Does the Mission explain how to accomplish the Vision? (If no, please explain.)	___	___

	Yes	No

12. Will the employees understand the Mission statement? (If no, please explain.) ___ ___

13. Is the Mission statement believable to the employees? (If no, please explain.) ___ ___

14. If we do the Mission well, will we be moving toward our Vision? (If no, please explain.) ___ ___

15. Is the Mission statement believable to the outside world? (If no, please explain.) ___ ___

16. Can the punctuation or wording be improved in the Mission statement? (If yes, please explain.) ___ ___

17. Are there any words that have a double meaning, which could result in misunderstanding of the Mission statement? (If yes, please explain.) ___ ___

18. Are there any fad words in the Mission statement whose meaning may change? (If yes, please explain.) ___ ___

19. Are you comfortable with the Mission statement? (If no, please explain.) ___ ___

20. Are the Guiding Principles in plain English? (If no, please explain.) ___ ___

21. Can the Guiding Principles be simplified without losing any ideas? (If yes, please explain.) ___ ___

	Yes	No

22. Are the Guiding Principles tools to help achieve the Vision? (If no, please explain.) ____ ____

23. Will the employees understand the Guiding Principles? (If no, please explain.) ____ ____

24. Are there any fad words in the Guiding Principles? (If yes, please explain.) ____ ____

25. Do the Guiding Principles present the values of the company? (If no, please explain.) ____ ____

26. Are you comfortable with the Guiding Principles? (If no, please explain.) ____ ____

27. Do the Requirements of Success accurately define the science of our business? (If no, please explain.) ____ ____

28. Will the employees understand the Requirements of Success? (If no, please explain.) ____ ____

29. Can the wording of the Requirements of Success be improved? (If yes, please explain.) ____ ____

30. Are there any words that have a double meaning in the Requirements of Success which could result in misunderstanding? (If yes, please explain.) ____ ____

31. Can the Requirements of Success be simplified without missing any ideas? (If yes, please explain.) ____ ____

	Yes	No

32. Are the Requirements of Success in plain English?
    (If no, please explain.)   ____   ____

33. Are you comfortable with the Requirements of
    Success? (If no, please explain.)   ____   ____

34. How is your personal performance measured by
    your employees?

35. How is your personal performance measured by
    your boss?

36. How is your personal performance measured by
    your peers?

37. How is our organization's performance measured
    by our customers?

38. How is our organization's performance measured
    by our vendors?

39. How is our organization's performance measured
    by our owners?

40. How is our organization's performance measured
    by our community?

41. How do you feel about the process to develop the
    Model of Success?

	Yes	No
42. Do you fully support the Model of Success? (If no, please explain.)	___	___
43. Do you feel comfortable in explaining the Model of Success to your staff? (If no, please explain.)	___	___

44. What barriers need to be overcome to pursue the Model of Success?

45. Are there any surprises in our Model of Success?

Appendix B
Examples of Team Charters

B.1 Charter for a Functional Work Team

CHARTER FOR THE SHEET METAL TEAM

TEAM SPONSOR   **James Arthur**

DATE: **January 6, 19XX**

Leadership Team Preliminary	February 8
Leadership Team Final	March 3
Sheet Metal Team Review	March 8
Sheet Metal Team Acceptance	March 22

I.   *Opportunity:* (What is the reason this team exists?)

The Sheet Metal Department is a critical first operation for over 50 percent of our parts. Assembly schedules are driven by the schedule adherence and quality of parts fabricated in sheet metal. Scrap and waste are both also very important, as is labor productivity. The goal, therefore, is to solve problems, improve performance, and make the Sheet Metal Department a center for ABC Company excellence.

II.   *Process:* (What are the steps to be followed, and what are the questions to be answered by this team?)

The Sheet Metal team will follow the ABC Company process of team-based continuous improvement as follows:

1. Orientation.
2. Accept/revise charter, and create ownership.
3. Data collection.
4. Assess status.
5. Define evidence of success.
6. Prioritize opportunities.
7. Brainstorm alternatives.
8. Identify improvement plans.
9. Evaluate improvement plans.
10. Define improvement plans.
11. Obtain improvement plan support.
12. Implement improvement plan.
13. Return to Step 3.

Issues to be considered include the following:

1. Is manpower staffing adequate?
2. Is employee education and training acceptable?
3. Are sheet metal facilities appropriate?

4. Are all required tools available when needed?
5. Are materials available
    a. On time?
    b. In proper quantities?
    c. Within spec?
    d. In good condition?
6. Are drawings
    a. Available on time?
    b. Correct?
    c. Uniform?
    d. Understandable?
7. Are support services available in a timely manner from:
    a. Engineering?
    b. Packaging?
    c. Warehouse?
    d. Computer operations?
    e. Human resources?
    f. Quality?
8. Are there safety hazards in need of corrections?

III. *Evidence of Success:* (What results are expected in what time frames for this team to be successful?)
1. Reduction of waste to 5 percent by June 1.
2. Reduction of scrap to 1 percent by July 1, and to .5 percent by December 1.
3. Increase schedule adherence by June 1.
4. SPC all operations by June 1.
5. Increase productivity 15 percent by August 1, and 25 percent by December 1.

IV. *Resources:* (Who are the team members, team leaders, and team liaison; who will support the team if needed; how much time should be spent both in meetings and outside of meetings; and what additional resources are available to the team?)

The team will have the Vice President of Manufacturing, the Materials Manager, the Chief Engineer, and the CAD Manager available as a resource. Word-processing support shall be done by HR secretary. The team will consist of the following people:

Team Members:	John Peters	Jill Harell
	Bob Smith	Norm Barnhill
	Harold Schwartz	Mike Finley
Team Leader:	Jim Reily	
Team Liaison:	Tim Prentice	

The team should meet one hour per week. The team leaders should spend an additional one hour per week.

V. *Constraints:* (What authority does the team have; what is the over-all time frame for the evolution of the empowerment process; what things cannot be changed; what items are outside the scope of the team; and what budget does the team have?)

1. No changes will be made to the layout of the sheet metal department
2. The CAD software cannot be changed
3. No new carts can be purchased without the approval of Bob Canada
4. Lot sizes cannot be changed without approval from Bob Jackson
5. No more than $2000 shall be spent without approval by Tim Prentice. To spend less than $2000, account code DIM4610 shall be used. The total year's budget for DIM4610 is $5000
6. No travel shall be charged to DIM4610. Any travel shall be done against the individual departments
7. No setups or drawing changes shall be made without routine approval through engineering
8. This team is a Suggestion Team and should remain so for three to six weeks. A natural evolution should occur, with the team becoming a Self-Managing Team in 12 to 18 months from the time of Charter acceptance

VI. *Expectations:* (What are the outputs from the team, when are they expected to be complete, and to whom should they be given?)

1. The team shall publish weekly minutes.
2. The team shall make a monthly presentation at the Communications Forum.
3. The team shall develop an effective training program for new employees by June 1.
4. Significant evidence of success progress will occur by July 1.
5. The team is expected to think outside the ongoing paradigms and to tackle the real issues.

B.2   Charter for a Cross-functional Work Team

CHARTER FOR THE MATERIALS TEAM

TEAM SPONSOR:	Tiffany Joy
DATE:	February 3, 19XX

Leadership Team Preliminary	March 6
Leadership Team Final	March 13
Materials Team Review	March 20
Materials Team Acceptance	April 3

I.   *Opportunity:* (What is the reason this team exists?)

Material availability and inventory turns are critical aspects of ABC's plan for cost reduction and improved customer service. This team shall ensure efficient and effective procedures for defining requirements, requisitioning, packaging, inspecting, receiving, storing, and dispatching materials in order to allow ABC to maximize production efficiency, capital utilization, and customer service.

II. *Process:* (What are the steps to be followed and what are the questions to be answered by this team?)

The Materials Team will follow the ABC Company process of team-based continuous improvement as follows:

1. Orientation.
2. Accept/revise charter and create ownership.
3. Data collection.
4. Assess status.
5. Define evidence of success.
6. Prioritize opportunities.
7. Brainstorm alternatives.
8. Identify improvement plans.
9. Evaluate improvement plans.
10. Define improvement plans.
11. Obtain improvement plan support.
12. Implement improvement plan.
13. Return to Step 3.

Issues to be considered include the following:

1. What inventory turns should be expected?
2. Have we implemented JIT?

---

3. Are there further opportunities for vendor certification or partnerships?

4. Is there a problem with engineering changes?

5. Are our promise dates realistic?

6. How can we improve customer service?

7. Are we organized for mutual effectiveness?

8. Are there opportunities for EDI?

9. Are our internal procedures efficient and effective?

10. How can we assure inventory accuracy?

11. Do our computer systems fully support materials?

12. Do we have the right people doing the right jobs?

III. *Evidence of Success:* (What results are expected, in what time frames, for this team to be successful?)

1. Achieve .5 percent stockouts by July 1.

2. Increase raw material turns to 12 by August 1, and 18 by December 1.

3. Inventory accuracy shall be above 99.9 percent by September 1.

4. In-house inspections shall be less than 30 percent by September 1, and 10 percent by December 1.

5. Material quality rejects shall be less than .2 percent on September 1.

6. On-time deliveries to first operation shall be 98 percent (four hours of plan) by August 1, 98 percent (two hours of plan) by December 1.

IV. *Resources:* (Who are the team members, team leaders, and team liaison; who will support the team if needed; how much time should be spent both in meetings and outside of meetings; and what additional resources are available to the team?)

The team will have the Materials Manager, Chief Engineer, and Customer Service Manager available as a resource. The team will consist of the following people:

Team Members:	Charles News	Mike Light
	Bub Case	Marge George
	Sue Purse	Jim Turner
Team Leader:	Shirley Nance	
Team Liaison:	Rob Jackson	

The team should meet one hour per week, and spend an additional one hour per week in preparation. The team leader should spend a total of three hours per week.

V. *Constraints:* (What authority does the team have; what is the overall time frame for the evolution of the empowerment process; what things cannot be changed; what items are outside the scope of the team; and what budget does the team have?)

1. The team shall complete its work by January 1, 19XX. The team should evolve from a Suggestion Team to an Improvement Team once its Materials Action Plan Report has been accepted by the Leadership Team.

2. The AMAPS software shall be base system.

3. The team shall interface with the ongoing DMR and Cost Reduction teams.

4. Inventory management systems must conform to corporate standards.

5. No more than $2000 shall be spent without approval by Harold Ristole. To spend less than $2000, account code DIM 4836 shall be used. The total year's budget for DIM 4836 is $4000.

6. No travel shall be charged to DIM 4836. Any travel shall be done against the individual departments.

VI. *Expectations:* (What are the outputs from the team; when are they expected to be complete; and to whom should they be given?)

1. The team shall publish weekly minutes.

2. The team shall make a monthly presentation at the Communications Forum. The team shall produce a Material Account Report by July 1.

3. The team shall produce a Materials Action Plan Report by September 15. This report shall present and justify a Materials path forward.

4. The team shall make the following presentations and obtain concurrence:
   - October 15: Plant Materials Staff
   - October 22: Corporate Materials and Information System Staff
   - November 1: Executive Committee

5. The team shall recommend the creation of a Materials Implementation Team by November 15. A draft charter of this new team should be submitted to the Leadership Team.

B.3 Charter for a
Leadership Team

CHARTER FOR THE LEADERSHIP TEAM

TEAM SPONSOR: **Jamie Ashley**

DATE: **January 16, 19XX**

Leadership Team Preliminary	March 11
Steering Team Final	April 17
Steering Team Review	April 17
Leadership Team Acceptance	April 24

I.   *Opportunity:* (What is the reason this team exists?)

The ABC Company has determined that a culture of team-based continuous improvement must exist to achieve our vision. The Leadership Team must ensure that this new culture exists, grows, and becomes our norm. The team must be proactive in this role by ensuring that the Model of Success is communicated to and understood by all employees, and that all employees are aligned. The team must also define and charter new teams as appropriate, provide direction for new and existing teams, motivate all teams, accept accountability for the performance and results of all teams, and recognize and reward teams and team members for their achievements when teams have completed their Evidence of Success and are disbanding.

II.   *Process:* (What are the steps to be followed and what are the questions to be answered by this team?)

The Leadership Team will follow the process of team-based continuous improvement as follows:

1. Orientation.

2. Develop charter, obtain Steering Team concurrence, and create ownership.

3. Obtain opportunities from Steering Team.

4. Obtain opportunities from all sources throughout the company.

5. Brainstorm opportunities.

6. Prioritize opportunities.

7. Develop a time-phased action plan for addressing opportunities, including communicating Model of Success to every employee.

8. Obtain Steering Team support for action plan.

9. Begin implementation of plan by creating and chartering teams as identified in action plan, or passing to appropriate areas.

10. Provide orientation and direction for teams.

11. Coordinate team activities, ensure proper direction, and resolve any cross-over issues.

12. Motivate and ensure progress from team.

13. Continuously monitor results, and address issues within the entire process.

14. Proactively update action plan.

III. *Evidence of Success:* (What results are expected in what time frames for this team to be successful?)

1. Clear communications from team to team.

2. Teams that function effectively and efficiently without the Leadership Team's intervention.

3. A Leadership Team that is truly an example of a successful team.

4. Strategy and work teams achieve their evidence of success in a timely manner.

5. Leadership Team is actively involved in the process, and visible to the teams.

6. Issues important to achieving our vision are being addressed in a team-based environment.

7. Model of Success is communicated, understood, and supported by every employee.

8. Company culture is one of continuous improvement.

9. Team expansion and activity is managed within effective limits.

10. Team charters are clear and concise.

11. Hourly work force will become much more involved and a part of its company.

12. More ideas will be generated from the floor.

13. Problems are solved without Steering Team members as active participants either directly or indirectly.

14. Create an effective means of identifying opportunities that the leadership team needs to address.

15. Documentation of all team activities and results.

IV. *Resources:* (Who are the team members, team leaders, and team liaison; who will support the team if needed; how much time should be spent both in meetings and outside of meetings; and what additional resources are available to the team?)

The team will consist of the following people:

Team Members:

Steve Hatt	Fred Abrams	Bob Laner	Sarah Bennette
Bennie Moss	Bill Parker	John Mahony	
Tiffany Thomas	Shari Harwell	Earl Smith	
	Jackie Hand	Mike Green	

Team Leader: Bruce Thompson
Team Liaison: Mary Jones

The team should meet every week initially, then biweekly, and devote no more than two hours per week outside of team meeting.

V. *Constraints:* (What authority does the team have; what is the overall time frame for the evolution of the empowerment process; what things cannot be changed; what items are outside the scope of the team; and what budget does the team have?)

1. Must work within department budgets.

2. High level of individual workloads outside of team process must be understood.

3. Seek approval of Steering Team for revisions to policy.

4. Must make recommendations to Steering Team on establishment of strategic objectives and directions.

5. Responsible to take strategic plans and develop detailed team-based implementation plans.

VI. *Expectations:* (What are the outputs from the team; when are they expected to be complete; and to whom should they be given?)

1. The team will publish weekly minutes and distribute to all team members and Steering Team members.

2. The team will make a monthly presentation at the Communication Forum.

3. The team will make recommendations to the Steering Team on improvements in the way we do business, on an ongoing basis.

4. The team will define and prioritize opportunities for improvement throughout company, and include in action plan what the path forward is for each.

5. Develop a method to involve Leadership Team members in process, and to show support for each work team. Plan should include which work teams to visit, who should visit, and how often members should be expected to visit teams (two per week, one per week, one per two weeks, etc.). Plan implemented by May 31.

6. Promote the Model of Success.

7. Foster and promote "team spirit."

8. Update Steering Team on team status and process evolution, monthly or as requested.

9. Provide a detailed, time-phased action plan (to include short- and long-term goals) to evolve our culture and achieve our Model of Success. Plan submitted to Steering Team by August 1.

10. Develop a method to monitor results of all teams and document achievements by June 1.

11. Provide direction for all teams and evolve empowerment process.

12. Develop a method to obtain input from entire company on opportunities for improvement.

13. Develop a plan to review current status of organization and team process, and develop path forward. Plan should include Steering/Leadership meeting schedule, duration, agenda, and objectives. Plan should be implemented by June 29.

14. Plan to involve all Steering and Leadership Team members in the process.

B.4 Charter for a Communication Team

CHARTER FOR THE COMMUNICATION TEAM

TEAM SPONSOR:	**Sharon Marie**
DATE:	**March 11, 19XX**
Leadership Team Preliminary	March 18
Leadership Team Final	March 25
Communication Team Review	April 4
Communication Team Acceptance	April 11

I. *Opportunity:* (What is the reason this team exists?)

Effective communications are essential for the team-based continuous improvement process to be successful. The company Model of Success must be clearly understood so that each employee knows how he/she fits into the company's direction. It is imperative that information and ideas accurately flow between employees and company leadership. In addition, our communication process must provide for recognition of team accomplishments. The opportunity for the Communication Team is to provide means of communication that are accurate and timely.

II. *Process:* (What are the steps to be followed, and what are the questions to be answered by this team?)

1. Orientation.
2. Accept/revise charter and create ownership.
3. Assess current communication means.
4. Develop communication plan.
5. Obtain leadership team support for plan.
6. Implement plan.
7. Monitor results.

III. *Evidence of Success:* (What results are expected, in what time frames, for this team to be successful?)

1. Use all existing means of communication.
2. Identify most effective means of communicating information.
3. Information flowing up and down organizations.
4. All employees are informed.
5. Hold Communication Forum each month, beginning May.

6. Model of Success communicated, and employees understand their role.

7. Right information disseminated on a timely basis.

8. Establish a self-measurement method by September 1.

IV. *Resources:* (Who are the team members, team leaders, and team liaison; who will support the team if needed; how much time should be spent both in meetings and outside of meetings; and what additional resources are available to the team?)

The team will consist of the following people:

Team Members:	Sue Maconchi	Harold Blue
	Robert Mathis	Dean Smith
	Ron Lewis	Bill Lawson
	Robert Porter	Mike Gimiski
	Pam Jackson	
Team Leader:	Bob Henry	
Team Liaison:	Bill Smith	

The team should meet one hour per week, and a maximum of two additional hours per week outside the meeting.

Human Resources will provide clerical support, as well as information on all existing areas of communication.

V. *Constraints:* (What authority does the team have; what is the overall time frame for the evolution of the empowerment process; what things cannot be changed; what items are outside the scope of the team; and what budget does the team have?)

1. Team must operate within HR Strategic Business Plan.

2. Team must operate within capital plan.

3. Disclosure of confidential information must adhere to company policy and guidelines.

4. Coordinate flow of information up and down the organization.

5. Authority to develop new methods of communication.

VI. *Expectations:* (What are the outputs from the team; when are they expected to be complete; and to whom should they be given?)

1. The team will publish minutes from their meeting, to be distributed to the Leadership Team.

2. The team will publish a monthly communication that will inform all employees what is happening within the organiza-

tion. The form and method of this communication will be decided by the Communication Team.

3. The team will establish regular and frequent opportunities to receive feedback and disseminate this feedback to and from all employees. Action plans and anticipated responses to the feedback should be published by June 1.

4. Evidence of Success will be determined by how knowledgeable employees are about the team-based activities. The method and frequency of this test will be determined by the Communication Team.

5. The Communication Team will recognize the success of other teams.

6. The Communication Team will be an ongoing team.

7. Coordinate Communication Forum monthly.

B.5   Charter for a Design Team

CHARTER FOR THE ORGANIZATION DESIGN TEAM

TEAM SPONSOR:	**Jack Wilkins**
DATE:	**February 6, 19XX**

Leadership Team Preliminary	February 16
Leadership Team Final	February 23
Organization Design Team Review	March 1
Organization Design Team Acceptance	March 8

I.   *Opportunity:* (What is the reason this team exists?)

ABC has undergone excellent growth. It has made good progress and has implemented a cultural transformation. It has a successful, ongoing process of Team-Based Continuous Improvement. ABC is practicing Winning Manufacturing.

A challenge that has resulted from the ABC success is the overloading of a number of people. This, when coupled with a culture of weak accountability, has resulted in some burnout, some frustration, and an excellent opportunity for both a present and a future upgrade of the ABC organizational structure. The responsibility of the Organizational Design Team is to define the $140 million, $170 million, and $200 million sales volume organizational structures that will allow ABC to be recognized as a leader in total customer commitment and a pioneer in the application of technology, while fostering an environment of high employee satisfaction.

It is realized that in the past the ABC organizational structure has been loosely followed, as this best allowed ABC to address the many tasks of the day. This loose structure has now become a liability, as it has added to the cultural problems of accountability, authority, and responsibility. The ABC organizational structure of the future shall require a more formal focus, in which accountability and lines of authority are more clearly defined. Additionally, the Organizational Design Team shall proceed, while fully understanding that the new structure must be superimposed upon the Winning Manufacturing team-based culture.

II. *Process:* (What are the steps to be followed, and what are the questions to be answered by this team?)

1. February 23:   Leadership Team finalizes charter. Rob Haynes makes March 1 assignments as follows:

Rob H.	Present Team Charter. Lead discussion.
Steve D./Dan K.	Define ABC key resources (people, customers, machinery, money, materials, information) and the organization chart that would follow from a resource perspective. Lead discussion.
Sue S./Dick T.	Define via a flow chart the flow through ABC, from receipt of a customer inquiry to the total satisfaction of the customer to the creation of a partnership, and the organization chart that would follow from a resource perspective. Lead discussion.
Steve M./Jack H.	Define the organization chart that would follow for the ABC Model of Success. Lead discussion.
Jerry M.	Do a needs assessment, focusing on the strengths and weaknesses of the present organizational structure. (Not people in positions, but positions themselves). What improvements should be made in the present structure? Lead discussion.

2. March 1 agenda:

9:00 — 9:30 AM	Introduction: Jim T.
9:30 — 9:45 AM	Charter: Rob H.
9:45 — 10:15 AM	Resource Organization Chart: Steve D./Dan K.
10:15 — 10:45 AM	Flow Organization Chart: Sue S./Dick T.
10:45 — 11:00 AM	Break
11:00 — 11:30 AM	Model of Success Organization Chart: Steve M./Jack H.
11:30 — 12:00 N	Needs Assessment Organization Chart: Jerry M.
12:00 — 12:30 PM	Thinking About $200 Million: Rob H. to lead discussion
12:30 — 1:30 PM	Pizza lunch to be brought in/phone calls
1:30 — 3:00 PM	Design $200 Million ABC Organization Chart: All
3:00 — 3:15 PM	Wrap-up and assignments for March 21

3. March 10: $200 million Organization Chart Refinement Questionnaire returned to Rob

4. March 21 agenda: A. Finalize $200 million Organization Chart

   B. Preliminary job descriptions

   C. $170 million Organization Chart

   D. $140 million Organization Chart

5. April 3: $170 million and $140 million Organization Chart and Job Description Refinement Questionnaire returned to Rob

6. April 7 agenda: A. Finalize Organization Charts and Job Descriptions

   B. Develop Implementation Strategy

   C. Develop Communication Plan for results

7. Pursue Communication Plan and Implementation Strategy

III. *Evidence of Success:* (What results are expected, in what time frames, for this team to be successful?)

The Organizational Design Team is to leave the paradigms of the past behind. The team is to develop its recommendations independent of the present ABC organizational structure and staff. This team is to establish the clean-sheet, blue-sky, green-field designs of the ABC organization of the future. The Organizational Design Team is to be innovative and creative in defining structure, titles, job descriptions, and implementation strategies. The team is to present its results to the Leadership Team by May 1.

IV. *Resources:* (Who are the team members, team leaders, and team liaison; who will support the team if needed; how much time should be spent both in meetings and outside of meetings; and what additional resources are available to the team?)

Team Leader:	Rob Haynes	
Team Members:	Sue Stein	Jerry Mickey
	Dick Tingel	Dan Klamp
	Steve Daniels	Jack Hoslin
	Steve Marit	
Team Liaison:	Jim Tackle	

The team should spend whatever time is required to accomplish the Organizational Design Team objectives by May 1. All clerical support should come from Dot Maston. Team deliberations should be held in strict confidence.

V. *Constraints:* (What authority does the team have; what is the overall time frame for the evolution of the empowerment process; what things cannot be changed; what items are outside the scope of the team; and what budget does the team have?)

The team is serving at the pleasure of the Leadership Team. The team has no authority to communicate any actions or to take any actions, other than to submit a final Organizational Design Team report to the Leadership Team by May 1. The team shall have a budget of $3000 to spend on off-site meeting space, lodging, and meals. This $3000 should be spent against account A6431.

VI. *Expectations:* (What are the outputs from the team; when are they expected to be complete; and to whom should they be given?)

1. No minutes or other documentation shall be distributed outside of the Organizational Design Team.

2. The sole output shall be a written report to the Leadership Team by May 1. If an oral presentation is desired, the Leadership Team shall so indicate. The written report shall include

   a. Three organization charts. One for a $140 million ABC, one for a $170 million ABC, and one for a $200 million ABC. These organization charts shall illustrate reporting relationships and job titles.

   b. For each of the organization charts, a description of the roles and responsibilities of each job title.

   c. An implementation strategy from now to the $200 Million ABC. This strategy will include the priority of filling jobs and the timing of transition between organization charts.

Appendix C

Assessing Team Progress

This appendix consists of the following three Team Assessment questionnaires:

TEAM ASSESSMENT I

This assessment questionnaire requests the team member to describe his/her present feeling about the frequency of truth (Never, Sometimes, Most of the Time, Always) of 30 team-related statements.

The lowest possible score ($30 \times 0 = 0$) would result if each statement was never true. The highest possible score ($30 \times 3 = 90$) would result if each statement was Always true.

TEAM ASSESSMENT II

This assessment questionnaire consists of 40 questions about a team that are to be responded to with a response of Not At All (0 points) to a response of To A Very Great Degree (5 points). The lowest possible score ($40 \times 0 = 0$) would result if each question was Not At All applicable to a team. The highest possible score ($40 \times 5 = 200$) was To A Very Great Degree to a team. In addition to this Team Assessment being used to assess the present status (How It Is Today), it can also be used to do a gap analysis by comparing the responses of the present status to the expectations of what should be (How It Should Be). This gap analysis will allow an assessment of how well the team is meeting the team members' expectations.

TEAM ASSESSMENT III

This assessment questionnaire consists of 14 questions, each of which has 5 possible answers. For each question, the first response is the least desirable and the last response is the most desirable. Therefore, the lowest possible score ($14 \times 1 = 14$) would result from a team member answering each question with the first response. The highest possible score ($14 \times 5 = 70$) would result from a team member answering each question with the fifth response.

The Team Liaison should select when and which Team Assessment questionnaires should be used. This assessment should be given to all team members, and the team leader, during a team meeting. The team should complete the questionnaire at the meeting and should give the completed questionnaire back to the Team Liaison. This should be done anonymously. The Team Liaison should summarize the results and discuss the results with the Team Leader, the team, and the Leadership Team. Corrective actions should be taken to resolve any identified problems or opportunities for improvement.

Figure C.1 illustrates how a team typically will score on these assessments. At time X of Fig. C.1, due to the plateau in Team Assessment scores, either an Oil Change or a Team Member Upgrade is needed. In Fig. C.1, an Oil Change took place and the Team Assessment score dropped. After the Oil Change, the Team Assessment scores increased again. If the Team Assessment II was used at time X, the "How It Is Today" score and the "How It Should Be" score would be the same. This is what is defined as *groupthink* in Sec. 6.4.5.

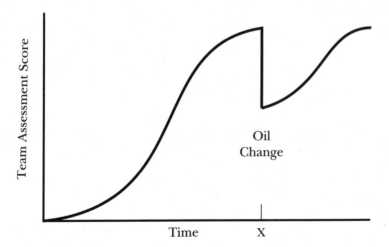

Figure C.1   Team development as viewed by team assessments

TEAM ASSESSMENT I

Instructions: Circle the number that best describes where the team is "now."

Scale: 0 = Never; 1 = Sometimes; 2 = Most of the time; 3 = Always

1. Trust between team members.	0	1	2	3
2. Members trust team leader.	0	1	2	3
3. Team leader trusts team members.	0	1	2	3
4. Team has support of company leadership.	0	1	2	3
5. Team members listen to each other.	0	1	2	3
6. Team leader is a good listener.	0	1	2	3
7. Team members openly and honestly communicate.	0	1	2	3
8. Team listens to my ideas.	0	1	2	3
9. Team uses my ideas.	0	1	2	3
10. Team has total amnesty for speaking openly.	0	1	2	3
11. Team receives information it needs to be effective.	0	1	2	3
12. Team receives technical training it needs.	0	1	2	3
13. Team receives interpersonal training it needs.	0	1	2	3
14. Team meetings are effective.				
▪ Team meets on a regular schedule.	0	1	2	3
▪ Time is well spent.	0	1	2	3
▪ Problems are solved.	0	1	2	3
▪ Actions are taken following the meeting.	0	1	2	3
▪ New ideas are encouraged.	0	1	2	3
▪ All members attend regularly.	0	1	2	3
▪ No one dominates meeting.	0	1	2	3
15. Everyone on team understands the team charter.	0	1	2	3
16. The team is productive.	0	1	2	3
17. Everyone is involved in making decisions.	0	1	2	3
18. Everyone supports decisions once they are made.	0	1	2	3
19. Team feels responsible for implementing decisions.	0	1	2	3
20. There is no "winner-loser" mentality between members.	0	1	2	3
21. Team members support each other.	0	1	2	3
22. Team leader supports team members.	0	1	2	3

Scale: 0 = Never; 1 = Sometimes; 2 = Most of the time; 3 = Always

23. Team members support team leader.	0	1	2	3
24. Risk-taking is encouraged.	0	1	2	3
25. I feel recognized for my efforts.	0	1	2	3
26. The team receives the recognition it deserves from leadership.	0	1	2	3
27. The team leader				
■ Teaches	0	1	2	3
■ Coaches	0	1	2	3
■ Counsels	0	1	2	3
28. The team has fun together.	0	1	2	3
29. I feel motivated by the process.	0	1	2	3
30. I feel committed to the process.	0	1	2	3

TEAM ASSESSMENT II

Instructions: Place a number in each of the columns to the right, using the response scale. The first column refers to how the team is functioning today. The second column refers to how the team should be functioning.

Response scale: 5 = To a very great degree; 4 = To a great degree; 3 = To some degree; 2 = To a small degree; 1 = To a very small degree; 0 = Not at all

	How it is today	How it should be
1. Do you feel proud to be a member of your team?		
2. Is your charter realistic?		
3. Does your charter support the organization's Model of Success?		
4. Are team members trusted to take reasonable risks?		
5. Do you feel there is pressure to do things just because they have always been done that way?		
6. Is necessary information available to your team in order to get the job done?		
7. Are team members' ideas sought after and considered by others?		
8. Are team members given immediate feedback on performance, when it clearly is not meeting necessary standards?		
9. Does my team function effectively with other teams?		
10. Have team members been given the necessary tools and resources to perform their jobs?		

Response scale: 5 = To a very great degree; 4 = To a great degree; 3 = To some degree; 2 = To a small degree; 1 = To a very small degree; 0 = Not at all

	How it is today	How it should be
11. Do you personally identify with your team's successes and failures?		
12. Do members of your team encourage each other to maintain high standards of performance?		
13. Are you aware of the reasons your organization is pursuing teams?		
14. Are you encouraged to take actions when outcomes are less than certain?		
15. Do unnecessary rules, policies, and procedures prevent you from getting your work done?		
16. Do team members seek information from each other?		
17. Are you included in decisions that will ultimately affect you?		
18. Are you recognized and appreciated for outstanding performance?		
19. Is the charter for your team aligned with the charters of other teams?		
20. Do team members have the necessary skills and knowledge to perform their assigned tasks?		

Response scale: 5 = To a very great degree; 4 = To a great degree; 3 = To some degree; 2 = To a small degree; 1 = To a very small degree; 0 = Not at all

	How it is today	How it should be
21. Is the morale on your team satisfactory?		
22. Is your charter challenging?		
23. Does your team understand the expectations from your team?		
24. Do you feel safe to exercise your own business judgment as a member of the team?		
25. Do unnecessary obstacles and barriers prevent you from successfully completing your assigned tasks?		
26. Do team members keep each other informed about important matters?		
27. Are you encouraged to participate on project teams?		
28. Do team members provide each other with immediate feedback on both good and bad performance?		
29. Does your team provide other teams with the necessary information and feedback for them to function effectively?		
30. Do team members have the knowledge and skill necessary to work as a highly functioning team?		
31. Is there a spirit of teamwork within the team?		

Response scale: 5 = To a very great degree; 4 = To a great degree; 3 = To some degree; 2 = To a small degree; 1 = To a very small degree; 0 = Not at all

	How it is today	How it should be
32. Does the team maintain high standards of performance?		
33. Does your team have a clear focus upon your charter?		
34. Do you feel free to express your opinions about how your operation should run?		
35. Does the team leader provide the team with necessary information?		
36. Are you given the opportunity to participate in decisions and solve problems?		
37. Are team members encouraged to coach each other?		
38. Is cooperation encouraged between your team and other teams?		
39. Is emphasis placed on doing one's best on this team?		
40. Does your team's charter's constraints restrict the performance of your team?		

TEAM ASSESSMENT III

Instructions: Circle the response that best reflects your feelings.

A. To what extent do the Vision, Mission, Requirements of Success, and Guiding Principles impact your daily performance?

   1. I don't know what you mean by Vision, Mission, Requirements of Success, and Guiding Principles.
   2. These have little impact on what I do.
   3. These are an undercurrent that are apparent in how [*company name*] works.
   4. They are guidelines that are thought of daily in doing my job.
   5. They are pervasive, and impact everything that occurs at [*company name*].

B. How has continuous improvement made a difference?

   1. It has made no impact at [*company name*].
   2. It seems to be a goal but not a reality at [*company name*].
   3. It is encouraged, but inadequate time exists to make it happen.
   4. It is having a significant impact at [*company name*].
   5. [*Company name*] has embraced continuous improvement, and it is well under way.

C. To what extent do you feel part of the team?

   1. On the outside, not really a part of the team
   2. Generally outside, except for one or two short periods
   3. On the edge; sometimes in, sometimes out
   4. A part, most of the time
   5. Completely a part, all of the time

D. How safe is it on this team to be at ease, relaxed, and yourself?

   1. A person would be a fool to be himself or herself on this team.
   2. I am quite fearful about being completely myself on this team.
   3. Generally, you have to be careful what you say or do on this team.
   4. I feel most people would accept me if I were completely myself, but there are some I'm not so sure about.
   5. I feel perfectly safe to be myself; they won't hold mistakes against me.

E. To what extent do you feel "under wraps"; that is, have private thoughts, unspoken reservations, or unexpressed feelings and opinions that you have not felt comfortable bringing out into the open?

   1. Almost completely under wraps
   2. Under wraps many times
   3. Slightly more free and expressive than "under wraps"
   4. Quite free and expressive much of the time
   5. Almost completely free and expressive

F. How effective are you, in your team, in getting out and using the ideas, opinions, and information of all team members, in making decisions?

1. We don't really encourage everyone to share their ideas, opinions, and information with the teams in making decisions.
2. Only the ideas, opinions, and information of a few members are really known and used in making decisions.
3. Sometimes we hear the views of most members before making decisions, and sometimes we disregard most members.
4. A few are sometimes hesitant about sharing their opinions, but generally we have good participation in making decisions.
5. Everyone feels that his or her ideas, opinions and information are given a fair hearing before decisions are made.

G. To what extent are the goals the team is working toward understood, and to what extent do they have meaning for you?

1. I really don't understand or feel involved in the goals of the team.
2. Much of the activity isn't clear or meaningful to me.
3. A few things we are doing are clear and meaningful.
4. I feel fairly good, but some things aren't too clear or meaningful.
5. I feel extremely good about the goals of our team.

H. How well does the team work at its tasks?

1. Coasts, loafs, makes no progress
2. Makes a little progress; most members loaf
3. Progress is slow, spurts of effective work
4. Above-average in progress and pace of work
5. Works well; achieves definite progress

I. How well does the team work at continuous improvement?

1. Not at all
2. Some
3. Progress is okay
4. Good, considering we are a new plant
5. Very well

J. Is there leadership support for continuous improvement?

1. No
2. Hard to say
3. Some
4. Yes
5. Yes, with much enthusiasm

K. Who is responsible for how your team operates?

1. One or two team members
2. A clique
3. Shifts from one person or clique to another

4. Shared by most of the members, some left out
5. Shared by all members of the team

L. What is the level of responsibility for work in your team?

1. Nobody (except perhaps one) really assumes responsibility for getting work done.
2. Only a few assume responsibility for getting work done.
3. Half assume responsibility, half do not.
4. A majority of the members assume responsibility for getting work done.
5. Each person assumes personal responsibility for getting work done.

M. How are differences or conflicts handled on your team?

1. Differences or conflicts are defined, suppressed, or avoided at all costs.
2. Differences or conflicts are recognized, but mostly remain unresolved.
3. Differences or conflicts are recognized, and some attempts are made to work them through by some members, often outside the team meetings.
4. Differences and conflicts are recognized, and some attempts are made to deal with them on our team.
5. Differences and conflicts are recognized, and usually the team is working them through satisfactorily.

N. Is continuous improvement a portion of [*company name*] culture?

1. No
2. To some people yes, some no
3. Yes, but not very active
4. Yes, actively pursued
5. Yes, a driving force

The Legal Aspects of Teams

THE SKY IS FALLING, THE SKY IS FALLING. This may not literally be the headline, but this has been the tone of many articles concerning the topic of team-based organizations and the National Labor Relations Board (NLRB). There have been hundreds of articles on this topic since January of 1993. The majority of these articles have dealt with a December 1992 NLRB ruling with regard to the Electromation, Inc. case, and a May 1993 NLRB ruling with regard to the E.I. DuPont de Nemours and Company case. At the outset in this discussion, it is important to point out the following:

1. In his concurring opinion on the Electromation case, NLRB member Clifford Oviatt, Jr., wrote:

   I find nothing in today's decision that should be read as a condemnation of cooperative programs. Indeed, in this age of increased global competition, I consider it of critical importance that management and employee be able—indeed are encouraged—to engage in cooperative endeavors to improve production methods and product quality.

2. Labor Secretary Robert Reich is a strong supporter of employee teams, and has said he would seek legislation if the NLRB takes a hard stand against teams.

3. NLRB head William Gould IV has frequently spoken in favor of worker-management teams.

So then, what's all the excitement about? Well, in my opinion, Electromation and DuPont made a few mistakes, and the NLRB, not having much latitude in enforcing a 60-year-old law, had to decide as they did. Nevertheless there *are* some issues here, so instead of pursuing the sensationalistic approach of "Teams Are Illegal," allow me to set forth the facts.

The story begins in the 1920s, when hundreds of American companies set up what were known as *work councils* or *company unions.* These company unions were to encourage shop-floor cooperation and to represent employee interests, but without any ties to organized labor. As the Great Depression approached, many companies used these company unions to thwart independent labor organizations. These company unions came to be known as *sham unions* or *captive unions.* Organized labor, quite understandably, felt that these company unions were unfair, and in 1935 a bill, sponsored by Senator Robert F. Wagner, was passed. This Wagner Act created the NLRB to protect the workers' right to join a labor union and to engage in union activities free from the interference of the companies. To be certain companies didn't try to skirt the law, the definition of *labor organizations* in the Act was purposely made very broad. In addition, to further preclude companies from circumventing the law, the term *unlawful employee domination* was defined very broadly. Interestingly, it is these two areas that are open for discussion today. In fact, before addressing the specific Electromation and DuPont cases, allow me to explain these two sticky issues first.

The issue at hand for the NLRB is to determine whether management exerts an unlawful domination of a labor organization. The two-part test used by the NLRB to decide this issue goes like this:

1. Is the entity in question a labor organization?

2. Is the entity unlawfully dominated by management?

Section 2(5) of the Act states:

> The term "labor organization" means any organization of any kind, or any agency or employee representation committee or plan, in which employees participate and which exists for the purpose, in whole or in part, of dealing with employers concerning grievances, labor disputes, wages, rates of pay, hours of employment, or conditions of work.

The four elements the NLRB will look at in deciding if an organization is a "labor organization" are

1. Employee participation

2. Whether the organization exists, at least in part, for the purpose of dealing with employees

3. Whether these dealings concern grievances, labor disputes, wages, rates of pay, bonus plans, hours of employment, and/or conditions of work

4. Whether the organization has a purpose of representing employees

Certainly, the teams in a Genesis Enterprise will have employee participation. Thus, the first condition of a team being a labor organization is
met. There are significant issues, however, with the second, third, and
fourth conditions of a team being a labor organization. The second issue
has to do with management "dealing" with employees. The NLRB has said
there will be no dealing if the team is governed by majority decision making (as opposed to consensus), management members are in the minority,
and the team has the power to decide matters itself rather than simply
make proposals to management.

Secondly, the NLRB has said there will be no dealing if the management members participate merely as observers or facilitators, without the
right to vote on team proposals. Thus it is clear that votes should be taken
and followed, that there exist no problems with self-managed teams, and
that team liaisons are fine, but should not vote. In many cases, teams in
Genesis Enterprises would not be considered labor organizations based
on the "dealing with employees" criterion. Sometimes teams would be
viewed as "dealing with employees," and thus viewed as labor organizations against the second condition.

The third and fourth conditions should further clarify that teams in a
Genesis Enterprise are not labor organizations. On the third condition,
teams should not be used to handle issues that typically are handled by
unions. Charters should not be involved with grievances, labor disputes,
wages, rates of pay, hours of employment, or conditions of work. Team
Leaders and Team Liaisons should be educated to understand these
restrictions. On the fourth issue, it should be made clear to Team Members that they represent themselves individually; that no Team Member
serves in a representative capacity, but speaks only for himself or herself.

The conditions stated here, which should preclude teams in Genesis
Enterprises from being classified as labor organizations, will not have any
negative impact on the team process, and in fact are good practices, irre-
spective of the NLRB, to esure the success of teams. So no efforts should
be made to circumvent the NLRB, and every effort should be made, if you
have a union, to involve the union in the process. If you have a union, a
good rule of thumb is that you should never allow a team to address the
issues covered in the contract. The "team" that should be consulted on
these issues is the union. If you don't have a union, the issues that typically
would be covered by the union (grievances, labor disputes, wages, rates of
pay, hours of employment, or conditions of work) should not be handled
by teams, but by the traditional hierarchical organization.

The issue of the labor organization being unlawfully dominated by management is covered in Section 8(a)(2) as follows:

> It shall be an unfair labor practice for an employer to dominate or
> interfere with the formation or administration of any labor organiza-

tion or contribute financial or other support to it: provided, that sub-ject to rules and regulations made and published by the Board ... an employer shall not be prohibited from permitting employees to confer with him during working hours without loss of time or pay.

The NLRB has defined the following factors which, when present in any combination, will support the findings of domination:

1. Financial support to the organization

2. Paying members for meetings during work time

3. Providing supplies and meeting places

4. Employer control of voting procedures

5. Employer selection of members

6. Employer control of the subjects of meetings

7. Supervisors chairing or participating in meetings

8. Employer conceived the idea for and created the organization

Since a Genesis Enterprise will be a leadership-driven, team-based process, it is clear that some of these factors would be present in the team process. Therefore the issue of domination is a given, and not really an issue. Nevertheless, once the Genesis Enterprise teams have been classified as not being labor organizations, the issue of domination is not relevant.

The first of the two cases getting most of the publicity has to do with the 200-employee, Elkhart, Indiana, company, Electromation, Inc. In 1989, after some financial problems, the Electromation management decided to cut its usual attendance bonus and its 1989 wage increases. Shortly after this action, 68 employees signed a petition expressing their unhappiness with the cuts. However, there were no union organization efforts ongoing, to the best of management's knowledge. Electromation set up five action committees to address the employee concerns. The five action committees were

1. Absenteeism/Infractions

2. No Smoking Policy

3. Communication Network

4. Pay Progression for Premium Positions

5. Attendance Bonus Program

Management decided the number of employees per committee and established the committee ground rules. The weekly committee meetings were held in a company conference room, the committee members were paid for their time spent in the meetings, and the company provided any materials the committee needed. The committee members were expected to talk "back and forth" with their coworkers, to solicit ideas from them and to discuss proposed solutions with them. Here is how the case was settled on the previously defined issues:

1. Were the action committees labor organizations?
   a. Employee participation? *Yes.*
   b. Dealing with employees? *Yes.*
   c. Dealing concerning grievances, labor disputes, wages, rates of pay, bonus plans? *Yes.*
   d. Representing employees? *Yes.*
2. Given that the action committees *are* labor organizations, were they dominated by management? *Yes.*

Thus, according to the Wagner Act, the Electromation action committees were declared an unfair labor practice.

The second highly publicized case has to do with DuPont and six safety committees and one fitness committee at their Deepwater, New Jersey, facility. In 1987, DuPont management decided to change the structure of the seven committees and to include nonmanagerial employees. These nonmanagerial employees were union employees and, at a prior union contract negotiation, the union had suggested employee involvement but management did not accept the suggestion. DuPont management decided the number of employees to serve on each committee, selected certain members, defined the workings of the committee, and had the power to veto any employee proposal. The DuPont committee approach was "decision making through consensus," and the committee's members were to convey employee complaints to the committee for correction. Here is how the DuPont case was decided:

1. Were the action committees labor organizations?
   a. Employee participation? *Yes.*
   b. Dealing with employees? *Yes.*
   c. Dealing concerning union issues? *Yes.*
   d. Representing employees? *Yes.*
2. Given that the committees *were* labor organizations, were they dominated by management? *Yes.*

Thus, according to the Wagner Act, the DuPont committees were declared an unfair labor practice.

The lessons to be learned from Electromation and DuPont are very important. Electromation, as a nonunion company, and DuPont, as a union company, both made mistakes which, in my opinion, resulted in their having the problems they had. It is *not* my opinion that these rulings or anything about the NLRB should have an impact on either union or nonunion companies moving forward with teams. The lessons to be learned are these:

1. If you have a union, actively involve the union in the entire team-based process.
2. Whether you have a union or not, your teams should
   a. Make decisions by voting, not by consensus
   b. Always have more nonmanagement employees than management employees on a team, unless the team is all management employees
   c. Not allow Team Liaisons to vote
   d. Never be used to handle the following issues: grievances, labor disputes, wages, rates of pay, hours of employment, or conditions of work
   e. Clearly indicate that employees represent only themselves, and do not serve in a representative capacity

Given the adherence to these lessons, Genesis Enterprises should not have a problem pursuing a team-based process. Nevertheless, stay tuned to the ongoing developments with the NLRB, to be certain there are not further cases that will require adjustments in the pursuit of becoming a Genesis Enterprise.

References

Case, J., "When Teamwork Is Un-American," *Inc.*, November 1993.

E.I. DuPont de Nemours and Company v. Chemical Workers Association, Inc., 311 NLRB, No. 88, May 28, 1993.

Electromation, Inc. v. International Brotherhood of Teamsters, 309 NLRB, No. 163, December 16, 1992.

Fink, R. L., R. K. Robinson and A. Canty, "DuPont v. Chemical Workers Association: Further Limits on Employee Participation Programs," *IM*, March–April, 1994.

Redeher, J. R. and D. P. O'Meare, "Safe Methods of Employee Participation," *HR Magazine*, April 1993.

Robinson, R. K., R. L. Fink and E. L. Gillenwater, "Do Employee Participation Programs Violate US Labor Laws?" *IM*, May–June, 1992.

Salwen, K. G., "DuPont Is Told It Must Disband Nonunion Panels," *The Wall Street Journal*, June 7, 1993.

Salwen, K. G., "NLRB Should Use Rule-Making Power, Says Clinton's Nominee to Head Board," *The Wall Street Journal*, October 4, 1993.

Customer Service Survey

CUSTOMER SURVEY

<u>Circle one</u>

Strongly disagree   Strongly agree

Internal Customers

1. A formal production schedule is used to coordinate our work with Department X.	1	2	3	4	5
2. Receipts from Department X are poorly identified, and there are frequent count discrepancies.	1	2	3	4	5
3. Department X is responsive to our emergency requirements.	1	2	3	4	5
4. Department X gives us advance notice when they anticipate unavoidable schedule problems.	1	2	3	4	5
5. We can count on Department X to keep their delivery promises.	1	2	3	4	5
6. We have a partnership relationship with Department X.	1	2	3	4	5
7. Department X's quality is substandard, and adversely affects performance.	1	2	3	4	5

<u>Circle one</u>

8. We are unable to get a reasonable
   response to inquiries of job status
   from Department X.   1   2   3   4   5

9. Are there any internal customer problems or opportunities for improvement that come to mind? _____
   _____
   _____

Product

1. Company X offers the range of
    products that our company
    requires.   1   2   3   4   5

2. Company X products meet our
    expectations.   1   2   3   4   5

3. Company X products perform
    well.   1   2   3   4   5

4. Company X products are
    durable.   1   2   3   4   5

5. Company X products provide
    useful and unique features. 1   2   3   4   5

6. Company X charges a reasonable
    price for its products.   1   2   3   4   5

7. Company X products are a good
    value.   1   2   3   4   5

8. The *overall* quality of Company
    X products is satisfactory. 1   2   3   4   5

9. Company X product packaging
    is easy to handle.   1   2   3   4   5

10. Company X products are usually
    damaged upon receipt.   1   2   3   4   5

11. Company X product packaging
    supports effective space
    utilization in our storage area. 1   2   3   4   5

12. Company X packaging causes
    housekeeping problems in our
    operation.   1   2   3   4   5

<u>Circle one</u>

13. Our company has packaging
    specifications, and Company X
    understands and satisfies our
    requirements for

Package size, weight, and count	1	2	3	4	5
Void fill/product protection	1	2	3	4	5
Labeling containers	1	2	3	4	5
Labeling individual items	1	2	3	4	5
Documentation of shipment	1	2	3	4	5

14. Are there any product problems, or opportunities for improvement,
    that come to mind? _____

    _____

    _____

    _____

Delivery

1. Company X provides reasonable
   ship promise dates.   1   2   3   4   5

2. Company X consistently meets
   our expectations on actual
   delivery dates.   1   2   3   4   5

3. Backorder levels at Company X
   are higher than we expect them
   to be.   1   2   3   4   5

4. Backordered items are shipped
   when promised.   1   2   3   4   5

5. Company X shipping errors are
   frequent.   1   2   3   4   5

6. The lead times for Company X
   products are:

Predictable	1	2	3	4	5
Reasonable	1	2	3	4	5

7. When there is a delay in
   shipment, Company X gives us
   advance notice.   1   2   3   4   5

<u>Circle one</u>

8. We often return Company X products due to:

Wrong item	1	2	3	4	5
Damaged or defective item	1	2	3	4	5
Inadequate substitute item	1	2	3	4	5
Late receipt of item	1	2	3	4	5

9. Packing slips from Company X facilitate our receiving process.   1   2   3   4   5

10. Receipts from Company X are:

Documented completely and accurately	1	2	3	4	5
Easy to process	1	2	3	4	5

11. Are there any delivery problems, or opportunities for improvement, that come to mind? _____

_____

_____

Responsiveness

1. Telephone communications with Company X are painless and productive.   1   2   3   4   5

2. Questions raised during calls for service are usually answered by the person that takes the call.   1   2   3   4   5

3. Company X typically is unwilling or unable to help us in an off-standard or emergency situation.   1   2   3   4   5

4. Returning an item to Company X is difficult.   1   2   3   4   5

5. Complaints are taken seriously and resolved promptly by Company X.   1   2   3   4   5

6. Our employees know whom to contact at Company X when they have a problem, complaint, or emergency requirement.   1   2   3   4   5

<u>Circle one</u>

7. Are there responsiveness problems, or opportunities for improvement, that come to mind? _____

_____

General

1. Company X's prices are competitive.	1	2	3	4	5
2. We have a positive relationship with Company X.	1	2	3	4	5
3. There is an effective system of information interchange between our company and Company X.	1	2	3	4	5
4. Company X stands behind its service and product guarantees and/or warranties.	1	2	3	4	5
5. Our employees rarely complain to Company X when they experience problems.	1	2	3	4	5
6. Company X invoices are consistently correct, with respect to invoice amount and terms of payment.	1	2	3	4	5
7. Customer service is a strength of Company X.	1	2	3	4	5
8. We are welcome to visit Company X, to observe their operations and offer suggestions.	1	2	3	4	5
9. Company X is welcome to visit our facility, to understand how we use their products.	1	2	3	4	5
10. We have plans to implement Electronic Data Interchange (EDI) for					
Order entry	1	2	3	4	5
Advance shipment notification	1	2	3	4	5

<u>Circle one</u>

Invoicing	1	2	3	4	5
Payment of invoices	1	2	3	4	5

11. Are there any other topics or additional feedback that you would like to provide to Company X? _____

_____

_____

12. Would you like Company X to contact you to discuss specific problems or opportunities in more detail?   ☐ Yes   ☐ No

    If yes, please state the topic: _____

    _____

    _____

Relationship Review Questionnaire

RELATIONSHIP REVIEW*

I.   Background information

A.   Company name: _____

Street address: _____

City, state, zip: _____

Phone number: _____

FAX number: _____

President/GM: _____   Engineering: _____

Sales VP/Mgr. _____   Quality: _____

B.   How many years have you been a supplier for this company? ___

C.   What volume of your business does our company represent in dollars? _____

D.   Who are your 10 largest customers, and what is their percent volume of total sales?

Customer	Percent volume of total sales
1. _____	_____
2. _____	_____

*So as not to create apprehension on the part of the potential partner, the following questionnaire does not mention the word "partner" but rather addresses the building of positive relationships.

3. _____ _____

4. _____ _____

5. _____ _____

6. _____ _____

7. _____ _____

8. _____ _____

9. _____ _____

10. _____ _____

E. Is there more than one manufacturing facility that could supply product?

❑ Yes   ❑ No

If so, what is their location and phone number?

Location	**Telephone number**
1. _____	_____
2. _____	_____
3. _____	_____

F. List the quality specifications that are included in your quality systems:

_____ _____ _____

_____ _____ _____

_____ _____ _____

G. Please submit a copy of your current Quality Control Manual with this completed form.

II. Relationship requirement

A. Do you have a formal drawing and change control system, which allows manufacturing and inspection access to adequate and up-to-date drawings?

❑ Yes   ❑ No

B. What is the status of your material traceability system?

_____

_____

_____

_____

_____

C. What is the status of your continuous improvement process?

_____

_____

_____

_____

_____

D. What is the status of teams at your facility?

_____

_____

_____

_____

_____

E. Do you have a formalized supplier rating/evaluation certification program?

❑ Yes   ❑ No

What evaluation criteria do you use?

_____

_____

F. How are incoming shipments inspected prior to storage? How does supplier certification change this process?

_____

_____

_____

_____

_____

G. What is the status of work instructions vis-à-vis being documented, up-to-date, available to operators, and followed?

_____

_____

_____

_____

_____

H. What is the status of setup qualification prior to the start of production?

_____

_____

_____

_____

_____

I. Are all outgoing products submitted for final inspect/test/audit? Over what time frame are these records retained?

_____

_____

_____

_____

_____

J. What is the status of statistical methods utilized for significant product characteristics and process parameters?

_____

_____

_____

_____

K. What is the status of process capability studies conducted for control/critical characteristics and process parameters?

_____

_____

_____

III. Relationship performance

A. Over the last year, what problems have existed in Quality?

_____

_____

_____

_____

Scheduling?

_____

_____

_____

_____

Product delivery?

_____

_____

_____

Communications between our organizations?

_____

_____

_____

_____

Price/cost?

_____

_____

_____

_____

B. What opportunities are there to improve our relationship?

_____

_____

_____

_____

C. What problems exist with our current relationship?

_____

_____

_____

_____

_____

Appendix **G**

Sample Letter of Intent for Cooperative Relationship between Company A and Company B

This agreement, entered into this _____ day of _____ 19____, by and between Company A of _____ and Company B of _____. For and in consideration of the mutual convenants and mutual agreements hereinafter contained, the receipt and sufficiency of which are hereby mutually acknowledged, the parties agree as follows:

1. It is the intent of the parties that this agreement will establish the framework for an ongoing business relationship between Company B, as a manufacturer of _____ and customer of Company A, who is a supplier of components and parts to Company B. This agreement is intended to cover _____, to be provided Company B by Company A, and to provide procedures for the addition of new items in the future. The agreement will be revised and extended on a periodic basis in order to facilitate the ongoing exchange of information, cooperation between the parties, and the establishment of a long-term partnership between Company A and Company B.

2. This agreement shall be in effect for an initial term of _____ years and will thereafter be reviewed and revised for extensions. Either party may terminate this agreement, with or without cause, by notifying the other party of an intent to terminate effective six (6) months from the date of written notice. Termination shall not, however, affect binding commitments made under the parameters of this agreement prior to the effective date of termination.

3. The parties agree to continuously exchange information necessary or appropriate, related to continuous improvement, to new product development plans, and to technological innovations. In order to protect proprietary data, the parties will execute a mutual nondisclosure agreement. The exchange of information will include:

   A. Each party providing the other with information, including relevant details as to each party's Model of Success and strategic plans.

   B. Each party providing the other with written specifications, drawings, and technical requirements relating to _____ to be designed, developed, or improved by the parties under this agreement.

   C. The designation by each party of a liaison person who will, respectively, be the single point of contact for handling technical, quality, and engineering issues and for receiving and communicating input from the other party.

    D. The establishment and conduct of meetings between appropriate quality, engineering, purchasing, and other personnel of both companies, to be held at mutually agreed locations each _____ weeks. At such meetings, an overview and update of relevant continuous improvement efforts and new product development projects will take place.

    E. Either company or the companies together may, from time to time, request changes, modifications, or alterations to existing or new _____. Such requests may include items intended to provide lower costs, better performance, improved reliability, or new markets to be addressed by revised or new items. The companies will respond to such requests in a timely fashion with estimated development costs and the time necessary to develop prototypes. Such responses also will include the assessment of the companies as to whether a given change request is desirable for items being presently sold/purchased.

    F. The establishment and conduct of meetings between Company A and Company B upper management every _____ months to evaluate, review, and upgrade the relationship to make sure the appropriate mutual interactions, activities, and actions are taking place to facilitate the evolution toward a mutually beneficial partnership.

4. This agreement shall initially cover the design, development, and supply by Company A _____ for Company B's _____. A general description of the components, the estimated volumes, availability dates, and suggested processes are as set forth in Addendum A. It is the intent of the parties to establish, over time, a single supplier relationship for _____ by Company B. To accomplish this, a target list of applications and products will be maintained in the form attached as Addendum B. Either party may suggest the addition of further applications to Addendum B, and for each such application, Company B will provide Company A with its technical requirements for the application, including any testing, estimated annual volume, and suggested schedules for conversion. As the parties mutually agree as to the implementation of items included on Addendum B, those approved applications and products will be added to and become a part of Addendum A.

5. The parties recognize that it is essential for Company A to maintain standards approval ratings on its products. Consequently, a joint task force will be established to include both Company B and Company A engineering resources to evaluate and develop action plans that will allow approvals to be obtained in a timely fashion.

6. It is the intent of Company A to provide Company B with a package of values, including prices, terms of sale, and other incentives, which, when taken as a whole, equals or exceeds those values given to any other customer. Likewise, it is the intent of Company B to increase the volume of business done with Company A as their business grows and more items are added to Addendum A.

7. All of the normal elements of the Company A warranty policy and technical customer support procedures will apply to this agreement. In addition, Company A will provide an instructor and course materials for a training school for Company B technicians at a time and place to be determined by Company B. Company A also will develop a self-teaching training course for Company B's use. Company A and Company B will work together to continuously improve such training and support efforts.

8. Company A and Company B mutually agree to work on joint continuous improvement efforts that will deal with both technical and business issues related to their cooperative efforts. Open and free communications shall occur on these efforts in such a manner as to support the ongoing evolution of a Company A/Company B partnership.

9. This agreement shall be binding upon the parties and their successors. The interest of either party shall not be assigned or transferred without the prior written consent of the other party. Any notice required under this agreement shall be provided in writing to the party as follows:

> Company B
>
> [address]
>
> Company A
>
> [address]

IN WITNESS WHEREOF, the parties have hereunto set their hands and seals on this day and year first written above.

WITNESSES:

_____	Company A
_____	By: _____
_____	Company B
_____	By: _____

Appendix **H**

Design of a Goalsharing Plan

If a goalsharing plan is to be designed for an organization, the following five questions must first be answered.

1. Who Is Goalsharing to Compensate?

To fully answer this question, the issue of "who" and "when" must be addressed. A decision needs to be made on the definitions and inclusion or exclusion of each of the following categories of employees:

1. Salaried
   a. Executive
   b. Management
   c. Professional
   d. Supervision
   e. Administration
   f. Other

2. Wage
   a. Full-time
   b. Part-time
   c. Temporary
   d. Other

In addition, it may not be beyond question whether partners should be included. Once a decision has been reached as to "who" is to be included in a goalsharing plan, the next issue to determine is when each category becomes eligible and when ineligible. In the case of losing eligibility, a variety of circumstances merit consideration. For example,

1. If a person dies, when does ineligibility occur? If death occurs at work, does this change the rule?

2. If a person retires, when does ineligibility occur? Does it matter if it is early retirement, forced retirement, or normal retirement?

3. If a person is laid off, when does ineligibility occur? What if a person is reduced from full- to part-time, or from full-time to temporary?

4. If a person is fired, when does ineligibility occur? Does it matter *why* they were fired?

5. If a person quits, when does the ineligibility occur? How is this impacted by the notice they give and the actual time they work?

Only after it has been determined who is to be compensated, and when their eligibility/ineligibility is effective, should the next question be pursued.

2. What Factors Define the Bonus?

The answer to this question will vary from organization to organization, and from time to time within the same organization. In consideration, use the following question to determine targets for stretch goals. In what areas is it critical that the organization achieve significant improvement? These targets or areas for stretch goals and improvements will most often be extracted from an organization's Model of Success. If an organization's Model of Success includes a focus on productivity, quality, customer service, energy, safety, waste, and scrap, the initial goalsharing plan may focus on productivity, quality, and customer service, with the other factors worked into the plan at some later time.

3. What Are the Goals upon Which Bonuses Will Be Paid?

To properly define the goals upon which the bonuses will be paid, the following factors need to be addressed.

   A. *Historical performance vs. targeted performance.* Historical performance typically is seen as the most fair baseline against which to set goals. After all, the historical performance is what actually took place. Unfortunately, a historical baseline sometimes may not exist. For example a new plant, a new product, a job-shop, and/or a new system may result in there not being a historical baseline, or the historical baseline may not be relevant. In these circumstances, the goal against which bonuses shall be paid is the targeted performance of the operation.

B. *Fixed goals vs. changing goals.* The use of a fixed goal over an extended period of time is unfair. The purpose of goalsharing is to pay for goal achievement, but not to continue to pay forever for these same goal achievements. The whole purpose of peak-to-peak performance is to continue to improve. Thus, the bonuses to be paid should be paid for goals achieved, not for prior goal achievement. The obvious challenge related to this issue comes in defining which are the recent goal achievements and which are the prior goal achievements. Often the approach taken is to calculate a goal several times a year, based upon a weighted average of historical performance. For example, consider the monthly productivity statistics given in Table H.1. A fair goal might be to do a weighted average of the six most recent average quarterly productivity rates. This would result in a productivity goal for the next quarter of

$$\frac{(1.59)1+(1.55)2+(1.47)3+(1.46)4+(1.43)5+(1.40)6}{21} = 1.45$$

Table H.1 Monthly and Average Quarterly Productivity Statistics for Calculating the Productivity Goal for the Next Quarter

Quarter	Month	Month productivity	Average quarter productivity
7	1	1.61	
	2	1.58	1.59
	3	1.57	
8	1	1.56	
	2	1.57	1.55
	3	1.51	
9	1	1.47	
	2	1.49	1.47
	3	1.44	
10	1	1.46	
	2	1.45	1.46
	3	1.47	
11	1	1.43	
	2	1.42	1.43
	3.	1.43	
12	1	1.42	
	2	1.41	1.40
	3	1.38	

C. *Substitution of capital for labor.* It is unfair and counterproductive if a major investment is made in new equipment or systems, while no adjustment is made in goals. It is clear, for example, that if a $1 million expenditure is made that results in sizable productivity and quality enhancements, then an adjustment should be made to the goals. By contrast, if a $500 capital expenditure is made, it isn't clear that an adjustment should be made in the goal. The challenge of addressing the issue of capital investment consists of attempting to answer the following three questions:

- What is the expenditure level above which an adjustment in the goal is warranted?
- When should the adjusted goal go into effect?
- How should the goal be adjusted?

A capital expenditure level of between $50,000 and $100,000 is generally used as a cutoff, below which no adjustment in the goal is made. Typically it is not considered fair if the new goal is applied immediately upon the utilization of the new equipment or system. A debug, adjustment, and learning period is standard, to allow the new equipment to be fully utilized. Sometimes this is a fixed time frame, but sometimes, it is based upon the performance of the new equipment or system. Also, once the goal has been adjusted, it is normal to adjust the goal not for the entire gain brought about by the equipment or system but for 80 percent of the increased performance, so that the people on the floor can share in the gains brought about by the new equipment or system.

D. *Product changes or product mix changes.* The issue of changes in product or in product mix should be handled in the same manner as the issue of substitution of capital for labor. If the changes in product or product mix are minor, no alteration should be made to the goal. If a change in product or product mix is significant, a change in the goal must be made. Therefore the following same three questions as for the substitution of capital for labor must be answered for product changes or product mix changes:

- What is the definition of significant product or product mix change?
- When should the adjusted goal go into effect?
- How should the goal be adjusted?

It is not desirable to continually change the goal for minor product or product mix changes. Often a product may have alternate material specifications, depending upon material availability. It is not desirable to apply different goals, as these alternate materials are used. Similarly, as changes in product mix continually occur, it is not desirable to continually change the goals. However, if there exist considerable differences in goals for different products, it most often *is* desirable to build these product mixes into the goal calculations. A typical definition of significant product or product mix changes is *a change greater than plus or minus 10 to 20 percent, or a change that has an impact greater than plus or minus 5 percent in the goalsharing bonus.* Contrary to the situation with the substitution of capital for labor, it is normal for any adjustment in goal to go into effect immediately upon the change in product being implemented or the product mix occurring. Likewise, the goal typically is adjusted not for a portion of the change but for 100 percent of it.

4. How Should the Bonus Be Shared?

This topic can be broken down into the following three questions.

A. *How to share the bonus between the organization and the employees?* Once a goal has been achieved, an excellent question is: "What percentage of the bonus should be given to the employees, and what percentage to the company as a whole?" Although plans have been created that give employees from as little as 10 percent of the bonus to as much as 100 percent, the concept of 50 percent to the company as a whole and 50 percent to the employees is consistent with the culture of a Genesis Enterprise. I am not in favor of the employees receiving less than 50 percent, or of the company receiving less than 30 percent. Thus, from a practical point of view, employees should receive somewhere between 50 and 70 percent.

B. *How to allocate bonuses between employees?* Once the size of the employee bonus pool has been determined, a method must be defined to establish how much to pay each employee. Some people believe the philosophy most consistent with a Genesis Enterprise is to pay all people the same bonus. Thus, if there were an employee bonus pool of $100,000 and 100 eligible employees, each employee would receive $1000. Yet this approach is illegal in the United States. The Fair Labor Standard Act says that hourly workers must be compensated at a rate of 1.5 percent for overtime, above their normal wage, plus other bonuses. Thus paying everyone an equal bonus would not be allowed, as this would not properly compensate people for their overtime hours. Therefore the choice for allocation of the bonus among employees is typically between a percentage of gross wages (where gross wages include overtime), and a flat amount per hour worked (where hours above 40 per week are counted as 1.5 hours).

An illustration of the first approach would be if there were an employee bonus pool of $100,000, and a total gross eligible employee payroll of $1 million, then each employee would receive a bonus of 10 percent of their gross pay. An illustration of the second approach would be if there were an employee bonus pool of $100,000, and a total of 1000 employees. If 900 employees worked 160 hours in a period (a total of 144,000 hours), and 100 employees worked 160 standard hours and 20 overtime hours (a total of $[100 \times 160] + [100 \times 20 \times 1.5]$ or 19,000 hours), then each employee would receive a bonus of 61 cents per hour of standard time worked and 92 cents per hour of overtime worked:

$$\frac{100,000}{144,000+19,000}$$

C. How to pay the bonus? All goalsharing bonus payments to employees should be made in separate checks, to ensure each employee's awareness of his or her bonus. The frequency of goalsharing bonus payments will depend upon the availability of the data, but almost always will be by the period, month, or quarter. The advantage of a more frequent payout is the reinforcement that occurs due to the frequency of the payment. The advantage of a less frequent payout is the reinforcement that occurs due to the magnitude of the payment and the reduced administrative cost.

A very important factor in defining the payment of the employee's bonus is the concept of a *reserve fund.* Many companies implement a reserve fund, as it protects against inconsistent performance and encourages a more long-term perspective. Reserve funds may vary from 25 to 75 percent of the payout bonus. A typical reserve would be 50 percent payout and 50 percent reserve.

To illustrate the importance of a reserve fund, consider the example given in Table H.2. The bonus for the entire year was $13,000, but due to the fluctuation from quarter to quarter, the employees who were supposed to receive a 50 percent share received a payout of $14,000. Obviously this is not right. Table H.3 presents the same example, but now with a reserve fund of 50 percent in place. The employee bonus with the

Table H.2 Employee Bonus with No Reserve Fund and a 50 Percent Share to Employees

	Quarter				
	1	2	3	4	Full year
Bonus	$16,000	($6,000)	$12,000	($9,000)	$13,000
Employee payout (50%)	$8,000	0	$6,000	0	$14,000

Table H.3   Employee Bonus with a 50 Percent Reserve Fund and a 50 Percent Share to Employees

	Quarter				Full year
	1	2	3	4	
Bonus	$16,000	($6,000)	$12,000	($9,000)	$13,000
Employee share (50%)	$8,000	($3,000)	$6,000	($4,500)	
Reserve withheld	$4,000	($3,000)	$3,000	($4,500)	
Employee payout	$4,000	0	$3,000	0	$7,000
Reserve balance	$4,000	$1,000	$4,000	($500)	

reserve account is much more fair. If the reserve balance at the end of the year is negative, typically it is absorbed by the company. If the reserve balance at the end of the year is positive, typically it is paid with the last payment for the year.

5. How May Certain Goals Be Emphasized?

There are three methods of emphasizing certain goals and thus impacting performance: company/employee bonus split, gates, and the magnitude of the bonus. The most subtle method of emphasizing a given factor in a goalsharing plan is to utilize different company/employee bonus splits for different factors. For example, for productivity, since employees have a major impact in this area, a likely split is 70 percent of the bonus to the employees and 30 percent to the company; for customer service, 50 percent to the employees and 50 percent to the company; and for energy, 30 percent to the employees and 70 percent to the company.

The second method of emphasizing certain goals is through the use of *gates*. A gate is a hurdle rate above which performance must be achieved before a bonus can be paid. For example, any of the following gates may be used:

1. No bonus will be paid if customer returns exceed 1 percent.

2. No bonus will be paid if a lost time accident occurs.

3. No bonus will be paid if customer service drops below 90 percent.

4. No bonus will be paid if absenteeism is above 4 percent.

5. No bonus will be paid if scrap exceeds 2 percent.

The third method of emphasizing certain goals is by increasing the magnitude of the bonus offered for a certain level of performance. For example, if a 2 percent bonus has been offered for a 20 percent reduction in scrap and scrap reduction isn't happening, an increase of the bonus to 4 percent for the same reduction in scrap may very well increase the emphasis placed upon this goal.

It is, then, by coming up with answers to these five questions that a goalsharing plan may be designed:

1. Who is goalsharing to compensate?

2. What factors define the bonus?

3. What are the goals upon which bonuses will be paid?

4. How should the bonus be shared?

5. How may certain goals be emphasized?

Index

About the Author

Jim Tompkins is a Genesis Leader. He has achieved great success and has tasted bitter failure. He has climbed to the peaks and fallen back to the valleys. He has helped large, medium, and small organizations achieve peak performance and then reinvent themselves while still on the top to reach new peaks. He has learned firsthand about success and failure and now has given us this book so we too may learn how to lead our organization on a peak-to-peak journey.

Several years in business, a military stint, and a Ph.D. in industrial engineering from Purdue University laid the foundation for Jim to simultaneously join the faculty of North Carolina State University and found a business with some of his students to serve as a laboratory for testing his hypotheses on creating business success. After a few years, he left the university and devoted himself full-time to Tompkins Associates, Inc., which has become a thriving engineering-based consulting firm that over the last two decades has grown to become a major international force in the areas of distribution, logistics, manufacturing, maintenance, warehousing, and organizational excellence. The author of several business books, Mr. Tompkins currently serves as the CEO of Tompkins Associates, Inc., which is headquartered in Raleigh, NC.